THE THEORY AND
PRACTICE
OF TRANSLATION

HELPS FOR TRANSLATORS

PREPARED UNDER THE AUSPICES OF THE

UNITED BIBLE SOCIETIES

VOLUME VIII

THE THEORY AND PRACTICE OF TRANSLATION

PUBLISHED FOR THE UNITED BIBLE SOCIETIES

BY E. J. BRILL, LEIDEN

1974

THE THEORY AND PRACTICE OF TRANSLATION

BY

EUGENE A. NIDA

AND

CHARLES R. TABER

PHOTOMECHANICAL REPRINT

PUBLISHED FOR THE UNITED BIBLE SOCIETIES
BY E. J. BRILL, LEIDEN
1974

Helps for Translators prepared under the auspices
of the United Bible Societies

———

Volume I

OLD TESTAMENT TRANSLATION PROBLEMS

Volume II

A TRANSLATOR'S HANDBOOK ON MARK

Volume III

OLD TESTAMENT QUOTATIONS IN THE NEW TESTAMENT

Volume IV

SECTION HEADING AND REFERENCE SYSTEM

Volume V

NEW TESTAMENT INDEX

Volume VI

ORTHOGRAPHY STUDIES

Volume VII

BIBLE TRANSLATIONS FOR POPULAR USE

Volume VIII

THE THEORY AND PRACTICE OF TRANSLATION

FIRST EDITION 1969

ISBN 90 04 03857 4

Copyright 1974 by E. J. Brill, Leiden, Netherlands

PRINTED IN THE NETHERLANDS

TABLE OF CONTENTS

PREFACE

This volume on *The Theory and Practice of Translation* is the logical outgrowth of the previous book *Toward a Science of Translating* (1964), which explored some of the basic factors constituting a scientific approach to translation. This second volume presents certain of these same theories in a pedagogically oriented order, designed to assist the translator to master the theoretical elements as well as to gain certain practical skills in learning how to carry out the procedures. Though this present book treats the problems of translating primarily in terms of a scientific orientation to linguistic structures, semantic analysis, and information theory, it does not lose sight of the fact that translating is far more than a science. It is also a skill, and in the ultimate analysis fully satisfactory translation is always an art.

In this volume the illustrative data are drawn primarily from the field of Bible translating. This reflects both the immediate concerns of those for whom the book has been specifically prepared and the background experience of the authors. There are, however, certain ways in which this may be a distinct advantage to the reader interested in the broadest possible aspects of translating, for Bible translating has a longer tradition (it began in the third century B.C.), involves far more languages (1393 languages by the end of 1968), is concerned with a greater variety of cultures (Bible translators have worked in all areas of the world), and includes a wider range of literary types (from lyric poetry to theological discourse) than any comparable kind of translating. Accordingly, even though the illustrative data may seem somewhat restricted, the total range of background experience is unusually wide, and hence the basis for observations on the essential problems of semantic analysis, discourse structures, and cultural transfers is particularly valid.

The first two chapters are essentially introductory, for they deal with certain of the broader issues and attempt to orient the reader with respect to the total task. The following chapters take up in a systematic order the fundamental procedures of translating: analysis, transfer, restructuring, and testing. Purely practical considerations of committee organization and procedures for carrying out the work of translating are treated in the Appendix. A glossary of technical terms is also added, as a kind of index, in which difficult words are briefly defined. The reader is then referred to that particular place in the text where the subject is discussed in greatest detail and thoroughness.

This volume is the result of three different drafts, prepared over a period of approximately four years, and used in varying form in a number of translators' institutes and seminars held in various places throughout the world. It has also benefited from the advice and counsel of a number of Translations Consultants working under the auspices of the United Bible Societies.

The Theory and Practice of Translation is not, however, to be considered exhaustive in the sense that it explores fully all the important areas and problems of the translator. In two respects especially there is need for further amplification: 1. the presentation of structural semantics, including componential analysis, and 2. discourse analysis. As regards the first kind of problems, another volume is now in preparation, tentatively titled *Introduction to Structural Semantics*, which will deal much more fully with the theoretical and structural aspects of semantics. The whole matter of grammatical meaning will be treated there, including especially the important notions of "case" and "role" as discussed in recent writings of Fillmore and Langendoen. In the second area, research is also being carried out by the technical staff of the Bible Societies, which will lead to publications in the not-too-distant future.

EUGENE A. NIDA and CHARLES R. TABER

New York, 1969

CHAPTER ONE

A NEW CONCEPT OF TRANSLATING

Never before in the history of the world have there been so many persons engaged in the translating of both secular and religious materials. It is estimated that at least 100,000 persons dedicate most or all of their time to such work, and of these at least 3,000 are engaged primarily in the translation of the Bible into some 800 languages, representing about 80 percent of the world's population.

Unfortunately, the underlying theory of translating has not caught up with the development of skills; and in religious translating, despite consecrated talent and painstaking efforts, a comprehension of the basic principles of translation and communication has lagged behind translating in the secular fields. One specialist in translating and interpreting for the aviation industry commented that in his work he did not dare to employ the principles often followed by translators of the Bible: "With us," he said, "complete intelligibility is a matter of life and death." Unfortunately, translators of religious materials have sometimes not been prompted by the same feeling of urgency to make sense.

THE OLD FOCUS AND THE NEW FOCUS

The older focus in translating was the form of the message, and translators took particular delight in being able to reproduce stylistic specialties, e.g., rhythms, rhymes, plays on words, chiasmus, parallelism, and unusual grammatical structures. The new focus, however, has shifted from the form of the message to the response of the receptor. Therefore, what one must determine is the response of the receptor to the translated message. This response must then be compared with the way in which the original receptors presumably reacted to the message when it was given in its original setting.

Even the old question: Is this a correct translation? must be answered in terms of another question, namely: For whom? Correctness must be determined by the extent to which the average reader for which a translation is intended will be likely to understand it correctly. Moreover, we are not concerned merely with the possibility of his understanding correctly, but with the overwhelming likelihood of it. In other words, we are not content merely to translate so that the average receptor is likely to understand the message; rather we aim to make certain that such a person is very unlikely to misunderstand it.

Posing the question of correctness in this manner naturally implies that there will be different translations which can be called "correct." In fact, for the scholar who is himself well acquainted with the original, even the most labored, literal translation will be "correct," for he will not misunderstand it. On the other hand, in most large linguistic communities, especially when they employ so-called international languages spoken by millions of people, there are a number of socioeducational levels of speech and comprehension. This means that several different levels of translation, in terms of vocabulary and grammatical structures, are required, if all people are to have essentially equal opportunities to understand the message.)

This test of comprehensibility is concerned primarily with discovering and eliminating two different types of expressions: (1) those which are likely to be misunderstood and (2) those so difficult and "heavy" (whether in vocabulary or grammar) as to discourage the reader from attempting to comprehend the content of the message. Such idioms as "children of the bridechamber" (Mark 2:19) and "heap coals of fire on his head" (Rom. 12:20) are typical of the first category. The average person un-acquainted with Semitic idioms is simply not going to understand that the "children of the bridechamber" are the friends of the bridegroom, or wedding guests, and that "heap coals of fire on his head" means to make a person ashamed of his behavior, and is not a way of torturing people to death.

When a high percentage of people misunderstand a rendering, it cannot be regarded as a legitimate translation. For example, in Romans 1:17 most traditional translations have "the righteousness of God is revealed from faith to faith," and most readers naturally assume that this is a reference to God's own personal righteousness. Most scholars are agreed, however, that this is not God's own righteousness, but the process by which God puts men right with himself (cf. Today's English Version). It is the act of "justification" (to use a technical, and generally misunder-stood word) and not the character of righteousness. But a translation which insists on rendering the Greek literally as "the righteousness of God" is simply violating the meaning for the sake of preserving a formal grammatical correspondence.

In addition to being quite misleading, a translation may also be so stylistically heavy as to make comprehension almost impossible. For example, in the American Standard Version (1901), 2 Corinthians 3:10 reads, "For verily that which hath been made glorious hath not been made glorious in this respect, by reason of the glory that surpasseth." The words are all English, but the sentence structure is essentially Greek. The New English Bible quite rightly restructures this passage to read, "Indeed, the splendour that once was is now no splendour at all; it is outshone by a splendour greater still."

Problem 1

Evaluate the following sets of renderings of Biblical passages in terms of how readily and correctly an ordinary reader or hearer is likely to understand them:

1. Matt. 3:15c: "Then he [John] suffered him [Jesus]" (KJV).

"So John agreed" (TEV).

2. John 1:14: "And the Word was made flesh, and dwelt among us, (and we beheld his glory, the glory as of the only begotten of the Father,) full of grace and truth" (KJV).

"So the word of God became a human being and lived among us. We saw his splendour (the splendour as of a father's only son), full of grace and truth" (Phillips).

"The Word became a human being and lived among us. We saw his glory, full of grace and truth. This was the glory which he received as the Father's only Son" (TEV).

3. Rom. 3:21-22: "But now the righteousness of God without the law is manifested, being witnessed by the law and the prophets; even the righteousness of God which is by faith of Jesus Christ unto all and upon all them that believe" (KJV).

"But, in these days, God's way of justification has at last been brought to light; one which was attested by the law and the prophets, but stands apart from the law; God's way of justification through faith in Jesus Christ, meant for everybody and sent down upon everybody without distinction, if he has faith" (Knox).

"But now God's way of putting men right with himself has been revealed, and it has nothing to do with law. The Law and the prophets gave their witness to it: God puts men right through their faith in Jesus Christ. God does this to all who believe in Christ" (TEV).

New Attitudes with Respect to Receptor Languages

Some of the basic difficulties in Bible translation can be traced to the fact that people often have quite wrong views of the receptor as well as of the source languages. Hence, to produce texts which will approximate the goal of equivalent response, translators often need to change their view of the languages in which they are working. This includes not merely a shift in some of the attitudes which tend to place the source languages on a theological pedestal and to bow down before them in blind submission, but it often requires quite a radical rethinking of one's attitude toward the receptor language, even when it is one's own mother tongue.

Each language has its own genius.

In the first place, it is essential to recognize that each language has its own genius. That is to say, each language possesses certain distinctive characteristics which give it a special character, *e.g.*, word-building capacities, unique patterns of phrase order, techniques for linking clauses into sentences, markers of discourse, and special discourse types of poetry, proverbs, and song. Each language is rich in vocabulary for the areas of cultural focus, the specialities of the people, *e.g.*, cattle (Anuaks in the Sudan), yams (Ponapeans in Micronesia), hunting and fishing (Piros in Peru), or technology (the western world). Some languages are rich in modal particles. Others seem particularly adept in the development of figurative language, and many have very rich literary resources, both written and oral.

To communicate effectively one must respect the genius of each language.

Rather than bemoan the lack of some feature in a language, one must respect the features of the receptor language and exploit the potentialities of the language to the greatest possible extent. Unfortunately, in some instances translators have actually tried to "remake" a language. For example, one missionary in Latin America insisted on trying to introduce the passive voice of the verb into a language which had no such form. Of course, this was not successful. One must simply accept the fact that there are many languages which do not have a passive voice. They merely choose to report actions only as active.

Rather than force the formal structure of one language upon another, the effective translator is quite prepared to make any and all formal changes necessary to reproduce the message in the distinctive structural forms of the receptor language.

Anything that can be said in one language can be said in another, unless the form is an essential element of the message.

For the average person the potential and actual equivalence of languages is perhaps the most debated point about translation. He does not see how people who have no snow can understand a passage in the Bible that speaks about "white as snow." If the people do not know snow, how can they have a word for it? And if they do not have a word for it, then how can the Bible be translated? The answer to this question is both complex and varied. In the first place, many people have a word for snow, even if they have not themselves experienced it, for they have heard about the phenomenon. Second, in other instances, people do not know snow, but they do have "frost" and they speak about the two with the same term. Third, many languages have equivalent idioms, *e.g.*, "white as egret feathers," or "white as fungus" (if there is an especially white form of fungus); or they may use a nonmetaphor to express the concept "white as snow," such as "very, very white." The point is that snow as an object is not crucial to the message.

Some persons may object, however, and insist that unless one has a word for snow, the translation is not adequate, for anything which does not communicate the precise meaning of the original is a distortion. Of course no communication, even within a single language, is ever absolute (for no two people ever understand words in exactly the same manner), and we certainly cannot expect a perfect match between languages. In fact, we do not have such a match even in translating from Hebrew or Greek into English, with all its wealth of vocabulary (more than a million words if one includes all the technical terminology). When the Hebrew word *ḥeṣed* is translated into English as "loving-kindness," or as "covenant love," there is much left unsaid, for this Hebrew term implies a whole social structure of mutual loyalty and support between the tribal chief and his followers, a relationship quite strange to us and almost unthinkable to many people. Similarly, when the Gospel of John uses the Greek word *logos*, "Word," in the prologue, there simply is no English word (and certainly not *Word* itself) which can do justice to the variety and richness of meaning of this Greek term.

It must be said, however, that if the form in which a message is expressed is an essential element of its significance, there is a very distinct limitation in communicating this significance from one language to another. It is usually impossible to reproduce this type of "meaning." For example, in the third chapter of John, Jesus speaks of the "wind" and of the "Spirit." In Greek a single word, *pneuma*, is used with both meanings. This results in a very significant play on words, but it cannot be reproduced in English. The best we can do under such circumstances is to use a marginal note to call the attention of the reader to the fact that in the source language one and the same word has both meanings.

In a similar way, we cannot reproduce the rhythm of Hebrew poetry, the acrostic features of many poems, and the frequent intentional alliteration. At this point, languages just do not correspond, and so we must be prepared to sacrifice certain formal niceties for the sake of the content.

To preserve the content of the message the form must be changed.

If all languages differ in form (and this is the essence of their being different languages), then quite naturally the forms must be altered if one is to preserve the content. For example, in Mark 1:4, the Greek employs a nominal construction, "baptism of repentance," but translated literally into English the resulting phrase really does not convey the meaning of the original. The average person is simply unable to describe clearly what is the **relationship** between **"baptism"** and **"repentance." Moreover,** in a high percentage of languages, terms which express events (and both "baptism" and "repentance" are events, not objects) are expressed more naturally as verbs, rather than as nouns. Even this Greek noun expression is really only a nominalization (or adaptation) of what occurs in Acts 2:38 in verbal form, namely, "repent and be baptized." In languages which either require that such events be expressed as verbs or normally use verb rather than noun phrases, it is not only right, but essential, that the nominal form of this Greek phrase be changed into a corresponding verbal expression.

The extent to which the forms must be changed in order to preserve the meaning will depend upon the linguistic and cultural distance between languages. Quite naturally the easiest transitions (those with the least amount of formal change), occur when one translates from a language such as English into German, or Fante into Ashanti, closely related languages. Moreover, English and German represent the same general cultural setting, Western technological, and Fante and Ashanti represent the same cultural setting, West African. On the other hand, if one is translating from English into Hungarian, or from Hausa to Fulani, the formal shifts are greater, for Hungarian is not a member of the Germanic branch of the Indo-European family of languages, but belongs to an entirely different family, the Finno-Ugrian, and Hausa and Fulani belong to different language families. However, Hungarian is still part of the same cultural setting as English, and Hausa and Fulani belong to the same basic cultural setting. Hence, the shifts are not so extreme.

If, however, one has to translate from English into Hindi, the formal changes are greater than from English to Hungarian, for even though English and Hindi belong to the same Indo-European family of languages, the cultural contexts, including many differences of world view, are so diverse that the formal structure patterns, both grammatical and lexical, must be altered more extensively in order to preserve the content. Finally, in translating from a language such as English into Zulu, which belongs to the so-called Bantu family of languages and represents quite a different culture, the formal modifications must be still more extreme.

Problem 2

After investigating the real meaning of the following expressions, recast them in a different form which better conveys the meaning:

1. "if she pass the flower of her age" (1 Cor. 7:36b).
2. "Bring forth therefore fruits meet for repentance" (Matt. 3:8).
3. "which devour widows' houses" (Luke 20:47).
4. "our fathers: who received the lively oracles to give unto us" (Acts 7:38b).

New Attitudes Concerning the Source Language

A new attitude concerning the receptor languages inevitably implies a new view of the source languages—Greek and Hebrew—and for some people, a new attitude toward secondary source languages, such as English, French, and Spanish, which are often used as substitute bases for translation.

Unfortunately some people have an exaggerated view of the Biblical languages. Hebrew is regarded as a special esoteric tongue for the theologians, and Greek is a "mystery," or "the finest instrument of human thought ever devised by man." On the contrary, Greek and Hebrew are just "languages," with all the excellencies and liabilities that every language tends to have. They are neither the languages of heaven nor the speech of the Holy Spirit. To recognize their true worth and significance it is important to understand three essential, theologically relevant implications about Greek and Hebrew and their use as vehicles of Biblical communication:

The languages of the Bible are subject to the same limitations as any other natural language.

Greek and Hebrew are simply languages, like any other languages, and they are to be understood and analyzed in the same manner as any other ancient tongues. They both possess extraordinarily effective means of communication, even as all languages do; and they also have their liabilities, even as all languages do. For example, in the Greek Gospels there are some 700 grammatical and lexical ambiguities, but of course, as in most languages, a high percentage of these are resolved by the linguistic context. But what is really important is that these languages, as used in the Bible, employ words which have meaning only in terms of the cultural contexts in which the languages were used. That is to say, for the message of the Bible the writers did not invent wholesale a number of unknown terms. Rather, they used words current at that time. They did, however, often use words in very special ways—just as one may do in any language when he wants to communicate some new insight—but the words of the Bible were all current terms. Our problem today is that many of the cultural contexts of Bible times which provided meanings for those words no longer exist and therefore we often cannot determine just what a word means. Nevertheless, all the vocabulary was itself rooted in the finite experience of men and women, and all of the expressions must be understood in terms of this type of background. Otherwise one becomes hopelessly enmeshed in arguments about the absolute character of symbols; and valid exegesis, that is, reconstructing the communication event with all its implications, becomes no longer possible.

The writers of the Biblical books expected to be understood.

Writing to be understood might seem to be a truism, but for some persons it is a startling revelation, for many individuals have assumed that the Bible is not a book to be understood. One person, for example, who began to read Today's English Version remarked, "This must not be the Bible; I can understand it."

The Bible is not a collection of cabalistic writings or of Delphic oracles. The writers of the Bible were addressing themselves to concrete historical situations and were speaking to living people confronted with pressing issues. It is not always possible for us to understand precisely what the writers meant, but we do injustice to them to assume that they were intentionally trying to be obscure.

If we assume that the writers of the Bible expected to be understood, we should also assume that they intended one meaning and not several, unless an intentional ambiguity is linguistically "marked." Of course, there are a number of such purposefully ambiguous expressions (which are clearly indicated by context), and it is important that the translator either reproduce the ambiguity in the same evident way or explain it in a marginal note. But one does not do justice to the intention of the writer if he tries to "ride the fence" in the case of those expressions which can have two or more meanings among which he cannot easily decide simply because he cannot reconstruct the cultural setting in which the writing first took place. In these instances it is better for the translator to select the meaning which seems best supported by all the evidence and to put this in the text, while placing the other in a marginal note. Otherwise he will give the impression to the reader that the original writer was constantly dodging the issue and was unwilling to make sense.

The translator must attempt to reproduce the meaning of a passage as understood by the writer.

The principle of attempting to reproduce the meaning of a passage as understood by the writer may seem so obvious as not to be worth saying, but there is much more here than one might suspect. For example, some persons insist that in translating the Greek of the New Testament one must go back to the Aramaic and understand Jesus' words in terms of what he must have said in Aramaic. But the translator is bound to ask himself: What was it that Luke, writing in his day, understood by the Greek that he used? If we are to make a faithful translation of Luke's Gospel, this is what must be our viewpoint. Otherwise, we will not only be involved in interminable controversy, but we will inevitably tend toward unwarranted harmonization. For example, in the Lucan form of the Beatitudes it is the "poor" who are blessed, but in Matthew they are the "poor in spirit" (or "those who recognize their spiritual poverty"). Luke employs an expression which is a direct reference to poor people, but Matthew puts it into a more "spiritual context." To try to reconstruct the Aramaic, and to reinterpret both Luke and Matthew on the basis of this reconstruction, is not the translator's task.

Similarly, many of the Psalms have important Ugaritic parallels, and much can be understood in the Psalms as the result of such studies, but one does not translate these Psalms as though they were Ugaritic ritual songs, but as hymns used in the temple worship of Yahweh.

Not only must we avoid going behind the writer; we must also avoid going ahead of the writer in exegeting and understanding his language. For example, the Greek term *pistis*, "faith," came to have the meaning "content of faith," or "creed," in the later parts of the New Testament and especially in the writings of the early Christian Fathers. But it would be quite wrong to read this meaning back into the Gospels, *e.g.*, in Luke 18:8. Similarly, we must not read back into the Genesis account of creation our own "world view" and translate the days as "geological ages," or the "dome of the sky" (wrongly translated in English as "firmament") as "the ionosphere."

PRACTICAL IMPLICATIONS OF A NEW CONCEPT OF TRANSLATING

The practical implications of a new concept of translating may be readily seen in the comparison of Romans 1:5 in the Revised Standard Version, the New English Bible, and Today's English Version:

RSV: "through whom we have received grace and apostleship to bring

about the obedience of faith for the sake of his name among all
the nations,"

NEB: "Through him I received the privilege of a commission in his
name to lead to faith and obedience men in all nations,"

TEV: "Through him God gave me the privilege of being an apostle, for
the sake of Christ, in order to lead people of all nations to
believe and obey."

The RSV represents a close formal correspondence to the original Greek
text, reflecting as it does the order of the Greek words and phrases and
also the corresponding word classes; that is to say, nouns are translated
as nouns and verbs as verbs. For the average reader there are, however,
some problems in understanding the RSV text:

1. "We" is quite ambiguous: Is Paul actually speaking about himself,
   in which case "I" would be clearer, or does he imply that other
   apostles are included?
2. Though "we" is the grammatical subject of "received grace," it is
   nevertheless the semantic "goal" of the process, and accordingly it
   is clearer in many languages to make it also the grammatical goal,
   as in the TEV.
3. In the RSV, "grace and apostleship" would seem to be two coordinate
   activities, while in reality the semantic goal of "grace" is the
   ministry of being an apostle, but the English coordinate phrase
   obscures this fact.
4. "The obedience of faith" is quite misleading in English, for we do
   not have in English this type of construction involving two nouns
   of action (we will be calling them by the more general term "event
   nouns"), in which the one which is chronologically second precedes
   the first (compare "baptism of repentance," a transform of "repent
   and be baptized").
5. The attachment of "among all the nations" to the phrase "obedience
   of faith" is unclear, for "all the nations" (or better, "all nations")
   is actually the semantic subject of both the obedience and the faith.
6. The position of the phrase "for the sake of his name" is misleading.
   Semantically it is related to the activity of being an apostle and
   therefore should be placed closer to the words with which it is
   meaningfully connected, if the reader is to understand fully what
   is intended.

Both the NEB and the TEV attempt to restructure this passage in order
to preserve the meaning of the original. Both translations, for example,
change "we" to "I" or "me." Both have related "grace" to "apostleship."
Similarly, "for his name's sake" is shifted in position, and "obedience
of faith" is correctly restructured in the right order, either as a noun
expression, "faith and obedience" (NEB), or as a verb expression, "believe
and obey" (TEV).

The TEV has gone somewhat further than the NEB in certain respects:

1. God is introduced as the subject of "grace," for this makes clear the fact that "through him" identifies the secondary agent.

2. "Me" is made the grammatical as well as the semantic goal.

3. The rather high-level word "apostleship" is restructured into the phrase "being an apostle." (One of the difficulties with "commission," as in NEB, is that it can be misleading, for to many people it seems to suggest a military commission.)

4. "For the sake of Christ" is employed instead of "for his name's sake," since modern English does not use "name" in the Semitic way as a symbolic substitute for the personality. In order to avoid confusion as to whether this was for "God's sake" or "Christ's sake," the TEV has used the noun rather than the pronominal substitute. This is, of course, made obligatory because "God" is introduced as the subject of the clause.

5. The relationship between the status of "being an apostle" and "the obedience of faith" on the part of all nations is made explicit by introducing the phrase "in order to lead."

6. The verb phrase "believe and obey" is chosen in place of the corresponding noun phrase, since it is more normal in straightforward language to employ verbs, rather than derivative nouns, for events.

7. Since "people among all nations" is the grammatical and semantic subject of the events of believing and obeying, this is made explicit in the TEV by the word order and by the subject-predicate structure, a relationship not so fully evident in the NEB.

Both the NEB and the TEV radically restructure the formal elements of this Greek clause, but it must be noted that they do not introduce any features not clearly implicit in the Greek. They also succeed in reproducing the message of the Greek in a form far more comprehensible than the more literal translation of the RSV. This is the type of faithfulness to the text of the source language which results in alterations of form in order to preserve the content.

Problem 3

In light of the principles stated in this chapter, evaluate the following sets of renderings of Biblical passages:

1. Matt. 3:15: "for thus it becometh us to fulfill all righteousness" (KJV).
"we do well to conform in this way with all that God requires" (NEB).
"For in this way we shall do all that God requires" (TEV).

2. Luke 1:1-2: "Forasmuch as many have taken in hand to set forth in order a declaration of those things which are most surely believed among us, even as they delivered them

unto us, which from the beginning were eyewitnesses"
(KJV).
"Many people have already written an account of the
events which have happened among us, basing their
work on the evidence of those who we know were
eyewitnesses as well as teachers of the message"
(Phillips).
"Many writers have undertaken to draw up an account
of the events that have happened among us, following
the traditions handed down to us by the original
eyewitnesses and servants of the Gospel" (NEB).

3. Gal. 2:6:   "And from those who were reputed to be something
(what they were makes no difference to me; God shows
no partiality)—those, I say, who were of repute added
nothing to me" (RSV).
"And as far as the leaders of the conference were
concerned (I neither know nor care what their exact
position was: God is not impressed with a man's
office), they had nothing to add to my gospel" (Phillips).
"But those who seemed to be the leaders—I say this
because it makes no difference to me what they were;
for God does not judge by outward appearances—those
leaders, I say, made no new suggestions to me" (TEV).

By comparing two or three versions find five additional examples
which illustrate the points made in this chapter.

CHAPTER TWO

THE NATURE OF TRANSLATING

Translating consists in reproducing in the receptor language the closest natural equivalent of the source-language message, first in terms of meaning and secondly in terms of style. But this relatively simple statement requires careful evaluation of several seemingly contradictory elements.

REPRODUCING THE MESSAGE

Translating must aim primarily at "reproducing the message." To do anything else is essentially false to one's task as a translator. But to reproduce the message one must make a good many grammatical and lexical adjustments. For example, the Hebrew idiom "bowels of mercies" (Col. 3:12) cannot be literally rendered into English if one really wants to communicate the message of the source language, for though we have the words "bowels" and "mercy" in English, we simply do not employ this combination. A meaningful equivalent is "tender compassion," and it is precisely in this manner that many translations attempt to reproduce the significance of this source-language expression.

EQUIVALENCE RATHER THAN IDENTITY

The translator must strive for equivalence rather than identity. In a sense this is just another way of emphasizing the reproduction of the message rather than the conservation of the form of the utterance, but it reinforces the need for radical alteration of a phrase such as "it came to pass," which may be quite meaningless. In fact, it is often misunderstood. Since in Greek *egeneto*, "it happened," is often only a "transitional word" to mark the beginning of a new episode, it is sometimes best not reproduced. In other instances, one may use some more natural transitions, *e.g.*, "and then," "now," "later."

In Mark 2:1 the Greek has *en oikō*, literally, "in house," but the real meaning of this phrase is "at home," and it is so rendered in many translations. This means a lack of verbal consistency, in not translating *oikos* as "house" always in the same manner, but one simply cannot translate in a completely concordant manner and at the same time accurately represent the meaning of the source-language text. In French, however, the Greek phrase *en oikō*, consisting of a preposition and a noun, is most idiomatically rendered as *chez lui*, a preposition and a pronoun, in which case *chez* carries the semantic components of both location and personal dwelling. Such a restructuring is fully justified, for it is the closest natural equivalent of the source-language text.

A NATURAL EQUIVALENT

The best translation does not sound like a translation. Quite naturally one cannot and should not make the Bible sound as if it happened in the next town ten years ago, for the historical context of the Scriptures is important, and one cannot remake the Pharisees and Sadducees into present-day religious parties, nor does one want to, for one respects too much the historical setting of the incarnation. In other words, a good translation of the Bible must not be a "cultural translation." Rather, it is a "linguistic translation." Nevertheless, this does not mean that it should exhibit in its grammatical and stylistic forms any trace of awkwardness or strangeness. That is to say, it should studiously avoid "translationese"—formal fidelity, with resulting unfaithfulness to the content and the impact of the message.

The Closest Equivalent

A conscientious translator will want the closest natural equivalent. It has been argued, for example, that in present-day English a natural equivalent of "demon-possessed" would be "mentally distressed." This might be regarded by some as a natural equivalent, but it is certainly not the "closest equivalent." Moreover, "mentally distressed" is a cultural reinterpretation which does not take seriously the cultural outlook of the people of Biblical times. (More will be said later (p. 134) about the differences between a linguistic and a cultural translation.)

The Priority of Meaning

As has already been indicated in the definition of translating, meaning must be given priority, for it is the content of the message which is of prime importance for Bible translating. This means that certain rather radical departures from the formal structure are not only legitimate but may even be highly desirable. For example, the NEB has rendered John 1:1b as "what God was, the Word was." This seems very different from the traditional "the Word was God," but it is an entirely legitimate translation, since it specifies unambiguously the predicate function of the term "God." To make this attributive function of the predicate noun quite clear, and thus to avoid the prevalent error of reversing the order, i.e., "God was the Word" (an interpretation which has been followed by some of the heretical sects in the history of Christendom), the NEB committee has departed from the form in order to make the content unambiguously clear.

The Significance of Style

Though style is secondary to content, it is nevertheless important. One should not translate poetry as though it were prose, nor expository material as though it were straight narrative. For example, the fast-moving, brisk style of Mark is quite different from the much more polished and structured style of Luke. Similarly, the First Epistle of Peter has some of the most elaborately organized sentence structure of the New Testament, while the Second Epistle of Peter is almost the exact opposite.

It is usually quite impossible to represent some of the stylistic subtleties of the original, e.g., plays on words (such as the meanings of certain

Old Testament names: Isaac, Abraham, Sarah, Cain, and Abel), acrostic poems (*i.e.*, poems in which successive lines or groups of lines begin with successive letters of the alphabet), rhythmic units (*e.g.*, phrases and lines of poetry). In many instances, one can indicate something about these stylistic peculiarities of the original by means of marginal notes, which will assist the reader to understand why the text reads as it does. This is particularly essential in the case of plays on words, where the meaning of a passage so often depends upon knowing the double meaning or the allusion.

In trying to reproduce the style of the original one must beware, however, of producing something which is not functionally equivalent. For example, Mark employs typical Semitic Greek in the use of the conjunction *kai*, "and," to begin many sentences. This is perfectly appropriate Semitized Koine Greek, in that it accurately reflects the corresponding use of the Hebrew conjunction *waw*. In the RSV, however, most of these conjunctions are reproduced literally, with the result that 26 sentences in Mark 1 begin with "And," producing a kind of style completely contrary to good English usage. In fact, it gives the impression of being "childish." This is, of course, not the case with the original Greek text of Mark. This means that reproducing style, even on a formal level, may not result in an equivalence, and it is functional equivalence which is required, whether on the level of content or on the level of style.

As may be clearly noted from the discussion of the definition of translating, one is constantly faced by a series of polar distinctions which force him to choose content as opposed to form, meaning as opposed to style, equivalence as opposed to identity, the closest equivalence as opposed to any equivalence, and naturalness as opposed to formal correspondence. In order to choose meaningfully between these opposing sets of defining features, it is necessary to set up certain fundamental criteria for guidance in the process. That is to say, one must establish a set of priorities, which can define translating from different perspectives: the perspectives of form and of comprehensibility.

A SYSTEM OF PRIORITIES

As a basis for judging what should be done in specific instances of translating, it is essential to establish certain fundamental sets of priorities: (1) contextual consistency has priority over verbal consistency (or word-for-word concordance), (2) dynamic equivalence has priority over formal correspondence, (3) the aural (heard) form of language has priority over the written form, (4) forms that are used by and acceptable to the audience for which a translation is intended have priority over forms that may be traditionally more prestigious. These four priorities reflect four different perspectives. The first views the translation in terms of its linguistic forms. The second is based upon the reactions of the receptors. The third deals with the typical circumstances of communication and is especially applicable to Bible translation since, the Bible is generally heard far more (as the result of its being read in worship services) than it is read personally. The fourth priority, which consists of a complex set of factors, *e.g.*, age, sex, education, and background experience, analyzes the problems of translation from the standpoint of the types of audience.

THE PRIORITY OF CONTEXTUAL CONSISTENCY OVER VERBAL CONSISTENCY

Since words cover areas of meaning and are not mere points of meaning, and since in different languages the semantic areas of corresponding words are not identical, it is inevitable that the choice of the right word in the receptor language to translate a word in the source-language text depends more on the context than upon a fixed system of verbal consistency, *i.e.*, always translating one word in the source language by a corresponding word in the receptor language. This can be conveniently illustrated by the translations of the Greek term *soma* (often spoken of as meaning "body") in several passages in the RSV, the NEB, and the TEV:

1. Matt. 6:25
   RSV: about your body
   NEB: clothes to cover your body
   TEV: clothes for your body
2. Mark 5:29
   RSV: she felt in her body
   NEB: she knew in herself
   TEV: she had the feeling inside herself
3. Luke 17:37
   RSV: where the body is
   NEB: where the corpse is
   TEV: where there is a dead body
4. Rom. 12:1
   RSV: present your bodies
   NEB: offer your very selves
   TEV: offer yourselves
5. Col. 2:11
   RSV: putting off the body of flesh
   NEB: divested of the lower nature
   TEV: freed from the power of this sinful body

The contrastive usages become all the more evident if we arrange these key terms in parallel columns:

	RSV	NEB	TEV
1. Matt. 6:25	body	body	body
2. Mark 5:29	body	herself	herself
3. Luke 17:37	body	corpse	dead body
4. Rom. 12:1	body	your very selves	yourselves
5. Col. 2:11	body (of flesh)	lower nature	(sinful) body

Can we justify different renderings, *i.e.*, departures from verbal consistency, such as are found in NEB and TEV? To answer this question, we must ask a further question: Is the literal rendering (the verbally consistent one) fully adequate, or is it possibly unnatural or misleading (in some cases both unnatural and misleading)?

In Matthew 6:25, the rendering of "body" is quite adequate, for there is no other equivalent term in English. In Mark 5:29, however, the use of "body" seems rather unnatural, for one does not "feel in the body" but "feel in oneself." In Luke 17:37, the rendering of "body" can be misleading, and in the RSV it is all the more so when the second clause has "eagles" instead of "vultures" (though the latter is in the margin). In Romans 12:1 the use of "body" is quite misleading and often results in wrong exegesis, for it is the total personality and not merely the physical part of man which is to be offered to God. In Colossians 2:11 the phrase "body of flesh" is unnatural and in the context also misleading. However, it is possible to interpret the Greek phrase in two different ways, either (1) as an identification of human nature, which is prone to sin, or (2) as the "lower nature," in contrast with man's higher nature. This latter view is defended by many scholars, but it is regarded by others as reflecting a Greek view of human personality (*i.e.*, into lower and higher elements) more than a strictly Biblical one. But regardless of the interpretation one prefers, the fact is that a literal rendering is both unnatural and misleading.[1]

The contrast between contextual consistency and verbal consistency becomes all the more evident in translations of the Greek term *sarks*, literally "flesh," in a number of passages in the American Standard Version (ASV), the NEB, and the TEV:

1. Luke 24:39
   ASV: a spirit hath not flesh and bones
   NEB: no ghost has flesh and bones
   TEV: a ghost doesn't have flesh and bones

2. 2 Cor. 7:5
   ASV: our flesh had no relief
   NEB: there was still no relief for this poor body of ours
   TEV: we did not have any rest

3. Rom. 11:14
   ASV: provoke to jealousy them that are my flesh
   NEB: to stir emulation in the men of my own race
   TEV: make the people of my own race jealous

4. Acts 2:17
   ASV: pour out my Spirit upon all flesh
   NEB: pour out upon everyone a portion of my spirit
   TEV: pour out my Spirit upon all men

5. Rom. 8:3
   ASV: what the law could not do, in that it was weak through the
        flesh, God...

---

[1] For a further discussion of the related problem of figurative meanings, see pp. 87-89.

NEB: what the law could never do, because our lower nature robbed
    it of all potency, God has done

TEV: what the Law could not do, because human nature was weak,
    God did

6. 2 Cor. 10:3

    ASV: for though we walk in the flesh, we do not war according to
        the flesh

    NEB: weak men we may be, but it is not as such that we fight
        our battles

    TEV: it is true we live in the world; but we do not fight from
        worldly motives

7. I Cor. 1:26

    ASV: not many wise after the flesh

    NEB: few of you are men of wisdom, by any human standard

    TEV: few of you were wise..., from the human point of view

The contrast between these different sets of renderings can be seen more
clearly by placing them in parallel columns:

		ASV	NEB	TEV
1.	Luke 24:39	flesh	flesh	flesh
2.	2 Cor. 7:5	flesh	poor body	we
3.	Rom. 11:14	flesh	men of my own race	people of my own race
4.	Acts 2:17	flesh	everyone	men
5.	Rom. 8:3	flesh	lower nature	human nature
6.	2 Cor. 10:3	flesh	weak men	world ... worldly
7.	I Cor. 1:26	flesh	human standard	human point of view

An analysis of the literal renderings of the ASV as good, unnatural, or
misleading produced the following results, based on the consensus of a
group of approximately fifty Bible translators who were asked to judge
these renderings. Though some persons may not agree with one or
another particular judgment, the problem is nevertheless evident:
Good: 1; Unnatural: 2; Misleading: 3, 4, 6; Unnatural and misleading: 5, 7.

The next question we must ask, however, is why one reacts unfavorably
to the verbally consistent translations in contexts 2 through 7. Basically,
the negative reactions are the result of recognizing that "flesh" in present-
day English does not fit these contexts, since for most persons "flesh" has
only three meanings: (1) meat which may be purchased at the butcher's
(but this is slightly obsolescent), (2) the flesh of a person, e.g., "She has put
on a lot of flesh," or "That person is fleshy," and (3) sex, which is becoming increasingly a central meaning. Quite obviously, therefore, only the
first context has a meaning of *sarks* which parallels a present-day use of
"flesh" in English, and it is for this reason that the average person can
rate such a translation as "good," for it seems to fit.

An examination of the translation of the Greek term *dikaioō* in certain
key passages in the New Testament further illustrates the problem of the
contrast between verbal consistency and contextual consistency.

1. Matt. 12:37
   RSV: for by your words you will be justified, and by your words
   you will be condemned
   NEB: for out of your own mouth you will be acquitted; out of
   your own mouth you will be condemned
   TEV: for your words will be used to judge you, either to declare
   you innocent or to declare you guilty
2. Luke 7:29
   RSV: all the people and the tax collectors justified God
   NEB: all the people, including the tax-gatherers, praised God
   TEV: all the people and the tax collectors heard him; they were
   the ones who had obeyed God's righteous demands
3. Luke 16:15
   RSV: you are those who justify yourselves before men
   NEB: you are the people who impress your fellowmen with your
   righteousness
   TEV: you are the ones who make yourselves look right in men's
   sight
4. Romans 3:4
   RSV: that thou mayest be justified in thy words
   NEB: when thou speakest thou shalt be vindicated
   TEV: you must be shown to be right when you speak
5. Romans 3:24
   RSV: they are justified by his grace as a gift
   NEB: all are justified by God's free grace alone
   TEV: by the free gift of God's grace they are all put right with him

The comparison of these renderings in parallel columns is likewise
instructive:

	RSV	NEB	TEV
1. Matt. 12:37	justified	acquitted	declared innocent
2. Luke 7:29	justified	praised (God)	obeyed (God's) right-eous demands
3. Luke 16:15	justify	impress ... with righteousness	make yourselves look right in man's sight
4. Rom. 3:4	justified	vindicated	be shown to be right
5. Rom. 3:24	justified	justified	are ... put right

In these passages verbal consistency in rendering *dikaioō* always by
"justify" is quite misleading, for in present-day English the verb "to
justify" has three meanings in popular usage. First, one may say, "He
was justified in doing that," implying that what he did may have ap-
peared to be wrong, but it was correct or right, despite such appearances.
One may also say, "He is always justifying what he is doing," implying
that what he is doing is basically wrong, and therefore he feels compelled
to make it appear all right. Second, one may speak of "justifying two different columns of type," thus making them both the same length. A third,

but very limited, usage of this term, may be found in the expression, "He justified his existence," *i.e.*, he did something worthwhile and constructive as a means of compensating the world for his presence. But none of these meanings conveys the concept of any change of state or relationship, as implied in Romans 3:24, or of acquittal as in Matthew 12:37. Certainly the Pharisees, mentioned in Luke 16:15, were not trying to show that they were innocent.

In technical theological writings the term *justify* does have a highly specialized meaning, but in this special theological sense, and as used in certain traditional translations in English, it is essentially Anglicized Latin. It is perfectly acceptable in a translation being made for persons who already know the Greek term *dikaioō* and understand its special range of meanings. That is to say, *justify* may serve the purposes of theological discussions between theologians, but it is not adequate as a term to be used in a translation for persons who are expected to understand the basic elements of the New Testament message from their knowledge of English alone.

THE REASONS FOR THE PRIORITY OF CONTEXTUAL CONSISTENCY OVER VERBAL CONSISTENCY

It is one thing to demonstrate in a practical way that strict verbal consistency may result in serious distortion of the meaning, but quite another thing to understand precisely why this is true. Basically, the priority of contextual consistency rests upon two important linguistic facts: (1) each language covers all of experience with a set of verbal symbols, *i.e.*, words to designate various features of experience, and (2) each language is different from all other languages in the ways in which the sets of verbal symbols classify the various elements of experience.

Each language covers the totality of experience with symbols.

One may liken the totality of experience to a large circle segmented completely into various parts, each corresponding to a particular word, which serves as a symbol of that area of experience, as in Figure 1:

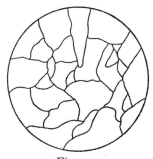

Figure 1

This means that people can always speak about anything that is in their experience, for their set of symbols covers their total world. But language is much more complex than a single "map" of experience, for this segmenting of experience is several layers deep. For example, one may use the term "terrier" in speaking of a particular house pet, but it is also possible to speak of the same object as a "dog." The word "dog," however, covers far more territory than "terrier," for it includes terriers, poodles, boxers, hounds, shepherds, etc. But a dog may also be referred to as a "mammal," a term which includes hundreds of different species but is distinct from amphibians. Finally, one may also speak of a terrier as an "animal," a word which has a very wide range of meaning.[2] Accordingly, if we were to diagram the way in which language segments the total experience of a people, we would need to describe numerous levels, each carefully segmented into larger and larger sections, with intricate patterns of inclusion and exclusion, as in Figure 2.

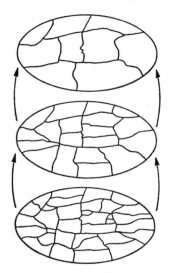

Figure 2

A useful analogy is that of the map of the political divisions of a country. Each higher-order division includes a number of lower-order divisions; that is, a state includes a certain number of counties, each of which may in turn consist of a certain number of towns, cities, townships, etc. This means that a given locality may be referred to as being in Chicago, or Cook County, or Illinois, or even in the United States of America, depending upon the perspective.

Each language has its own system of symbolizing meaning.

As long as one is dealing with merely one language, the problems of semantic areas are not so acute. What makes the problems infinitely more difficult is that each language has a distinctive way of segmenting its

---

[2]   See also p. 68.

experience by means of words. Moreover, the ways in which these words are related to each other are also very different. For one thing, there is often a one-for-many relationship between languages. The English word *corner* is translated into Spanish as *esquina* (an outside corner) and *rincón* (an inside corner), while the Spanish word *radio* corresponds in part to English *radio*, *radium*, and *radius*. Actually, however, these terms represent not merely a system of one-to-many meanings, for though *corner* in English corresponds to two different Spanish words, *corner* also has meanings in English which could not possibly be translated by either *esquina* or *rincón*. If languages were related merely by one-to-many relationships, that would not be too difficult, but in reality one usually encounters many-to-many relationships, in almost endless chains of related meanings, as in the following set:

| English: | faucet | key | key (solution) | code (Morse) | code (legal) |
| Spanish: | llave | llave | clave | clave | código |

In addition to these chains of many-to-many meanings, one must also reckon with differences of classification. For example, in some languages one can speak of bamboo as a tree, as we do in English, but in many languages bamboo is only grass. In some of the languages of New Guinea a cassowary is not considered a bird, for though it does have feathers and lays eggs, it does not fly. On the other hand, bats, which do fly, are classed with birds, not with mammals. In the Hebrew classification of plants in Genesis 1:11, there is a general designation of "plants," but then a subdivision of "trees bearing fruit" and "grasses bearing seed." In Chibemba, a language of Zambia, the classification is somewhat parallel, but it is based on the veins of the leaves. If the veins branch, the plant is in one class, but if they are parallel along the entire length of the leaf, the plant belongs to another class, regardless of size or shape.

All this means that not only do languages have a distinct way of segmenting their most concrete, specific layer of existence, but they also have very different ways of distinguishing the classes in the upper layers. In fact, languages tend to be more alike on the specific concrete level and increasingly different on the higher levels. This is true because the distinctions made on the lower levels depend primarily on "perception" (the shape and size of things), while the upper layers of classification depend essentially upon "conception" (the way people think about objects, events, and qualities). In other words, each language classifies things, that is, groups them as similar in some way, on the basis of certain qualities which they share, while features in which they differ are ignored as incidental. But which features are crucial and which are incidental is basically a matter of arbitrary choice within each language and culture.

When we speak of verbal consistency in translating, we focus primary attention upon the way in which specific words are translated, but words are not the only formal features involved in formal consistency. One may, for example, have formal consistency of word, phrase, and clause order (word order is, however, more difficult to retain than phrase or clause order), length of sentences, and classes of words, *e.g.*, translating nouns by nouns and verbs by verbs. All of these formal features combine to produce what is called "formal correspondence," of which verbal consistency is merely one element.

Problem 4

For each of the following words, give one word which is on a *higher* level and another which is on a *lower* (more specific) level (*e.g.*, given *rodent*, a higher-level word might be *mammal* or *animal*, a lower one might be *rat* or *mouse*): *automobile, child, table, walk, red, look.*

The Priority of Dynamic Equivalence over Formal Correspondence

If we look at translations in terms of the receptors, rather than in terms of their respective forms, then we introduce another point of view; the intelligibility of the translation. Such intelligibility is not, however, to be measured merely in terms of whether the words are understandable and the sentences grammatically constructed, but in terms of the total impact the message has on the one who receives it.

Traditionally the way in which translations were judged may be diagrammatically represented by Figure 3.

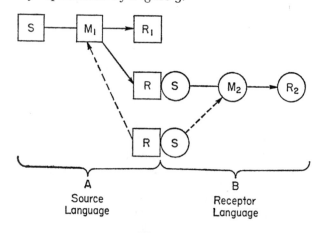

Figure 3

The first box represents the source (S), who communicates the message (M₁), which is received by an original receptor (R₁). The translator, who is both receptor and source, first receives M₁ as if he were an R₁, and then produces in a totally different historical-cultural context a new message M₂, which he hopes will be understood by the final receptor, R₂. The differences between the two languages and the two cultural settings are represented by the different shapes. The squares represent the source-language factors and the circles represent the receptor-language factors. Both the translator and the scholarly judge of the translation combine both types of factors. In the past critical examination of a translation was usually carried out by someone who simply examined the two messages (M_1 and M_2) and compared their formal and meaningful structures, and on the basis of this decided whether the translation was "faithful."

This is, of course, one way to judge translations, but it does involve a built-in problem, for the scholarly person is often too familiar with the source (M_1), and he almost instinctively judges the forms of M_2 in terms of what he already knows about M_1. If, however, we focus attention, not upon the formal correspondence as judged by the scholar but upon the manner in which the two receptors (R_1 and R_2) understand the corresponding messages, we oblige the critic to inquire from R_2 just how he understands M_2, and on this basis he is in a much better position to evaluate the dynamic equivalence. The critic must compare the real or presumed comprehension of M_1 by R_1 with the comprehension of M_2 by the average receptor R_2, as diagrammatically represented in Figure 4:

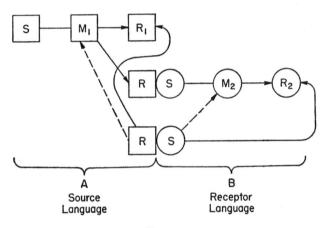

A
Source
Language

B
Receptor
Language

Figure 4

The first message (M_1) was designed not for the bilingual person (the translator-critic), but for the monolingual R_1, and it is his comprehension which is to be compared with that of R_2. Moreover, it is the comprehension of M_2 by R_2 which must ultimately serve as the criterion of correctness and adequacy of M_2.[3]

[3] We must assume that there is at least some basic relationship between the intention of the source and the response of the first receptors. Otherwise, of course, the communication has utterly failed. But in general we can assume that the source had in mind the backgrounds of his receptors and prepared his message in such a form as to obtain the highest degree of comprehension. To measure dynamic equivalence we can only rightly compare the equivalence of response, rather than the degree of agreement between the original source and the later receptors, for we cannot presume that the source was writing for this "unknown audience" or that the monolingual receptors in the second language have enough background to understand the setting of the original communication. Of course, we could study the extent to which the translator and his source exhibit similarities of purpose, intent,

Dynamic equivalence is therefore to be defined in terms of the degree to which the receptors of the message in the receptor language respond to it in substantially the same manner as the receptors in the source language. This response can never be identical, for the cultural and historical settings are too different, but there should be a high degree of equivalence of response, or the translation will have failed to accomplish its purpose.

It would be wrong to think, however, that the response of the receptors in the second language is merely in terms of comprehension of the information, for communication is not merely informative. It must also be expressive and imperative if it is to serve the principal purposes of communications such as those found in the Bible. That is to say, a translation of the Bible must not only provide information which people can understand but must present the message in such a way that people can feel its relevance (the expressive element in communication) and can then respond to it in action (the imperative function).

The Informative Function

The informative function in language can only be served by a translation which is thoroughly understandable. This means that a phrase such as "the God of peace" (Heb. 13:20) must be rendered so that people will realize that this is a reference not to "a peaceful God," but to "God who makes peace" or "causes peace." Similarly, "he opened his mouth and taught the multitude" (Matthew 5:2), must not be interpreted as some strange way of speaking with the mouth open. If people do tend to misunderstand, one must change the expression, *e.g.*, "he began to teach." In Matthew 5:17, one must make certain that "fulfill the law" really makes the proper sense. If "fulfill the law" means only to do precisely what the law demanded, then it is neither true of Jesus' ministry nor meaningful in this context, for Jesus consistently violated many of the ritual interpretations of the law. A more contextually justifiable rendering is "to give the Law real meaning" (TEV).

Problem 5

How effectively do the following renderings fulfill their informative function?

1. Heb. 2:2b: "every transgression and disobedience received a just recompense of reward" (KJV).
"every transgression or disobedience received a just retribution" (RSV).
"anyone who did not follow it [the message given by the angels] or obey it received the punishment he deserved" (TEV).

and techniques, but ultimately the adequacy of the translation must be judged in terms of the way people respond to it. Or, to put the same idea in a different perspective, if Paul had been writing directly for us *rather than* for his original audience, he would no doubt have said the same things differently, and the differences would not have been only linguistic.

2. Jude 8b: "despise dominion" (KJV).
                "reject authority" (RSV).
3. 1 Cor. 4:13: "Being defamed, we entreat" (KJV).
                "they slander us, and we humbly make our appeal"
                (NEB).
                "when we are insulted, we answer back with kind
                words" (TEV).

THE EXPRESSIVE FUNCTION

[Dynamic equivalence in translation is far more than mere correct communication of information. In fact, one of the most essential, and yet
often neglected, elements is the expressive factor, for people must also
feel as well as understand what is said.] The poetry of the Bible should
read like poetry, not like a dull prose account. Similarly, the letters
of Paul should reflect something of the freshness of a general letter, and
not sound like a theological dissertation.

One of the most interesting "expressive" problems of Bible translation
is the Hebrew tetragrammaton (literally, "four letters") YHWH, the
name for God, often transliterated as *Yahweh*, and traditionally represented as *Jehovah*. The Jewish people themselves regarded this name as
so holy (*i.e.*, taboo, in the technical sense of the word) that it was not to
be uttered except at the most sublime occasions. For the oral reading of
the Scriptures, they usually substituted *Adonai*, "Lord," as reflected in
later voweling of the text by the Masoretes. In terms of the expressive
value of language, the use of *Adonai* meant a much more intimate,
personal, and direct relationship.

In the Greek translation of the Old Testament, made a couple of
centuries before Christ, Jewish scholars used the Greek term *kurios* to
render both *Adonai* and YHWH. This use was carried over into the Greek
New Testament, with the result that there is a kind of divine ambiguity
in the use of the same term to apply both to God and to Jesus Christ.

It is interesting that in the English tradition, the term "LORD" has
consistently been preferred to "Jehovah" (the use of "Jehovah" in the
Revised Version and the American Standard Version never proved
especially popular), and the RSV has returned to the King James use of
"LORD." In French, the Protestant tradition has used *l'Eternel*, "the
Eternal," but more recently there has been a strong movement in the
direction of *le Seigneur*, "the Lord." In Spanish, *Jehová* has been traditional for many years in the Protestant constituency, but one of the most
recent translations is using *el Señor*, "the Lord."

Buber and Rosenzweig, in their German translation of the Old Testament, have in many instances translated YHWH by personal pronouns:
Ich (and its inflected forms) when YHWH is the speaker; *Er* (and its
inflected forms) when he is referred to; the intimate *Du* (and its inflected
forms) when he is addressed. These pronouns, especially *Du*, reflect the
very personal relationship between the worshiper and his God.

Despite all the arguments for YHWH being a proper name, there has

nevertheless been this persistent "feeling" that there must be something
more intimate and personal, *i.e.*, more "expressive," than is communicated
in a strange personal name.

Problem 6

Evaluate the expressive effects of the following sets of renderings of
Biblical passages; do they carry the same impact as the original?

    1. Acts 8:20: "Thy money perish with thee" (KJV).
                   "You and your money, ... may you come to a bad
                   end" (NEB).
                   "To hell with you and your money!" (Phillips; see
                   translator's note).
                   "May you and your money go to hell" (TEV).
    2. Gal. 1:9:   "let him be accursed" (KJV, RSV).
                   "may he be damned!" (Phillips).
                   "let him be outcast!" (NEB).
                   "may he be condemned to hell!" (TEV).
    3. John 2:4:   "Woman, what have I to do with thee?" (KJV).
                   "Your concern, mother, is not mine" (NEB).
                   "Is that your concern, or mine?" (Phillips).
                   "You must not tell me what to do, woman" (TEV).

THE IMPERATIVE FUNCTION

Language is not restricted to mere informative and expressive functions; it must also be clearly imperative, especially in the sort of document
the Bible is, which claims not only to describe the acts of God, but to
announce guiding principles for proper human conduct, *i.e.*, a "way of
life." To do this, however, the renderings must be sufficiently clear
that one can understand not merely what they must have meant to people
in ancient times but also how they can be applied in the present-day
context. In line with this type of principle for a "dynamic equivalent
translation," the TEV has rendered "do not let your left hand know what
your right hand is doing" (Matt. 6:3, RSV) as "do it in such a way that
even your closest friend will not know about it." Not only do some persons
misinterpret the idiom about not letting one's left hand know what the
right hand is doing (in fact, they often use it in speaking of covering up
illicit deals), but for many individuals this is an obscure statement which
does not seem to make any tangible reference to present-day circumstances or life.

An even more evident illustration of the need for an imperative element
in language is found in Matthew 7:1, which contains in the Greek one of
the so-called "passive avoidances of God." "Judge not that ye be not
judged" does not mean that one is not to criticize others in order not to
be criticized. Rather, one should not judge others in order not to be
judged by God, or as in the TEV, "Do not judge others, so that God will
not judge you." Any failure to understand precisely what is meant in this

passage means that the imperative function of such a communication has been seriously impaired.

Problem 7

How well would an ordinary speaker of modern English understand what is expected of him in the following passages?

1. I Peter 2:12: "Having your conversation honest among the Gentiles" (KJV).
"Maintain good conduct among the Gentiles" (RSV).
"Let all your behaviour be such as even pagans can recognize as good" (NEB).

2. I Peter 3:3: "Whose adorning, let it not be that outward adorning of plaiting the hair, and of wearing of gold, or of putting on of apparel" (KJV).
"Your beauty should not be dependent on an elaborate coiffure, or on the wearing of jewelry or fine clothes" (Phillips).

A COMPARISON OF FORMAL CORRESPONDENCE AND DYNAMIC EQUIVALENCE

Philippians 2:1-2 in the RSV and the TEV illustrate quite well some of the essential differences between a formal-correspondence translation (F-C) and a dynamic-equivalent translation (D-E):

(1) So if there is any encouragement in Christ, any incentive of love, any participation in the Spirit, any affection and sympathy, (2) complete my joy by being of the same mind, having the same love, being in full accord and of one mind.

(1) Does your life in Christ make you strong? Does his love comfort you? Do you have fellowship with the Spirit? Do you feel kindness and compassion for one another? (2) I urge you, then, make me completely happy by having the same thoughts, sharing the same love, and being one in soul and mind.

Certain distinctive features of these two translations are illustrative of the contrast between formal correspondence and dynamic equivalence:

1. The RSV's employment of a single sentence makes the utterance seem somewhat heavier and more formal than the corresponding TEV translation, which has five sentences.
2. The RSV phrases "encouragement in Christ," "incentive of love," and "participation in the Spirit" are somewhat vague and obscure, for there is no clear indication of how the receptors of this letter are involved. In contrast the repeated use of *your* and *you* in the TEV make these relationships specific and personal.
3. Words such as "affection" and "sympathy" in the RSV lack some-

thing of their expressive and imperative sense, for they do not indicate to whom such attitudes are directed.

4. In the TEV the use of somewhat simpler expressions, *e.g.*, *make ... strong* (vs. *encouragement*), *comfort* (vs. *incentive*), *fellowship* (vs. *participation*), *kindness* (vs. *affection*) and *compassion* (vs. *sympathy*), makes the communication likewise seem more personal and less "theological."

5. The RSV phrases "complete my joy" (vs. "make me completely happy") and "being in full accord and of one mind" (vs. "being one in soul and mind") seem somewhat strange and artificial, a kind of translationese. On the other hand, the TEV expressions not only communicate the information equally as well but provide a more fitting stylistic medium.

It can, of course, be argued that in the first part of this Greek sentence one does not have a series of questions. This is true, but there is a series of conjunctions *ei*, meaning "if," followed by *tis* or *ti*, "some," "any," and this very striking stylistic device is actually lost in the RSV series. To that extent, therefore, the TEV does attempt to do greater justice to the rather emphatic series of introductory clauses.

The purpose of comparing this passage in the RSV and the TEV is not to defend or to criticize, but merely to illustrate some of the differences between a formal correspondence translation and a dynamic equivalent translation. Of course, persons may insist that by its very nature a dynamic equivalent translation is a less "accurate" translation, for it departs further from the forms of the original. To argue in this manner, however, is to use "accurate" in a strictly formal sense, whereas accuracy can only be rightly determined by judging the extent to which the response of the receptor is substantially equivalent to the response of the original receptors. In other words, does the dynamic equivalent translation succeed more completely in evoking in the receptors responses which are substantially equivalent to those experienced by the original receptors? If "accuracy" is to be judged in this light, then certainly the dynamic equivalent translation is not only more meaningful to the receptors but also more accurate. This assumes, of course, that both the formal correspondence translation and the dynamic equivalent translation do not contain any overt errors of exegesis.

THE PRIORITY OF THE HEARD LANGUAGE OVER THE WRITTEN LANGUAGE

The priority of the heard form of language over the purely written forms is particularly important for translations of the Bible. In the first place, the Holy Scriptures are often used liturgically, and this means that many more people will hear the Scriptures read than will read them for themselves. Second, the Scriptures are often read aloud to groups as means of group instruction. Third, in some areas of the world people employ a kind of "oral" reading. That is to say, the people tend to read everything aloud, and "listen to what they have said." In such situations, it is particularly important that people understand the Bible correctly from the oral form. Last, the Scriptures are employed increasingly in such media as radio and television, which means that the oral form must be fully intelligible if the audience is to comprehend.

Some persons assume that a translation which is well done in the aspect of its printed form will be quite easily read aloud, but this is by no means always true. In fact, if one is to anticipate the problems of the hearer, it is necessary to bear in mind a number of very essential matters:

Capitalization is not sufficient to correct the meaning of otherwise ambiguous or misleading translations.

For example, in Mark 1:12 the use of "Spirit," with capitalization, will still be misleading in the oral form of languages in which the term is likely to imply an evil as well as a good spirit, for the action of "driving out into the wilderness" suggests much more the deed of an evil spirit or demon than the action of the Holy Spirit. In such instances, it is not only legitimate but even obligatory to employ "Holy" as a qualifier of "Spirit," so that the hearer will understand. Similarly, one cannot expect the capitalization of pronouns to correct otherwise ambiguous or misleading references to God. People simply do not signal in their speech the existence of caps in the printed text.

One must not depend upon the spelling to correct otherwise misleading pronunciations.

For example, in 1 Chronicles 25:1, the RSV reads, "prophesy with lyres," but people will almost inevitably think of *liars* and not *lyres*, since the latter is such an uncommon term. The problem of the written form of language is very acute in the case of Chinese, in which a written text may be quite clear, but a spoken text of the same passage can be very ambiguous.

Terms which are vulgar in pronunciation should not be used in the text, even when the written form does not seem vulgar.

For example, in American English the word *ass* does not seem so vulgar in a printed text, but in pronunciation the term carries strongly unfavorable connotations.

The punctuation should not be employed in an arbitrary manner to correct otherwise misleading grammatical arrangements.

The connections of words should be clear from their arrangements and order, and one should not have to employ marks of punctuation in an arbitrary way to clear up an otherwise misleading combination of words. In other words, punctuation marks should be employed to "reinforce" the proper interpretation rather than to restructure it. People actually pay very little attention to punctuation unless it supports what is already the evident grammatical structure. They certainly do not look to the punctuation to correct what is otherwise misleading.

Answers to rhetorical questions must often be provided, so that the hearer will not misunderstand what is involved.

For example, in Romans 8:33-34 the listener may be misled by the set of rhetorical questions, for the question, "Who shall bring any charge against God's elect?" is immediately followed by a sentence which begins, "It is God. . . ." Similarly, in the following verse, "Who is to condemn?" is followed in some translations by a statement beginning, "It is Christ. . ."

Because of the awkwardness of some rhetorical questions, these may be restructured as emphatic statements, e.g., in Hebrews 1:5, "For to what angel did God ever say. . .," is rendered in the TEV as, "For God never said to any of his angels."

Unintentional oral puns should be carefully avoided.

In some languages, *e.g.*, Portuguese, it is quite common for people to listen for combinations of sounds (usually the endings of words combined with the initial portions of following words) which have vulgar or obscene meanings. This means that one must carefully read all translations of the Bible so as to avoid any combination of sounds which can be reinterpreted as a different and unacceptable word.

The forms of proper names should be completely adjusted to the phonological system of the receptor language so as not to provide special problems for those who must read the Scriptures.

In order to preserve some of the special phonological contrasts in Hebrew and Greek, some languages have employed artificial sound distinctions and combinations of sounds, which are very misleading to the average reader. As a result, many persons hesitate, or even refuse, to read the Scriptures in public, for they do not know how to pronounce these unusual letters or combinations of letters.

Meaninglessness should be avoided in a text.

For example, in the RSV, 1 Chronicles 26:18 reads: "and for the parbar on the west there were four at the road and two at the parbar." There is a footnote indicating that the meaning of *parbar* is uncertain. But to retain complete meaninglessness in the text is not satisfactory. It would be much better to attempt at least some of the plausible conjectures as to the meaning of *parbar* and to make sense of the passage. One could always caution the reader that the meaning of the verse is uncertain. But as a principle it is best at least to make sense in the text and put the scholarly caution in the margin, rather than to make nonsense in the text and offer the excuse in the margin.

Overloading of the translation should be carefully avoided .

If a translation is relatively literal (*i.e.*, a formal correspondence translation), it is likely to be overloaded to the point that the listener cannot understand as rapidly as the reader speaks. This is particularly true in the case of expository materials. For this reason it is not only legitimate, but also necessary, to see that the rate at which new information is communicated in the translation will not be too fast for the average listener.

One of the decided advantages in giving priority to the heard form of language is that one can always be certain that if it can be understood by the average hearer it is more likely to be fully intelligible when it is read silently.

THE PRIORITY OF THE NEEDS OF THE AUDIENCE OVER THE FORMS OF LANGUAGE

The priority of the audience over the forms of the language means essentially that one must attach greater importance to the forms understood and accepted by the audience for which a translation is designed than to the forms which may possess a longer linguistic tradition or have greater literary prestige.

In applying this principle of priority it is necessary to distinguish between two different sets of situations: (1) those in which the language in question has a long literary tradition and in which the Scriptures have existed for some time and (2) those in which the language has no such literary tradition and in which the Scriptures have either not been translated or are not so set in their form as to pose serious problems for revisers.

As will be seen in Chapter 7, in which the basic problems of style are considered for languages with a long literary tradition and a well-established traditional text of the Bible, it is usually necessary to have three types of Scriptures: (1) a translation which will reflect the traditional usage and be used in the churches, largely for liturgical purposes (this may be called an "ecclesiastical translation"), (2) a translation in the present-day literary language, so as to communicate to the well-educated constituency, and (3) a translation in the "common" or "popular" language, which is known to and used by the common people, and which is at the same time acceptable as a standard for published materials.

In languages which have no literary tradition and no Biblical text which is so rooted in the life of the church as to be "untouchable," one must usually accept as the norm the oral form of speech used in formal discourse, e.g., the speech of a chief explaining some important matter or the discussions of the elders about some significant event. Even then, there will be certain differences between oral and written language, as is indicated in Chapter 7. But apart from the level of speech, i.e., formal rather than technical, informal, casual, or intimate, one must also consider the type of audience to which a translation is directed. In setting up these priorities the following are usually of primary consideration:

Non-Christians have priority over Christians.

That is to say, the Scriptures must be intelligible to non-Christians, and if they are, they will also be intelligible to Christians. Not only is this principle important in making the translation of the Bible effective as an instrument of evangelism, but it is also necessary if the language of the church is to be kept from becoming an esoteric dialect—a symbol of belonging and identification or a semimagical means of imploring God.

The use of language by persons twenty-five to thirty years of age has priority over the language of the older people or of children.

Because of the rapid changes affecting so many languages in the world, the forms used by the older people are becoming obsolescent. If in translating, one insists on using primarily the speech of the elders, many of the words and expressions are likely to be unknown or to appear odd within a few years. Moreover, putting them in the Scriptures is likely neither to preserve such forms nor to resurrect them. One cannot so easily reverse linguistic history. At the same time, one should not accept the language of children or teenagers as a norm, for this does not have sufficient status to be fully acceptable. Such forms often including slang and fad words, are generally rejected by the young people themselves, who may be offended by being addressed in a style which seems substandard or paternalistic.

In certain situations the speech of women should have priority over the speech of men.

This is true in places in which men have many more advantages of linguistic contact than women; *e.g.*, they may go off to work in mines or on plantations in which other languages are spoken. Men therefore may acquire a number of expressions quite unknown to the women; nor are they likely to be shared with the women, for such terms are used almost exclusively in the "foreign" places of work. It is true that the language of the men indicates the direction in which the language is likely to change, but if one gets too far ahead of such developments, comprehension by women will be relatively low and the probability of women learning to read will be severely reduced, with the result that the children are very unlikely to have any significant instruction in Biblical content. On the other hand, in those languages which have special forms of language used by women, i.e., distinctive women's speech in contrast with men's speech, but with both sets of forms completely known to everyone, it is usually important to correctly represent this women's speech when the Scriptures report the words of women.

This new concept of the nature of translating, especially as it is related to Bible translating, suggests an approach to the problems of translation quite different from what has been traditionally employed. This approach naturally calls for certain new techniques, especially in the stages of analysis, and fortunately developments in linguistic science, in the areas both of grammar and of semantics, provide us with some very important tools.

CHAPTER THREE

GRAMMATICAL ANALYSIS

Basically there are two different systems for translating. The first consists in setting up a series of rules which are intended to be applied strictly in order and are designed to specify exactly what should be done with each item or combination of items in the source language so as to select the appropriate corresponding form in the receptor language. Some theoreticians have contended that this automatic selection process is best accomplished by working through an intermediate, neutral, universal linguistic structure. This go-between language into which the source is translated and from which the finished translation is derived may be either another natural language or a completely artificial language. But whether or not such an intermediate stage is used, this approach is based on the application of rules to what linguists call the "surface structure" of language, that is, the level of structure which is overtly spoken and heard, or written and read. This approach may be diagrammed as in Figure 5.

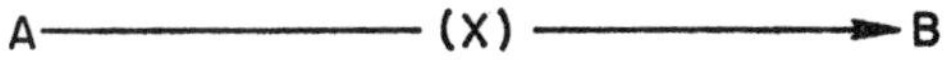

A———————— (X) ————————▶ B

Figure 5

In Figure 5, A represents the source language and B represents the receptor, or target, language. The letter X in parentheses stands for any intermediate structure which may have been set up as a kind of universal structure to which any and all languages might be related for more economic transfer.

The second system of translation consists of a more elaborate procedure comprising three stages: (1) analysis, in which the surface structure (*i.e.*, the message as given in language A) is analyzed in terms of (a) the grammatical relationships and (b) the meanings of the words and combinations of words, (2) transfer, in which the analyzed material is transferred in the mind of the translator from language A to language B, and (3) restructuring, in which the transferred material is restructured in order to make the final message fully acceptable in the receptor language. This approach may be diagrammed as in Figure 6.

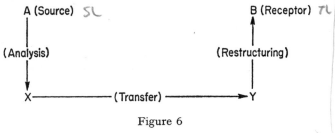

Figure 6

At first glance, this sytem seems much more complicated and cumbersome than the other. But the more linguists learn of the structure of languages and of messages expressed in linguistic forms, the more they realize that a single-stage procedure is inadequate. The seemingly roundabout route actually reflects much better the real nature of linguistic structures, and therefore reflects much more accurately what happens in good translation and represents a much more efficient method for the mastery of translation technique than the first system. In effect, the remainder of this book is an exposition of Figure 6, of the justification for it, and of the methods and procedures by which it may be implemented. A useful analogy is that of crossing a broad, deep, swift river. If one does not know how to swim, and does not have a boat, it is necessary to go up or down the bank of the river until a place is found which is shallow enough to serve as a ford. The time and effort spent walking along one side of the river is not only not wasted; it is absolutely essential to the crossing.

As indicated above, there are three major steps in analysis: (1) determining the meaningful relationships between the words and combinations of words, (2) the referential meaning of the words and special combinations of words (the idioms), and (3) the connotative meaning, *i.e.*, how the users of the language react, whether positively or negatively, to the words and combinations of them. In this chapter we shall be dealing only with the analysis of the meaningful relationship between words on a grammatical level.

GRAMMAR HAS MEANING

When one thinks of meaning, it is almost inevitably in terms of words or idioms, for we generally take grammar for granted, since it seems to be merely a set of arbitrary rules about arrangements—rules that must be followed if one wants to be understood, but not rules that in themselves seem to have any meaning. A close look at the poem "Jabberwocky" in *Through the Looking Glass* will soon convince us that grammar does carry some meaning.

> 'Twas brillig, and the slithy toves,
>   Did gyre and gimble in the wabe;
> All mimsy were the borogoves,
>   And the mome raths outgrabe.

Almost immediately we can decide what the grammatical classes of the meaningless words probably are: *e.g.*, *brillig*, *slithy* (adjectives), *toves* (noun), *gyre*, *outgrabe*, and *gimble* (verbs). Moreover, we can readily make up some further sentences, such as (1) *the toves were slithy*; (2) *the toves were in the wabe*; (3) *Toves can gyre and gimble*; (4) *Gyring and gimbling take place in the wabe*; (5) *The wabe is a place*; (6) *The borogoves are mimsy*; and (7) *The raths are mome*.

Even from the grammar itself we can make some highly probable guesses about the referential meaning of some of these terms: (1) *brillig* either characterizes a general quality of the circumstances in which the *toves gyre and gimble,* or it expresses the general time of the action, (2) *toves* are objects (perhaps animate) which can engage in some type of action, (3) *wabe* is a place in which actions can take place, (4) *mimsy* is a quality with various degrees, (5) the *borogoves* are objects which can possess certain qualities, (6) the *raths* are objects which can participate in an event such as *outgribing,* and (7) the *raths* are objects which may have a quality such as *mome.* Of course, it would be possible to assign to these nonsense terms in the Jabberwocky poem such meanings as would make such deductions untenable, but if we accept the "meaning" of the various forms used in this poem in terms of their highest probabilities of usage, then the deductions which we have made are not unfounded, for the grammatical markers, such as *'twas, and, the, did, in, all, were, -s,* all provide the necessary clues.[1]

Even a comparison of *John hit Bill* and *Bill hit John* should convince us that grammar has some meaning, for it is the first word which performs the action of the second word, and the third word identifies the goal of the action specified by the second word. This meaningfulness of grammar can also be illustrated by such a contrasting pair as *Naturally he did it* and *He did it naturally,* in which *naturally* has two quite different meanings because it is used in two quite different grammatical constructions. Even the combinations *Did you go* and *You did go* can be uttered with the same intonational pattern, but the grammatical differences of order provide quite different meanings.

THE SAME GRAMMATICAL CONSTRUCTION MAY HAVE MANY DIFFERENT MEANINGS

The fact that what is generally regarded as the same grammatical construction may represent a number of different relationships, and thus be said to have many different meanings, is no better illustrated than by the grammatical construction consisting of two nouns or pronouns connected by *of.* The following phrases (from KJV) are typical of some of the different relationships expressed by the structure "A of B":

1. the will of God (Eph. 1:1)
2. the foundation of the world (Eph. 1:4)
3. the God of peace (Rom. 15:33)
4. that holy Spirit of promise (Eph. 1:13)
5. the word of truth (Eph. 1:13)
6. the riches of his grace (Eph. 1:7)
7. Jesus of Nazareth (Matt. 26:71)
8. the lake of Gennesaret (Luke 5:1)
9. the land of Judaea (John 3:22)
10. the Lord . . . of the sabbath (Mark 2:28)
11. the day of the preparation (Matt. 27:62)
12. servant of all (Mark 9:35)
13. the book of Moses (Mark 12:26)

---

[1] The syntactical meanings here indicated are subsequently confirmed in *Through the Looking Glass* by Humpty Dumpty, who, in answer to Alice's enquiry, also assigns a lexical meaning to each of the items concerned.

14. baptism of repentance (Mark 1:4)   15. the remission of sins (Mark 1:4)

In order to determine precisely the relationship of the components A and B in these phrases, we ask ourselves: Just what is the relationship, for example, between *God* and *will* in the phrase *the will of God*? Obviously, it is God, the second element, which "wills", the first element. Or we may say it is B which does A, *i.e.*, "God wills." In the case of *the foundation of the world* (2) there is an immediate confusion, for *foundation* normally identifies an object, *e.g.*, the foundation of the house, but we know that this is not what is meant in Ephesians 1:4. *Foundation* can also, in modern usage, mean an organization or institution, especially one which gives away money (*e.g.*, the Rockefeller Foundation), but in view of the time when Ephesians was written and the cultural patterns that prevailed then, we can, of course, discount this meaning. We conclude, therefore, that *foundation* must in this instance not be an object, but an event, and that it should actually be translated as "creation." This interpretation is further strongly supported by the presence of the preposition *before*, which expresses time relations between events. We can then readily understand the relationship between the parts as "creating the world"; that is to say, the second element B is the goal of the first. But the first element also implies a subject, namely, God, so that the entire expression is really equivalent to "(God) creates the world." And an appropriate formula could be "X does A to B," or "B is the goal of A."

In the phrase *the God of peace* (3) we are not speaking of a peaceful God, but God who causes or produces peace. Thus the relationship between A and B in this instance is almost completely the reverse of what it is in *the will of God*, for in *the God of peace* A causes B. In *the Holy Spirit of promise* (4) the Holy Spirit is the object which is promised, and in this instance God must be understood as the implicit subject. But again the order is entirely the reverse of what exists in *the foundation of the world* (2), for the Holy Spirit (A) is the goal of the promise (B).

We are forced to the conclusion that the construction *Noun + of + Noun* can "mean" many different things, depending on what nouns are involved and what meanings we assign to them. In other words, this *construction* means not one relation, but many: it is ambiguous. Our efforts must therefore be aimed at discovering and then stating unambiguously exactly what the relation is in each case.

If we proceed to analyze all of these phrases in terms of their simplest and most unambiguous relationships, we come out with the following series:

Biblical Phrase	*Unambiguously Marked Relationships*
1. the will of God	God wills
2. the foundation/creation of the world	(God) creates the world
3. the God of peace	God causes/produces peace

4. the Holy Spirit of promise	God promised the Holy Spirit
5. the word of truth	the word is true
6. the riches of his grace	he shows grace richly/abundantly [2]
7. Jesus of Nazareth	Jesus came from Nazareth
8. the lake of Gennesaret	the lake is in Gennesaret
9. the land of Judea	the land is Judea
10. the Lord of the sabbath	one who commands the Sabbath [3]
11. the day of the preparation	the day when (people) prepare (for the Sabbath) [4]
12. servant of all	he serves all (people) [5]
13. the book of Moses	Moses wrote the book [6]
14. baptism of repentance	(people) repent and are baptized [7]
15. remission of sins	(God) forgives (the people's) sin [8]

We have, at one time or another, already made use of the terms *object, event, abstract,* and *relation*. It becomes crucial at this point to explain just what we mean by these terms. In the first place, they refer to basic semantic categories, in contrast with the more familiar terms *noun, verb, adjective, preposition*, etc., which refer to grammatical classes. Second, these four categories include exhaustively all the semantic subcategories of all languages, even though various languages have quite different sets of grammatical classes; in other words, they are universal. This means that the entire universe of experience is divided among these four categories: (1) *Object* refers to those semantic classes which designate things or entities which normally participate in events, *e.g., house, dog, man,*

[2] If we examine closely the meaning of *grace*, we will realize that God's grace is neither a thing (substance) nor a quality of God, but that it expresses a kind of action or behavior on the part of God: God does something, and it is this action (event) that we call grace. Because English lacks a verb to express this semantically simple notion, we use the expression *show grace*. Similarly, *riches* does not here designate an accumulation of material things but an abstraction, basically an expression of quantity or degree, which describes the way in which God shows grace. For this reason we use an adverb in the unambiguous expression.

[3] The term *Lord* is structurally complex in that it combines two types of elements: (1) an object, *i.e.,* a person, and (2) an event, the act of lording, commanding, or controlling. *The Lord of the Sabbath* may be interpreted to mean "the one who determines what should be done on the Sabbath."

[4] *Preparation* designates an event, but there are participants implied, namely, the people.

[5] *Servant*, like *Lord*, is structurally complex, for it implies both a person (an object), and an event, the act of serving. *All* is therefore the goal of the event of serving, but it also functions as a substitute for, or modifier of, an implied substantive, such as *people*.

[6] If one employs the normal possessive construction, *Moses' book*, then it is the book that Moses had in his possession, rather than the one he was regarded as having written.

[7] It is also possible to state this relationship as *people repent and John baptizes them*, but in this context the phrase is a transform of the imperative phrase, "Repent and be baptized."

[8] When there are two events, such as *forgiveness* and *sins*, there may be two different implied subjects, and one event (the sinning) may be the goal of the other (the forgiving).

sun, stick, water, spirit, etc. (2) *Event* is the semantic class which designates actions, processes, happenings, *e.g., run ,jump, kill, speak, shine, appear, grow, die*. (3) *Abstract* refers to the semantic class of expressions which have as their only referents the qualities, quantities, and degrees of objects, events, and other abstracts. For example, *red* is nothing in and of itself; it is only a quality inherent in certain objects, *e.g., red hat, red binding, red face*. From these objects, the quality *red* is abstracted and named as if it had separate existence. Similarly, *quickly* is a quality of certain events, such as *run quickly*, but it can be conceptually abstracted and named. Abstracts of quantity include *two* and *twice, many, often, several*, etc. The abstracts which serve to mark the degree of other abstracts, *e.g., too* and *very*, belong in this general subclass. (4) *Relations* are the expressions of the meaningful connections between the other kinds of terms. Often they are expressed by particles (in English many are prepositions and conjunctions); some languages make extensive use of affixes, such as case endings, for similar purposes; and many languages, including English, use the order of parts extensively to signify meaningful relations, *e.g.*, the subject and the predicate in *John ate the peanut*. Finally, some languages use special verbs such as *be* and *have* (in some of their uses only) to express relations, *e.g., John is in the house, John is a boy, John has a brother* (but not in "He that cometh to God must believe that he is," where *be* is a verb of existence).

How a word is to be understood, that is, what category it will be assigned to, depends entirely upon each particular context. For example, in the sentence *he picked up a stone, stone* represents an object; in *they will stone him*, it functions as an event; and in *he was stone deaf*, it serves as an abstract.

It is important to realize that there is a kind of "fit" between these semantic categories and certain grammatical classes. For instance, objects are most typically expressed by nouns or pronouns, events by verbs, and abstracts by adjectives and adverbs. It is this intuitively felt "fit" that gave rise to the traditional semantic definitions of the grammatical parts of speech. But the fact that most languages also provide ways of shifting the class membership of terms (*e.g.*, by expressing events by nouns) causes the downfall of these traditional definitions and makes it impossible for us simply to place an = sign between the two sets of terms.

Problem 8

Compare Philippians 2:1-2 in the RSV and the TEV:

RSV	TEV
"So if there is any encouragement in Christ, any incentive of love, any participation in the Spirit, any affection and sympathy, complete my joy by being of the same mind, having the same love,	"Does your life in Christ make you strong? Does his love comfort you? Do you have fellowship with the Spirit? Do you feel kindness and compassion for one another? I urge you, then, make

being in full accord and of one
mind."

me completely happy by having
the same thoughts, sharing the
same love, and being one in soul
and mind."

Compare the following corresponding phrases (*cf.* discussion of this
passage in the previous chapter).

RSV	TEV
1a. encouragement	1b. make you strong
2a. incentive of love	2b. his love comfort you
3a. participation in the Spirit	3b. you have fellowship with the Spirit
4a. affection	4b. you feel kindness
5a. sympathy	5b. compassion for one another

Answer the following questions:

1. What makes the verb expressions in 1b, 2b, 4b, and 5b clearer than
   corresponding noun expressions in 1a, 2a, 4a, and 5a?
2. What is the value of the use of pronouns *you, his,* and *one another*
   in the phrases of the TEV series?
3. What is the justification, if any, for using these verbs and pronouns?

KERNEL SENTENCES

Now if we examine carefully what we have done in order to state the
relationships between words in ways that are the clearest and least ambiguous, we soon discover that we have simply recast the expressions so
that events are expressed as verbs, objects as nouns, abstracts (quantities
and qualities) as adjectives or adverbs. The only other terms are relationals, *i.e.,* the prepositions and conjunctions.

These restructured expressions are basically what many linguists call
"kernels"; that is to say, they are the basic structural elements out of
which the language builds its elaborate surface structures. In fact, one
of the most important insights coming from "transformational grammar"
is the fact that in all languages there are half a dozen to a dozen basic
structures out of which all the more elaborate formations are constructed
by means of so-called "transformations." In contrast, back-transformation, then, is the analytic process of reducing the surface structure to its
underlying kernels. From the standpoint of the translator, however, what
is even more important than the existence of kernels in all languages is the
fact that languages agree far more on the level of the kernels than on the
level of the more elaborate structures. This means that if one can reduce
grammatical structures to the kernel level, they can be transferred more
readily and with a minimum of distortion.[9] This is one justification for the

---

[9] For this book on the theory and practice of translation we are not advocating
that the translator go below the level of the kernels to the underlying bases, the
"deep structure." There are certain theoretical interests in such an approach, but

claim that the three-stage process of translation is preferable, and the basis for the river-ford analogy (see Figure 6 and p. 33).

The actual kernel expressions in English from which the more elaborate grammatical structures can be constructed consist of the following illustrative types:

1. John ran quickly.   5. John is sick.
2. John hit Bill.   6. John is a boy.
3. John gave Bill a ball.   7. John is my father.
4. John is in the house.

Certain features of these kernel expressions should be noted:

1. The subject *John* stands for any object word which can serve as a subject of a subject-predicate expression.
2. The adverbial attributive, such as *quickly*, can of course be attributive to any kernel expression, e.g., *John hit Bill quickly*.
3. The phrase *in the house* is representative of any type of prepositional phrase expression involving an object, e.g., *with a stick*, *through the fence*, and *over the mountain*.
4. In kernel 5, *sick* is grammatically a predicate adjective and semantically a qualitative abstract characteristic of the subject, and *is* merely permits the attribution of this quality to be made the grammatical predicate of the sentence, in contrast with *sick John*.
5. Kernels 6 and 7, which appear very similar, are in reality profoundly different. This fact can perhaps best be highlighted by contrasting *John is a father* and *John is my father*. In the first case, the predicate noun, with *indefinite* determiner, designates a class of which the subject is a member among others, and it is impossible to reverse the sentence: one cannot very well say, *A father is John*, which would reverse the roles of the definite and indefinite references. In the type-7 kernel, on the other hand, both subject and predicate noun are definite, and the *is* serves as an identity sign between them: *John = my father*, which by the rules of mathematics can be inverted to *My father = John*, with no change of meaning.
6. Though grammatically *is* is a verb, which permits it to serve its predicate role, in these contexts it is semantically a relation (or, rather, a distinct relation in each kernel).
7. Included in our scheme in kernel 6, though possibly distinct, is the part-whole predication, such as *this liquid is water*. The difference is in the nature of the nouns involved: *John* is a proper name designating an isolatable and countable object, and *boy* designates an entire class of such countable objects; in contrast, *liquid* and *water* designate masses of which one can have more or less with

practically, the bases are neither useful nor advisable, since these bases cannot be readily manipulated. When the message is transferred, it is not, however, on precisely the kernel level, for if this were the case, the connections between the kernel elements would be lost or obscured. Therefore, the transfer is made at a near-kernel level, in which the relevant connections between the kernels are explicitly marked.

indefinite gradation. Closely related to this is the fact that one says *one of the boys* but *some of the water* (note that *some of the boys* is quite distinct, since it is the indefinite plural of *one*).

Problem 9

1. In reading John 1, Colossians 1, and Hebrews 11 in the KJV or the RSV, list the nouns that express events, and then see how many of these have been rendered by verbs in NEB, Phillips, and TEV.

2. Do the same thing for nouns that express abstracts.

3. Rewrite the following "of" phrases (from RSV) as kernel expressions to show the relationship between the parts:

hardness of heart (Mark 3:5)	*Example*: the heart is hard
a flow of blood (Mark 5:25)	*Example*: the blood flows
the prophets of old (Mark 6:15)	
the washing of cups (Mark 7:4)	
the precepts of men (Mark 7:7)	
the commandment of God (Mark 7:9)	
the eye of a needle (Mark 10:25)	
Mount of Olives (Mark 13:3)	
the master of the house (Mark 13:35)	
the King of the Jews (Mark 15:9)	
the day of Preparation (Mark 15:42)	
men of little faith (Matt. 8:26)	
men of violence (Matt. 11:12)	
fishers of men (Mark 1:17)	

WORDS WITH COMPLEX STRUCTURES

As has been noted in the previous analysis of the "of" phrases in English, some words have complex semantic structures. *Servant* and *Lord*, for example, in the contexts *servant of all* and *the Lord of the sabbath* identify both objects and events, for the kernels underlying these expressions are: "He serves all," or "one (who) serves all," and "He commands/controls the sabbath."

Some phrases may seem quite similar in structure, but because of terms having complex structures, the relationships between the parts turn out to be quite different. The phrases *our beloved ruler, his old servant*, and *three good bakers* would all seem to be quite similar in structure, but they actually go back to quite different kernels. Note the diagrammatic analysis of these three phrases in Figure 7.

In *our beloved ruler*, the object (*our*) performs the event (*beloved, i.e., love*), of which the goal is the object element in *ruler*. But this same object performs the event of ruling the first object, *our*. This may be paraphrased as "we love the one who rules over us."

In *his old servant*, the first object (*his*) may be said to "command" or "direct" the object element in *servant*, but this same object also is the subject of the event of *serving* the first object (*his*). At the same time the

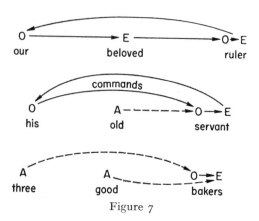

Figure 7

abstract (*old*) may be described as attributive to the object contained in *servant*.[10] It is also possible for *old* to designate the length of time during which the serving was done or to specify that it was the one who served at a previous time, in which case *old* is attributive to the event element in *servant*.

In *three good bakers*, however, *three* qualifies the three objects, but *good* qualifies not the men but their capabilities in baking.[11]

Classes of Structurally Complex Terms [12]

There are numerous types of combinations of elements which occur with single terms, but those which are most frequently encountered in English are:

[10]   In the relationship *his servant*, there is an implied relationship of superior to inferior, suggested by the added event word "commands" or "directs," for it is the first object which tells the second object what to do. (Compare *his ruler*, where the relationships are very different.) At the same time, the second object performs an event (serving) which has as its goal the first object. The second relationship is explicit in the event element of the term *servant*, but the first relationship is only implicit in the phrase as a whole.

[11]   In almost all such expressions, *e.g.*, *good carpenter, fine artist, capable executive,* and *bad dancer*, the attributive qualifies the event, not the object component, in the terms *carpenter, artist, executive,* and *dancer*. In Dutch, the grammatical usage permits in certain cases a distinction between relations: *een vlotte spreker* can mean both "a sociable man who is a speaker" and "a man who speaks fluently"; but *een vlot spreker* can have only the second meaning, in which the abstract qualifies the event.

[12]   The linguistic bases for analyzing certain terms as complex are of two types: (1) the existence of analytical expressions which are regarded as synonymous (readily substitutable without appreciable change of meaning), in which the different elements are each represented by separate lexical items, *e.g.*, *player* (one who plays), *doctrine* (that which is taught or believed), and (2) the manner in which the complex terms function within the total grammatical structure. For example, *heir* is morphologically simple, but it functions in relationship to a "goal" in the same way as does a morphologically complex term such as *owner*. Compare, for example, *heir to the property* and *owner of the property*. In the latter case *property* may be described as the goal of the event of *owning*. Similarly, in *heir to the property*, the property is likewise the goal of the implied event of inheriting.

1. O-E (the object element performs the event): *disciple* (one who learns), *player* (one who plays), *heir* (one who will inherit), *sinner* (one who sins).
2. E-O (the object element is the goal of the event): *gift* (that which is given), *apostle* (one who is sent), *doctrine* (that which is taught or believed).
3. E-A (the abstract qualifies the implied goal of the event): *sanctify* (to make holy), *justify* (declare innocent).
4. O-E-A (the object element performs an event to an implicit goal which acquires a particular quality): *sanctifier, justifier.*
5. E-R (an event with an implied relationship): *mediate, reconcile* (to act as an agent between others).[13]

It is also important to recognize that so-called event words may represent either simple events or complex ones. For example, in the phrase "I am the resurrection and the life," both *resurrection* and *life* are events, but these do not refer to intransitive actions, such as "rising" and "living," as one might at first presume, but rather to causative transitive events, *i.e.,* "to cause to rise" and "to cause to live." Hence, this sentence actually means "I am the one who causes people to rise from the dead and who causes people to live."

Problem 10

What are the components (O, E, A, R) in the terms *governor, decree* (Luke 2:1), *shepherd, brother, apostle, purify, mediator, teacher, reconciliation, forgiveness*?

THE RELATIONSHIP OF SURFACE STRUCTURE TO KERNELS

As has been indicated above, one of the most effective ways to determine the underlying relationships between elements in a phrase is to go beneath the surface structure, by the process of back-transformation, and to determine what is the kernel from which the surface structure is derived. This provides the clearest and most unambiguous expression of the relationship. But to do this successfully, it is important to bear in mind constantly the types of kernels to which such structures may be related. Compare, for example, (1) some of the phrases with "of" analyzed in a previous section with (2) the list of basic kernels:

Phrases with *of*	Kernels in English
1. "the will of God" God wills (K. 1)	1. John ran (quickly)
2. "the foundation of the world" (God) creates the world (K. 2)	2. John hit Bill
3. "the Holy Spirit of promise" (God) promised the Holy Spirit (K. 2)	3. John gave Bill a ball

[13] One can, of course, also have terms such as *mediator* and *reconciler*, which would be O-E-R.

or (God) promised (the people) the
   Holy Spirit (K. 3)
4. "the word of truth"   4. John is in the house
   the word is true (K. 5)
5. "the riches of his grace"   5. John is sick
   he shows grace richly (K. 1)
6. "Jesus of Nazareth"   6. John is a boy
   Jesus comes from Nazareth (K. 4) [14]
7. "the lake of Galilee"   7. John is my father
   the lake is in Galilee (K. 4)
8. "the land of Judea"
   the land is Judea (K. 7)
9. "One of the soldiers" [15]
   he was/is a soldier (K. 6)

Relationship of Elements in So-Called Possessive Constructions

The so-called possessive construction provides even more striking contrasts in the relationship between the elements of the construction. Compare, for example, the phrases in the following set (from KJV):

    O   E
1. his   sins (Heb. 7:27): he sins: A does B
    O   E
2. his   destruction (Prov. 18:7): X [16] destroys him: X does B to A
    O   E
3. his   calling (Eph. 1:18): he (God) calls (him): A does B to X
    O   A
4. his   glory (Matt. 6:29): he is glorious: A is B
    O (E) O
5. thy   way (Mark 1:2): thou (goest on) the way: A goes on B
    O (E) O
6. my   burden (Matt. 11:30): I (provide) a burden: A provides B
    O (E) O
7. my   God (John 20:28): I (worship) God: A worships B
    O (E) O
8. his   father (Matt. 2:22): he (possesses) a father, and the father
             (possesses) him (as a son): A and B are lineally
             related in contiguous generations
    O (R) O
9. his   arm (Luke 1:51): he (has) an arm: B is a part of A
    O (E) O
10. his   house (Matt. 9:7): he (owns) a house: A owns B

---

[14] "Comes from" is the idiomatic equivalent of "is from" rather than designating a directional movement such as is usually expressed by *come*.

[15] It is an interesting fact that almost the only "of" expressions based on kernel 6 are those beginning in either *one of* or *some of*, which underlines the member-of-a-class and the part-of-the-whole nature of this type of kernel, noted on p. 40.

[16] The symbol X specifies an agent which is implied, but not explicitly named, in the context.

It should be noted that in this series there is little or no difficulty involved as long as an object is related to an event or an abstract, for these relationships are clearly indicated in the corresponding kernels. There are problems, however, with two objects, for they may be related in so many different ways. That is to say, objects may be related to one another by so many different events and in so many different manners. In *thy way* (5) it is obvious that B is the way on which A is to travel, but this may be actually *walk, pass, go, come, travel, journey*, etc. Similarly, in *my burden* (6) A may be said to provide B, but it may be *placed on, given to, bound on, given to carry*, etc. In the phrase *my God* (7) the problem becomes even more complex, for this is not a possessive relationship since A does not possess B. Rather, it is A which worships B or is *loyal to, believes in, follows, commits himself to*, etc.

There is little or no problem in *his house* (10), for this is the one clear case of "possession," or "ownership," but in *his father* (8) there is a reciprocity of relationship which cannot be analyzed as mere possession in the sense of *his house*. In fact, in many languages, kinship-possession is expressed quite differently from thing-possession. Similarly, *his arm* (9), though normally considered as a kind of possession, is actually a relationship of a part to the whole: B is a part of A. In many languages this kind of possession is obligatory, in the same way that kinship possession may be obligatory, and is very different from the possession of material objects.

Some of the problems of determining relationships between elements in phrases derive from the unexpected significance of one of the elements. As noted above, *the grace of God* tends to be understood by some people as the gracious character of God rather than what he does for men; that is, these people analyze *grace* as an abstract rather than as an event. Similarly, the expression *the kingdom of God* is often misunderstood. Because *kingdom* is a noun, people assume it must refer to an object, that is, a place. As a matter of fact, its primary reference is to the rule of God, that is, an event. The problem becomes acute in the phrase *the kingdom of heaven*, in which *heaven* (usually considered a kind of place term) is used as a substitute for *God* (a result of the Jewish taboo on the term for God). The tendency is strong but erroneous to interpret this phrase as meaning "the kingdom which is in heaven." Languages display various patterns for such shifts in category membership and substitutions of one term for another. Closely related are all the problems of what is called figurative meaning, which will be discussed in detail in the next chapter (p. 87-89).

Also related to these difficulties are problems resulting from those specialized expressions which we call idioms. Idioms are typically constructed on quite normal grammatical patterns of phrase structure, but the meaning of the whole idiom is not simply the sum of the meanings of the parts, nor can one segment the meaning (in the many cases where it is complex) and assign a definable portion of the meaning to each grammatical piece (*e.g.*, a morpheme). In other words, idioms are expressions in which the semantic and grammatical structures are radically different. Hence it is idle to attempt to determine the "meaningful relation of the parts" as discussed in this chapter; one must treat the entire expression as a semantic unit, even though in the surface structure of the grammar it obeys all of the rules applicable to the individual pieces. A more extensive discussion of idioms and related expressions will be found in the next chapter (p. 89).

Problem II

Analyze the actual meaning of the possessive expressions from Luke 2 (RSV): *his city* (vs. 3), *Mary, his betrothed* (vs. 5), *her first-born son* (vs. 7), *their flock* (vs. 8), *her heart* (vs. 19), *their purification* (vs. 22), *thy servant* (vs. 29), *thy word* (vs. 29), *thy salvation* (vs. 30), *thy people* (vs. 32); for each expression determine what is the underlying kernel.

Problem 12

Determine the semantic classification of the following expressions from the RSV: *world* (Luke 2:1), *authorities* (Rom. 13:1), *glory* (Rom. 15:7), *tongues* (1 Cor. 13:1), *knowledge* (1 Cor. 13:8), *commandments* (1 John 5:2).

Problem 13

Rewrite the following "possessive" constructions from Matthew (RSV) as kernels so as to show the relationship between the parts:

his household (10:36)   my yoke (11:29)
a prophet's reward (10:41)   his life (10:39)
his disciples (11:2)   kings' houses (11:8)
their playmates (11:16)   his mighty works (11:20)
thy gracious will (11:26)

DETERMINING THE STRUCTURAL ROLE OF ELEMENTS BY MEANS OF THE CONTEXT

Determining the function of the elements in a phrase, and hence their relationship to the other elements, can only be done by a careful examination of the context. This involves not merely the immediate context but also the wider context of the entire communication. In the case of *dominion of darkness* (Col. 1:13), we might think of this phrase as consisting of an object followed by an abstract, but in parallelism with *kingdom of his beloved Son*, it is evident that *dominion* is also an event (the rule), and *darkness* is a title for Satan, *i.e.*, the one who is dark.

A phrase such as *weapons of righteousness* (2 Cor. 6:7) may be particularly difficult, unless one carefully examines the context and the parallels which occur in Ephesians 6. It is then quite clear that *righteousness* is the weapon the Christian possesses. In Ephesians 2:20 *the foundation of the apostles and the prophets* can be interpreted as the foundation which is the apostles and the prophets, or better, the foundation which is laid by the apostles and the prophets.

The phrases *the gospel of God* (Rom. 1:1) and *the gospel of Christ* (2 Cor. 10:14) are also subject to easy misinterpretation, and only by a comparison of the total contexts in which the *gospel* and the *proclamation* are discussed can one fully understand the ways in which the two phrases are to be understood. *The gospel of God* should undoubtedly be interpreted as "the good news which comes from God," but *the gospel of Christ* is "the good news about Christ." God is the source of the gospel, but Jesus Christ is the substance or the message of the Good News.

BACK-TRANSFORMATION AS A TYPE OF PARAPHRASE

Back-transformation of a surface structure to the underlying kernels may be regarded as a form of paraphrase, and it is pertinent to ask in what respects this kind of paraphrase differs from certain other kinds. The word "paraphrase" has sometimes been used to mean a quite loose and inaccurate translation, in which the translator has injected uncontrolled subjective judgments and thus biased the result. "Paraphrase," as we are using it at this point in referring to back-transformation, is a technical term from linguistics and related disciplines, and is characterized by three specific features: (1) it is intralingual rather than interlingual, *i.e.*, it is "another way of saying the same thing" in the *same* language; (2) it is rigorous, in that there are no changes in the semantic components: no additions, no deletions, no skewing of relationships, only a different marking of the same relations between the same elements; (3) specifically as it relates to back-transformation, it is aimed at restatement at a particular level, that of the kernels.

Of course, one may paraphrase without regard to the underlying kernels. For example, J. B. Phillips' translation of the New Testament admits a great deal of paraphrase, but it is on a very "high level" of surface structure and is interlingual. Mr. Kenneth Taylor, who has translated *Living Letters*, published by Tyndale House, has used extensive paraphrase, but without significant shifts in the direction of the kernel structures. What makes *Today's English Version*, published by the American Bible Society, so popular and so helpful to translators is that it is frequently restructured in the direction of kernel expressions, and is thus more readily understandable and provides a useful basis for transfer to other languages.

It must be emphasized, however, in anticipation of a fuller discussion in Chapter 6, that the kernel expressions themselves are not to be translated literally. Such back-transformations are not to be used as a model for translation, nor are they to be carried over wholesale into any translation into a receptor language. They are only the basis for transfer into the receptor language, since they provide not only the clearest and least ambiguous statements of the relationships but also constitute forms which correspond most closely with those expressions likely to occur in receptor languages.

In this process of back-transformation it would be very easy for the translator to lose sight of the subtle stylistic features of the source-language text were it not that in the analysis of the connotative meanings of words and combinations of words, he returns to study those formal features of the source-language text which are so essential to the communication of its message. It is at this point that one picks up any important elements in the style which may have been overlooked in the processes of back-transformation.

DIFFERENT CONSTRUCTIONS MAY EXPRESS THE SAME MEANINGFUL RELATIONSHIP BETWEEN THE PARTS

Whereas in the previous sections we have dealt with the fact that the same constructions, when viewed as surface structure, have involved quite different relationships between the constituent parts, in this section it is necessary to recognize the converse of this situation and to deal with different surface structures which go back to essentially the same kernels. We are, in other words, developing the notion of back-transformation, and hence of transformation (since these are simply the same mechanism applied in opposite directions), as a kind of paraphrase. This is the formal and rigorous way of explaining what is meant when we say that "every language has different ways of saying the same thing."

In the following series of expressions the relationship between the parts is the same:

1. She sings beautifully.
2. the beauty of her singing
3. Her singing is beautiful.
4. her beautiful singing

In each instance the object element is expressed by *she* or *her*. The event element is *sings* or *singing*, and the abstract element is *beautifully, beauty,* or *beautiful.* Both *of* and *is* serve as relationals.[17]

The basic kernel of this series is *She sings beautifully,* and the other three expressions are simply transforms. But if, as is true, the relationship between the constituent parts is basically the same in each of these four expressions, the essential question is then: What are the reasons for the obvious differences of meaning? In the first place, expressions 1 and 3 differ from 2 and 4 in that the former are complete utterances and the latter are merely topics (subjects), to which must be added something to make them complete. But there is another equally significant aspect, namely, the differences in the focus of attention. In the expression *She sings beautifully,* the focus is upon the object (*she*), while in *Her singing is beautiful,* the focus shifts to the *singing.* On the other hand, in phrase 2, the focus is upon the *beauty,* even though the construction is still only a topic, and thus incomplete, but in phrase 4 the focus has shifted to the *singing.*

This recognition of the fact that in English as well as in all languages the same kernel can give rise to a number of different surface structure expressions with different features of focus is essential if we are to handle

---

[17] The definite article *the* may be considered as a type of abstract, but it is often simpler and more relevant to regard it as a kind of "grammatical word," in the same way that auxiliaries are regarded as a part of the following verb with which they are related.

source materials properly in a receptor language. For example, the phrases *the glory of God* and *the God of glory* express essentially the same relationships between the constituent parts, but there are obvious differences in meaning. This is because of the focus. In *the glory of God* the focus is on *glory*, but in *the God of glory* the focus is upon *God*. The same relationships exist in the phrases *the God of peace* and *the peace of God*.

The variety of transforms from a single kernel may be rather numerous, as in the following series, all derived from *Jesus rebuked Peter* (the basic kernel):

1. Jesus rebuked Peter.
2. Peter was rebuked by Jesus.
3. Jesus' rebuking of Peter
4. Peter's being rebuked by Jesus
5. the rebuke of Peter by Jesus
6. Peter's rebuke by Jesus
7. the rebuking of Peter by Jesus
8. It was Jesus who rebuked Peter.
9. It was Peter who was rebuked by Jesus.

Such a series of transforms, all of which go back to the same kernel, only illustrate what has already been said, that one can say the same thing in many ways. The fact that this is possible provides the structural basis for diversities in style, and it is the sensitivity with which one deals with such issues that determines in large measure the effectiveness with which one is able, in the last step of translation, to restructure materials in a receptor language in such a way as to provide the closest natural equivalent in style.

Problem 14

For each of the following expressions from Philippians, (1) determine what is the underlying kernel, (2) see how many other transforms you can derive from each kernel, and (3) explain the nature of the difference between the various transforms:

1. my remembrance of you (1:3)
2. my imprisonment (1:14)
3. my eager expectation (1:20)
4. if there is any encouragement in Christ (2:1)
5. in the beginning of the gospel (4:15)

GRAMMATICAL TRANSFORMATIONS FROM KERNELS

In order to handle most of the problems of back-transformation in the processes of analysis, it is not necessary to deal with all the technical problems treated in transformational grammars or to employ the numerous detailed procedures with rigorous precision (though one must not be any less precise in the handling of the structural relationships). But it is important to have a general idea of some of the more common types of forward-transformations in order to appreciate the implications of the system and the ways in which it can be applied to the problems of relationships between words.

Forward-transformations are essentially of two types: (1) those involving the restructuring of single kernels and (2) those involving the combining of two or more kernels. In English the restructuring of single kernels is of three principal kinds: (a) active to passive, e.g., *John hit Bill* to *Bill was hit by John*, (b) positive to negative, e.g., *John hit Bill* to *John did not hit Bill*, and (c) statement to question, e.g., *John hit Bill* to *Did John hit Bill?* At the same time, of course, both active and passive constructions can be negativized, and both active-passive and positive-negative contrasts can be changed from statements into questions.

The process of combining two or more kernels results in two kinds of surface structure expressions: (1) those in which all the essential components of both kernels remain explicitly and overtly expressed and (2) those in which some of the elements of at least one of the kernels are left implicit or covert. In English, there are three types of combinations which retain in the surface structure all of the elements of the kernels: (a) those in which the relation between the two kernels is marked by a conjunction, e.g., *Because they were angry, we left*; *These people slept while the others watched*; *He said that we should go*; (b) those in which the relation of one kernel to a part of another is marked by a relative pronoun, e.g., *The man whom we hired is lazy* and *We found the boat which had sunk*; and (c) those in which one of the kernels has been transformed into a "dependent" form without a connective marker, e.g., *We saw him go* (from *we saw him* and *he went*) and *His leaving irked everyone* (from *he left* and *(this) irked everyone*).

In many instances, on the other hand, one or more of the kernels may undergo the loss of one or more of its parts when two kernels are combined into a complex structure. For example, the sentence *Having left, he never returned* is derived from the kernels *he left* and *he never returned*; and *He came back after wasting a fortune* is derived from the kernels *he came back* and *he wasted a fortune*; similarly, in the sentence *Though sick he carried on* we find the kernels *he was sick* and *he carried on*. In this type of combination, however, the "loss" is actually only apparent, since all that happens is that both kernels share the same subject component which need not be expressed twice in the resulting surface structure: one overt expression suffices for both kernels, and it is quite easy to state a rule for such sentences which permits the unambiguous recovery of the "lost" element. This is why we can say that the loss is only apparent. But it is not only a single subject element which may be so "lost." In a sentence such as *Peter is bigger than John* we find two kernels, *Peter is bigger* and *John is big*, and in the combination it is the entire predicate of the subordinate clause that is dropped because it is identical with that of the principal clause. In *He liked the song, and so did she* we combine two kernels with identical predicates, *liked the song*, and all that remains of this in the second clause is the pro-form *did*.

Though these arrangements of kernels are by no means the only types of transformations, they provide at least some of the more important clues as to the ways in which kernels combine in series to constitute the complex surface structures.

THE ANALYSIS OF SERIES OF KERNELS

The analysis of the grammatical relationships between words cannot be restricted to simple combinations of words in single constructions, for the most important problems arise when series of kernels are combined into semantically heavy expressions. In Mark 1:4 there is an apparently simple expression, which nevertheless illustrates a number of the basic problems.

In analyzing the relationships between words in the sentence *John . . .* [*preached*] *a baptism of repentance for the forgiveness of sins* (Mark 1:4, RSV), there are five basic steps in procedure: (1) identifying the basic structural element(s) of each word, *i.e.*, object, event, abstract, and relational, (2) making explicit any implicit structural elements which are required to complete the kernels, (3) determining the basic kernels which combine to constitute the surface structure of the sentence, (4) grouping the kernels into related sets, and (5) stating these relationships in a form which will be optimal for transfer into the receptor language.

The basic structural element of each word may be indicated as follows (step 1):

O   E   E   R   E   R   E   R E
John . . . [preached] a baptism of repentance for the forgiveness of sins.

There are, however, two implicit elements which should be made explicit in order to complete the analysis (step 2), namely, (1) *people*, which serves as the goal of *baptism*, the subject of *repentance*, one of the goals of *forgiveness*, and the subject of *sin*, and (2) *God*, which is the subject of *forgiveness*.

The basic kernels which make up this sentence (step 3) are:

1. John preached X (in which X stands for the entire indirect discourse).
2. John baptizes the people.
3. The people repent.
4. God forgives X.
5. The people sin.

In determining the relationship between the kernels (step 4), it is essential to examine not only the explicit markers such as *unto* and *of*, but also the positional relationships. If we do this, we find the following sets of relationships:

1. The goal of *preached* is kernels 2-5. (In many languages it is, therefore, appropriate to put this into the form of direct discourse, introduced by the verb "to preach.")
2. Kernel 3 precedes kernel 2 in time, as two related events combined

by *and*. This set of kernels is equivalent to the expression "repent and be baptized." (Compare *obedience of faith* back-transformed into "believe and obey.")

3. Kernel 5 is the goal of the verb of kernel 4.
4. Kernel 4 (with its goal, kernel 5) is the purpose of kernels 3 and 2. That is to say, *the forgiveness of sins* is not related merely to *repentance* but to the combined expression "repent and be baptized."[18]

The manner in which we formulate a "near-kernel" statement of these elements and relationships (step 5) depends in very large measure on the way in which we know that a particular expression can be effectively transferred into the receptor language. For example, we may know that some languages prefer direct discourse, in which case, a readily transferable statement might be: "John preached, 'Repent and be baptized, so that God will forgive the evil you have done'." Such a restatement, of course, presumes that a passive may be used for *baptize*. If, however, the language has no such passive formation, it may be necessary to employ "I will baptize you," or "You will receive baptism" (if there is such a verb-noun substitute for the passive expression). If the receptor language requires an indirect form of discourse, one could use "John preached that the people should repent and be baptized in order that God would forgive their sins" (or "the evil they had done").

The particular form which the translation will take in the receptor language will, of course, be greatly modified in the processes of restructuring, so as to conform to the stylistic requirements for the various language levels.

The same five steps in procedure, namely, (1) identification of the object, event, abstract, and relational role of each term, (2) explicit mention of the implied elements, (3) statement of the kernels, (4) determining the relationships between kernels, and (5) restatement on a near-kernel level, may also be applied to a more complex passage, such as Ephesians 1:7 (KJV):

Step 1

R   O   O   E   R   O   O-E   E   R
"in whom we have redemption through his blood, the forgiveness of

E   R   A   R   O   E
sins, according to the riches of his grace"

Step 2

Implicit items which need to be added: *God* (as the subject of *redemption* and *forgiveness*) and *we* (as the subject of *sins*).

Step 3

The basic kernels consist of:

---

[18] *Forgiveness* actually has the entire kernel 5 as the goal, for God forgives the sins of the people.

1. God redeems us.
2. Christ dies (sheds his blood). [19]
3. God forgives.
4. We sin.
5. God shows grace richly.

Step 4
1. Kernel 2 is the means of the event of kernel 1, but it may also be associated with the event in kernel 3 (*cf.* the NEB).
2. Kernel 3 is supplementary to kernel 2, or possibly, even in apposition to it.
3. Kernel 4 is the goal of the event in kernel 3.
4. Kernels 3 and 4 may be regarded in apposition to kernel 1, but it is more likely that this is an amplification rather than an apposition. Hence it is frequently connected with the preceding by *and* (cf. NEB and TEV).
5. Kernel 5 states the basis for kernel 1 and its amplification in kernel 3.

Step 5
The near-kernel statement of Ephesians 1:7 may be given as follows:

"God redeemed us through Christ's shedding of his blood, and God forgave our sins. All this indicates how richly God showed his grace."

The problems of analysis and back-transformation become even more acute in a passage such as Ephesians 2:8 (KJV), in which the system of reference is complex and the need for supplying implicit participants is much greater than in many contexts:

Step 1
　　R　R　E　　　O　E　　R　　E　　R　(E)　A　R　　　O
"For by grace are ye saved through faith; and that not of yourselves:
(E) R　　　E　R　O　　A　R　E　R-A　A　　O　　　　E
it is the gift of God: not of works, lest any man should boast."

Certain features in this marking of basic structural elements should be noted:

1. Expressions such as *are . . . saved* and *should boast* are considered to be units, and are identified merely by E.
2. The symbol (E) indicates that the term in question refers to an event indirectly. The words *that* and *it* are pronominal references to an event identified by another word.
3. The word *not* can be considered a part of the negative transform and designated by T. However, it may equally well be classified as an abstract.

---

[19]　*Blood* is literally an "object word," but it refers here not to an object, but to an entire event, with which the object *blood* is associated. That is to say, though it is literally an object, it really refers to an event.

Step 2

Several implicit elements should be added: *God* (as subject of *grace* and *saved*), *you* (as subject of *faith*), *saved* (as predicate with *yourselves* as subject), *you* (as goal of *gift* and as subject of *works*).

Step 3

The kernels of Ephesians 2:8 are:

1. God showed grace.
2. God saved you.
3. You believed.
4. You did not save yourselves.
5. God gave it.
6. You did not work for it.
7. No man should boast.

Step 4

1. Kernel 1 is the means of the event in kernel 2.
2. Kernel 3 expresses an attendant circumstance or instrumentality of the event in kernel 2.
3. Kernel 4 stands in contrast with kernel 2.
4. Kernel 5 is in contrast with kernel 4, and is a confirmation and reemphasis of kernel 2.
5. Kernel 6 is a further amplification of kernel 4.
6. Kernel 7 states the result of this entire process.

Step 5

"God showed his grace to you, and in this way he saved you through your trusting in him. You yourselves did not save yourselves. Rather, God gave you this salvation. You did not earn it by what you did. Therefore no one can boast about what he has done."

In many ways it is instructive to compare the translation of Ephesians 2:8 in the New English Bible, for as will be noted immediately, the important advantages of this translation over the KJV consist in the extent to which some of the implicit elements, especially certain participants, have been supplied:

"For it is by his grace you are saved through trusting him. It is not your own doing. It is God's gift, not a reward for work done. There is nothing for anyone to boast of."

Several features of this NEB translation should be noted:

1. By adding *his* before *grace* the implied subject of this event is made clear.
2. *Trusting him* clarifies the meaning of "faith," not only in terms of a more meaningful term (*i.e.*, *trusting* in contrast with *faith*) but also by the addition of *him* as the goal of the *trusting*.

3. *Your own doing* supplies the components of the kernel, which are not fully represented in *not of yourselves* (KJV).
4. The phrase *gift of God* (KJV) can be misleading, since it could be interpreted as objective, but by reversing the order and changing the construction, God is clearly implied as the subject of the event.
5. *A reward* has been added in order to highlight the contrast between *gift* and *work done*, for it is *reward* which stands in direct contrast with *gift*.
6. *Work done* indicates the feature of event more clearly, than merely *works*, which has such a different value in present-day English, *e.g., steelworks, gasworks*, and *works of art*.
7. The avoidance of the obsolescent term *lest* makes the translation somewhat more contemporary and also makes the kernel structure more evident.

Problem 15

Analyze the following passage in terms of the 5 steps of procedure:

1 Peter 1:3b-4 (RSV): "By his great mercy we have been born anew to a living hope through the resurrection of Jesus Christ from the dead, and to an inheritance which is imperishable, undefiled, and unfading, kept in heaven for you. . . ."

1. Identify the basic structural element of each word: O, E, A, or R.
2. Identify any implied structural elements.
3. List the basic kernels of this passage.
4. Group the kernels into meaningful sets, showing the relationship between the kernels.
5. Restate the passage in such a form as will lead to the best and easiest transfer.

You may use the following translations as a basis for comparison:

NEB: "who in his mercy gave us new birth into a living hope by the resurrection of Jesus Christ from the dead! The inheritance to which we are born is one that nothing can destroy or spoil or wither. It is kept for you in heaven. . . ."

TEV: "Because of his great mercy, he gave us new life by raising Jesus Christ from the dead. This fills us with a living hope, and so we look forward to possess the rich blessings that God keeps for his people. He keeps them for you in heaven, where they cannot decay or spoil or fade away."

Problem 16

For further practice in the analysis of passages involving relatively complex combinations of kernels, employ the five steps of procedure for the following passages: Luke 2:1-5, Luke 1:1-4, Matthew 5:1-7, Matthew 7:1-2, Romans 1:1-7, Hebrews 1:1-4. In each of these passages the types of difficulties encountered are quite different.

CHAPTER FOUR

REFERENTIAL MEANING

Having analyzed the meaningful relationships between words, we must now study the meanings of the words or linguistic units themselves. Such a study must be divided into two parts: (1) the words as symbols which refer to objects, events, abstracts, relations (the referential meaning), and (2) the words as prompters of reactions of the participants in communication (the connotative meaning), treated in Chapter 5.

THE MARKING OF MEANING

In view of the fact that people are expected to speak about a staggering variety of experiences with only a limited number of words or semantic units (perhaps 25,000 to 50,000 for the average person), it would seem that language would be incredibly ambiguous and obscure. Nevertheless, people do succeed quite well in using this very limited inventory of words to identify, describe, and talk about literally millions of elements in their world, as well as many concepts, ideas, and beliefs which seem to bear no resemblance to anything earthly. The mechanism by which this is accomplished is one of the really remarkable features of language.

In most studies of semantics, or the science of meaning, the emphasis is upon the relative ambivalence of terms, *i.e.*, their capacity to have many different meanings. For example, words such as *red*, *chair*, and *man* are discussed in terms of the great variety of possibilities. While this is undoubtedly quite true, the real point of all this is that in the actual usage of language there is no such prevailing ambivalence. In fact, in most instances the surrounding context points out quite clearly which of these basic meanings of a word is intended. And it is perhaps from this standpoint that we can best understand the true nature of the semantic structure of language.

But when we speak about the contextual specification of the meanings of words, we are not talking in vague, nebulous terms. Rather, the linguistic context in the sense in which it is referred to here has two very definite aspects: (1) In many cases, the particular meaning of a word that is intended is clearly specified by the grammatical constructions in which it occurs; this is what we will refer to as *syntactic* marking. (2) In other cases, the specific meaning of a word which is intended is marked by the interaction of that term with the meanings of other terms in its environment. That is, the fact that term A is found in the context of term B means that only sense *x* of term A will fit. This conditioning by the meanings of surrounding terms we will call *semotactic* marking. In each case, we will describe something of the kind of classes and categories which are involved. And, as we shall see, in a great many cases both syntactic and semotactic marking are involved in a single expression.

Marking of Meaning by the Syntax

In many instances the meaning of terms is clearly indicated by the syntactic constructions in which they occur. Compare, for example, the following sets:

A	B
1. He picked up a *stone*.	1. They will *stone* him.
2. He saw a *cloud*.	2. The quarrel will *cloud* the issue.
3. She has a beautiful *face*.	3. He will *face* the audience.
4. He fell in the *water*.	4. Please *water* the garden.

The distinct meanings of the terms *stone, cloud, face,* and *water* are very clearly marked by the occurrence of these terms in quite different constructions, *i.e.,* as nouns in contrast with verbs. In this sense the grammar itself points to the correct intended meaning.

In some instances, however, the syntactic marking is not simply a distinction in word classes. For example, the term *fox* may occur in the following contexts, with three quite different meanings:

1. It is a fox.
2. He is a fox.
3. She will fox him.

In the first sentence, the presence of *it* identifies *fox* as an animal, because that is the only sense of *fox* for which *it* is a legitimate substitute; *fox* in this sense belongs to the same grammatical class as *animal, what the hunters are chasing, that mammal,* etc. In the second sentence, the presence of *he* forces us to take a sense of *fox* that applies to a person, since *he* in this construction, as an anaphoric substitute for a "male human," [1] is a legitimate substitute only for a class of terms, including *the man, the young fellow, that politician,* etc., which identify male persons; and the only sense of *fox* that applies to a person is "cunning person." In the third sentence, *fox* is a verb, as can be seen from its position between the auxiliary *will* and the object pronoun *him*; the verbal sense of *fox* is "deceive by clever means."

Another frequently occurring grammatical marker of meaning is the intransitive-transitive contrast: *he ran* vs. *she ran him*. Certainly *run* as an intransitive verb has quite different meanings from those situations in which it occurs as transitive (this will become even clearer in the discussion of this verb in a following section).

As can be seen from the above examples, the syntactic classes which help in the selection of specific meanings of words are determined by grammatical functions. These syntactic classes, such as verb, noun, and adjective, animate or inanimate, transitive or intransitive, etc., are generally large, comprehensive, and clearly contrastive; they are often formally marked, as, for example, by the presence of certain endings, typical of such a grammatical class of words.

---

[1] In a discourse *he* would only be used as an anaphoric substitute for a contextually identified referent.

Problem 17

In Matthew 5 (RSV), show how the syntactic marking determines the meaning of *meek* (vs. 5), *evil* (vs. 11), *stand* (vs. 15), *prophets* (vs. 17), *causes* (vs. 30).

MARKING OF MEANING BY SEMOTAXIS

In addition to the syntactic marking which has been described above, in many instances the semotactic environment of words is also essential to differentiate meanings. Here we are dealing not with functional grammatical classes but with categories of meanings which can be said to be compatible or incompatible, and which mutually select or eliminate each other. Here, because we are dealing with semantics, which is far more complex than grammar, the semotactic classes are very numerous, often quite small and even arbitrary, often overlap in multidimensional ways, and are seldom formally marked. A good number of them are highly specific. But, as we shall see, it is possible at least in part to describe the components of meaning that are involved in particular selections of meanings. As a matter of fact, quite often the syntactic and the semotactic markings interact to pinpoint specific meanings. But they remain in essence quite distinct.

This distinction between syntactic and semotactic functions will become more evident as special examples and problems are studied. Compare, for example, the following sentences:

1. He cut his *hand*.
2. He cut off a *hand* of bananas.
3. *Hand* me the book.

Sentence 3 is clearly distinguished from the other two by syntactic marking, in that *hand* is used as a verb (as seen from the presence of the indirect and direct object), whereas the other two are both nouns. What differentiates these two? In sentence 1, the presence of *his* makes it quite clear, in the absence of any contradictory features in the environment, that we should understand the commonest sense of *hand* as a part of the body at the end of the arm. However, *of bananas* quite specifically marks the area or domain in which *hand* is being used: it is the quite specific one relating to bananas, in which *hand* means "a number of bananas in a single or double row and still fastened to each other at the base."

Certain problems of semotactic marking may be illustrated by the use of *chair* in a number of different contexts.

1. He bought a *chair* at the furniture store.
2. He was condemned to the (electric) *chair*.
3. Please address the *chair*.
4. He will *chair* the meeting.
5. He was appointed to the *chair* of philosophy at the university.

In these sentences, one stands out from the rest by syntactic marking: in sentence 4, *chair* is a verb, as seen by the presence of subject and object, whereas all the rest are nouns. Of these, the commonest sense is understood in sentence 1, and would be even in the absence of the word *furniture*, since it is marked as a countable concrete object and nothing in the context *requires* a different sense. In sentence 2, the *chair* remains a concrete object, but the presence of *condemned* and (optionally) of *electric* forces us to a specialized understanding of *chair* as an instrument of execution.

In sentence 3, we are no longer dealing with an inanimate concrete object but rather with an object which can be *addressed*, that is, spoken to. The only sense of *chair* which fits, and which is especially appropriate with this particular verb of speaking, is "person who presides at a meeting." Incidentally, the verbal sense in sentence 4 is otherwise semantically related to sense 3. As for sentence 5, this special sense of "faculty position" can be understood only when there is in the immediate environment an expression such as *of philosophy*. Beyond that, the reference to the *university* is the only supplementary confirmation of this interpretation.

The importance of contextual conditioning may also be illustrated by certain meanings of the word *father*, for in this instance the range of syntactic and semotactic differentiations is somewhat different from the case of *chair*. Compare the following four meanings of *father*:

1. my father, the father of Tim Smith, the father of the girl
2. our Father in heaven, the heavenly Father
3. Father Murphy
4. father of the idea, father of the invention, father of his country

In meaning 1 we are dealing with the so-called literal meaning [2]; and in such instances there are always at least two persons specified or implied, and these stand in a biological and social relationship of contiguous generations and in direct descent.

With meaning 2 some term such as *heaven, divine,* or *everlasting* (to designate something supernatural), or the very context of the utterance (*e.g.*, in church), or the type of intonation (some persons have a special intonation for prayer) marks the meaning.

In meaning 3 there is a syntactic distinction, as well as a semotactic one. In the first place, *father* in such contexts is essentially a title and occurs in the same syntactic positions as a word such as *mister*. Moreover, *father* in meaning 3 would not be used except with a proper name or in direct address where the practical context completely defines the range of possibilities.

In meaning 4 there is always the specific meaning of the "goal" of the implied process of "fathering." Otherwise, this meaning is not understood.

The manner in which semotactic classes mark the meanings of words may be readily illustrated by the use of verb *run* in four sets of meanings:

1. The horse runs.   2. The water runs.
   The man runs.   The tap runs.
   The dog runs.   His nose runs.

[2] For a further discussion of literal and figurative meanings, see pp. 87.

3. The motor runs.   4. The vine runs over the door.
    The business runs.   The line runs abruptly up on this graph.

For these four meanings of *run* in these intransitive usages, we immediately sense that the specific meaning in each instance is determined by the
type of subject term. With meaning 1 the subject is an animate object,
and the meaning is the so-called literal meaning (*i.e.*, the central meaning).
With meaning 2 the subject is either a mass, *e.g.*, *water, oil, flour*, or *salt*,
or an object associated with a mass, *e.g.*, *tap, nose, spout*. With meaning 3
the subject element is a complex mechanism or organization with parts
which function in relationship to each other, and with meaning 4 the
object is a projection which has the capacity of extension, either naturally
(by growth) or artificially (by some outside agency). It is no good reason-
ing that these differences of meaning are merely "natural" and that any
language could and would do the same, since French, for example, simply
cannot say that a motor runs. Rather it walks: *Le moteur marche*. Similar
differences exist in the case of a number of different combinations which
seem so natural in English that we simply do not question them.

When *run* is used as a transitive verb, it is causative, with an interesting set of correspondences:

1. He ran the animal in the last race, *i.e.*, he caused the animal to
   run.
2. She ran the water into the tub, *i.e.*, the water did the running.
3. He ran his business well, *i.e.*, he caused the business to function
   efficiently.
4. He ran the vine over the trellis, *i.e.*, he caused the vine to grow
   over the trellis.

In some cases, the extreme complexity of the sets of semotactic classes
which interact to select the intended meanings can be conveniently sum-
marized by means of formulas, which may then serve to explain some of
the reduced but diagnostic features of contexts marking particular
meanings. The English verb *charge* illustrates a number of the problems
associated with such complex patterns [3]:

1. He charged the man ten cents for the pencil.
2. He charged the battery.
3. He charged them to do their duty.
4. He charged it to the man's account at the store.
5. He charged into the enemy.
6. He charged the man with murder.

The formulas for these meanings may be listed as follows:

[3] There are, of course, a number of nominal parallels, *e.g.*, *a charge for the
pencil, his charge account*, and *the charge against him*, but since these may be better
described as derivative from the verb expressions, it is preferable to analyze the
verb phrases first, and then describe the nominal adaptations.

Subject	Verb	First Goal	Second Goal	Predicate Phrases
1. person	*charge*	person	amount	*for* object or event
2. person or mechanism	,,	*battery, gun, hole,* etc.		*with* powder, dynamite, etc.
3. person	,,	person		socially approved deed (infinitive or *with* plus noun)
4. person	,,	purchasable object		*to* person
5. moving person or object	,,	thing or person		
6. person	,,	person		*with* (reprehensible deed)

In the first formula, the subject is always a person or a human institution, *e.g., The store charged him ten dollars for the service.* The first goal is a person (or human institution), followed in some instances by the amount (the second goal) and often by a prepositional phrase introduced by *for*, and followed by an object or event, *e.g., charged him three dollars for the string,* or *charged him five dollars for the ride.*

In the second formula the subject is a person or a limited type of mechanism, *e.g., This machine will charge your battery quickly,* but the first goal position is very restricted in the types of words which may occur, *e.g., battery, gun* (*they charged the gun*) or *hole* (*The miners charged the hole with dynamite*). The predicate phrase may be introduced by *with*, followed by a limited number of terms denoting power, *e.g., dynamite, electricity, gunpowder,* etc.

The third formula contains a person or human institution as subject and in the first-goal position also a person, usually followed either by an infinitive introduced by *to* or by an event noun introduced by *with*.

The fourth formula consists of a person (or human institution) as subject and in the first-goal position a purchasable object, frequently followed by a specification of the person involved, introduced by *to* followed either by a direct reference, *e.g., to the man,* or an indirect reference, *e.g., to the man's account.*

The fifth formula consists of some moving object such as a person (*e.g., The soldiers charged the enemy*), an animal (*The lion charged the hunter*), or a mechanism capable of "intentional movement" (*The tanks charged into the fortifications*). The first-goal position is occupied by either a person or a thing which is locationally relatable to the subject. That is to say, A (the subject) moves toward B (the goal).

The sixth formula means that the subject is a person or human institution, *e.g., The judge charged him with the crime,* or *The court charged him with murder,* and a person (or human institution) is in the first-goal position, usually with a second position occupied by *with* followed by an event word naming some reprehensible behavior. In this aspect, the sixth formula is entirely different from the third in that in the sixth meaning the event involved is socially disapproved while in the third meaning the event is a socially approved one, *e.g., The general charged him to carry out the task.*

An examination of these formulas indicates quite clearly that certain of these meanings are much more closely related than others. For example, meanings 1 and 4 are closely associated, in that they involve commercial transactions; meanings 3 and 6 are also closely related, for they involve the charging of a person with future responsibilities or with past reprehensible deeds. Meanings 2 and 5 might also be combined on the basis that they share at least a component of "power" or "energy."

These formulas do not need in every case to have every part explicitly identified in the surface structure. In some of them, one or more items is obligatory and the others optional. In other cases, any one of the items would be sufficient by itself to select the proper meaning. For example, the first meaning is fully identified if one says, *They charged a dollar*, or *They charged for the service*, in which only the second object and the predicate phrase positions are filled respectively. The second frame must have the first-goal position but can dispense with the predicate phrase. The third frame must specify not only the goal but also the event in which the goal is to participate. In frame 4 one can often eliminate the predicate phrase, *e.g., She charged the dress.* No reduction is possible in the fifth frame, and likewise in the sixth frame it is necessary to have both post-verb features.

Certain reductions are also possible in the passive transforms of these expressions, *e.g.,* frame 1 (*Fifty cents was charged for each ticket; He was charged one dollar*); frame 2 (*The battery was charged*); frame 3 (*He was charged with the task*); frame 4 (*The dress was charged*); frame 5: in general, no reduction in constituent elements is possible, since both agent and goal must be specified; and frame 6 (*The man was charged with the crime,* and *to be charged with a crime*).

There are a corresponding number of noun phrases employing substantive forms of *charge*: frame 1, *a charge for the admission, a charge of ten cents*; frame 2, *a charge of dynamite, put a charge in the hole*; frame 3, *a charge from the assembly, The minister received his charge from the synod, He has charge of it*; frame 4, *his charge account, a charge against his account*; frame 5, *the charge of the light brigade, a lightning charge against the embankment*; and frame 6, *the charge of murder, The court refused to review the charge, a serious charge against him.*

Problem 18

Show how the meanings of *head* are marked, syntactically or semotactically or both, in the following contexts: (1) The hat fit his head; (2) Here is the head of the parade; (3) He is the head of the firm; (4) I bought a head of cabbage; (5) He was at the head of his class; (6) I will head him off; (7) He will head the department.

Problem 19

Identify the syntactic and semotactic elements which help to identify the different meanings in the following series:

(a) *case*

(1) They had a case against him; (2) He bought a case of fruit; (3) The robbers always case a place ahead of time; (4) In case you come, be sure to let us know.

(b) *point*

(1) He never gets the point of the story; (2) They arrived at the point of land; (3) He will point it out; (4) Please sharpen the point of the pencil.

(c) *corner*

(1) He tried to corner the market; (2) It was a corner store; (3) They put him in a corner; (4) Never corner him, unless you are prepared to fight.

(d) *change*

(1) Please change this bill; (2) He wants to change his clothes; (3) He has some change in his pocket; (4) We will have a change of weather.

(e) *air*

(1) He pumped too much air into his tire; (2) He has a proud air about him; (3) The air is very stuffy here; (4) He played an air on the flute; (5) Please air the bedclothes.

Problem 20

In Matthew 5 (RSV) show how the proper meanings of the following words are marked semotactically: *bushel* (vs. 15), *works* (vs. 16), *prophets* (vs. 17), *court* (vs. 25), *members* (vs. 29).

Problem 21

In the language in which you are working, how many different meanings are there for the word you have selected to translate (in Matthew 5) *heaven* (vs. 3), *mourn* (vs. 4), *meek* (vs. 5), *merciful* (vs. 7), *pure* (vs. 8)? What are these meanings, and how will you specify the right meaning by context?

The Analysis of Related Meanings of Different Words

Though the analysis of related meanings of a single term is important, especially for the exegesis (interpretation) of a passage, the analysis of the meanings of words having related (or competing) meanings is even more important. Actually, the different meanings of a single word are rarely in competition, for they not only have relatively well-defined markers which help to differentiate the meanings, but so often they are so diverse as not to compete with one another for the same semantic domain. It is for this reason that one should focus attention primarily upon those specific meanings of different terms which tend to occupy the same semantic field and hence are likely to be regarded as closely synonymous or as competing.

This means, for example, that it is not so important for us to analyze all the different componential features of the meanings of *chair*, as it is to contrast one of the meanings of *chair* (meaning 1) with other words which occur in the same semantic field, *i.e.*, *stool*, *bench*, and *hassock* (a cushionlike seat, usually made of leather and stuffed with relatively firm material). It should be very clear, however, that in comparing *chair, stool, bench*, and *hassock*, we are only comparing "comparable meanings"; that is to say, we are not comparing all the meanings of *chair* with all the meanings of *stool, bench*, or *hassock*. We must select only those meanings which compete in the same semantic field, that is, *chair, stool, bench*, and *hassock* as manufactured articles to sit on, and not *chair* in the other meanings mentioned above, nor *stool* in the meaning of toilet bowl or feces, or *bench* in the meaning of position of judge (*He was elected to the bench*). It is precisely these basic components "manufactured object" and "for sitting" which are the common components of this set. There is, in fact, a single term which covers precisely this and no more: one of the meanings of the word *seat*.

If we contrast *chair, stool, bench*, and *hassock* in terms of their minimal contrasting features we obtain the following set of contrasts:

chair	*stool*	*bench*	*hassock*
a. with legs	a. with legs	a. with legs	a. without legs
b. with back	b. without back	b. with or without back	b. without back
c. for one person	c. for one person	c. for two or more persons	c. for one person

With these three sets of diagnostic components it is possible to contrast the essential elements of meaning in these competing terms. There are, however, other components not listed here. For example, there are the common components shared by all of these terms, namely, "manufactured article" and "used for sitting." But these common components do not distinguish between the words, though they may be important and hence diagnostic on another level of contrast; for example, in distinguishing a rough stone on which a person might sit from the central meanings of these four words (the stone is not manufactured) and also in distinguishing the meaning of a *dresser* from one of these meanings (the dresser is not made to be sat on).

There are also many supplementary components in each of these meanings. For example, *chairs* may be made in many shapes and sizes, with or without arms, with different number and arrangement of legs, plain or fancy, hard or overstuffed. Similarly stools occur in many different forms. Likewise, *chairs, stools*, and *hassocks* are normally movable, whereas benches may be movable or built in.

Certain further implications of the componential structures of terms in a related semantic area may be illustrated by the series *walk, skip, hop, crawl, run*, and *dance*. Again, however, these terms are to be analyzed only in terms of their specific, so-called central meanings involving physical movement by a living being, and more specifically by a person, for the sake of simplifying the description of some of the types of movement involved. We are not concerned, for example, with *skip* in *skipping class*; *hop* as a dance; *crawl* as *the car was crawling through traffic*; *run* in the sense of *running one's business*; and *dance* in the meaning of *belly dance*.

For the specific sense of each of these words which fits into the set, there must be at least one common component (which, incidentally, is shared by a good many other verbs): movement by an animate being. It is this component which places these meanings in a set and makes of the total semantic area a definable domain.

Next, there are in the meaning of each of these words a number of components which, either singly or collectively, are distinctive. These we may represent in the following columns:

1 *walk*	2 *skip*	3 *hop*
a. pedal b. 121212 c. one foot on ground at any time	a. pedal b. 11221122 c. not one foot on ground at any time	a. pedal b. 1111 or 2222 c. not one foot on ground at any time

4 *crawl*	5 *run*	6 *dance*
a. all four limbs b. 1-3 2-4 1-3 2-4 c. one foot and hand on ground at any time	a. pedal b. 121212 c. not one foot on ground at any time	a. pedal b. different patterns but rhythmically repeated c. one foot may or may not be on ground at any time

By means of these three sets of related components we are able to distinguish the essential features which contrast these six different meanings. We have not, however, described all the elements in any one of these terms. There are many different types of walking. Zulu, for example, has 120 different ideophones to characterize numerous varieties, *e.g.*, like a fat man, like a pregnant woman, sauntering, briskly, etc. The same is also true for the other terms.

The contrastive features may be said to include those particular components which are "necessary and sufficient" to define the differences between the respective meanings. By this is meant that if even one of the components is absent, the particular meaning could not exist: the components are necessary. Further, no other components are necessary to distinguish a particular meaning from others in its set: these components are sufficient. For example, in the case of triangle, rectangle, and square, the common components are (1) enclosed geometrical figures and (2) sides consisting of straight lines. The contrastive features are:

triangle	*rectangle*	*square*
a. three-sided	a. four-sided	a. four-sided
	b. corners of 90-degree [4] angles	b. corners of 90-degree angles
	c. length and width not the same	c. length of all four sides identical

The supplementary features would include a description of the great variety, both in shape and size, of triangles, rectangles, and squares.

Problem 22
1. Examine the following English words referring to various kinds of sexual misconduct, and analyze their related meanings componentially: *fornication, adultery, rape, homosexuality.*
2. Do the same with three or four terms covering the same domain (sexual misconduct) from the language with which you are working. See how the two analyses are similar and how they are different.

Problem 23
Examine the following English words, isolate any common component(s), and then analyze them componentially (remember to take only the one sense of each word which belongs to the domain): *swear, promise, vow.* Then do the same with the set *swear, curse, blaspheme.*

Such closely related words as *repentance, remorse,* and *conversion* provide a number of additional insights into the problems of describing related meanings of different words.

repentance	*remorse*	*conversion*
1. bad behavior	1. bad behavior	1. bad behavior
2. sorrow	2. sorrow	2. — — — — — —
3. change of behavior	3. — — — — — — —	3. change of behavior

These three terms share the common components of psychological experience and behavioral event. They also include a number of supplementary components which are important, but not contrastive. For example, *repentance* is often associated with penance in the thinking of many persons. It is also primarily "religious" in connotation. *Remorse* shares with *repentance* a component of sorrow for what one has done, but repentance indicates some change in the direction of proper behavior, while remorse has a dead end of sorrow, often of a highly egocentric, morbid nature.

The general component "bad behavior" is included here, not only

---

[4] The component of 90-degree angles presupposes a four sided-figure, but the "extra" component is listed because of the contrast with three-sided figured triangles.

because it stands in contrast with "bad condition," a component of *salvation*, to be considered below, but because in these terms the events involve a historical sequence of components, something which is not true of words such as *walk, run, dance,* etc. In all event-words involving a change of state or condition one must take into consideration such ordering of the components.

In most instances the various components of meaning have exactly the same rank, *e.g.*, the components of the word *walk*. Similarly, the word *father*, in contrast with *grandfather, mother,* and *uncle*, has the components of one prior generation, male, and direct descent, but no one of these features has any logical or temporal priority over the others. But in the case of the components of *repentance, remorse*, and *conversion*, there is a system of temporal priority, for as in *repentance*, there is first the bad behavior, then the sorrow for this, and finally the change of behavior.

It is rare that a language will be explicit about all the essential components. Rather, there is a tendency to focus upon one or another feature. In Greek the focus of *metanoeō* (traditionally translated "to repent") is "to change one's ways," rather than merely "to change the mind," for in English to change the mind is a relatively inconsequential event. In some languages, however, the equivalent term means "sorrow for sin," with the subsequent change implied. In some instances the equivalent expression is "to leave sin behind," with a focus upon components 1 and 3. In still other cases one encounters "to change in the heart," which not only concentrates primary attention upon the change of behavior, but by the use of "heart" implies a strong emotive element, thus suggesting the second component. Whatever expression is employed, it is essential that the principal component, namely, the change of behavior, is not overlooked, for this not only occurs in the final position of temporal priority, but it certainly is the principal component.

It may be argued that *repentance* should differ from *conversion* in more than the mere sorrow for sin, and of course this is true. Repentance may focus upon the negative aspect of turning away from sin, while at least one of the supplementary components of conversion is the positive aspect of turning toward a new and different form of behavior. At the same time, however, repentance may be said to imply the same, especially if one views this event in terms of the Greek expressions used, rather than the meanings which have been read into the corresponding English equivalents. To express this contrast some languages have used "to turn from sin" (for repentance) and "to turn to God" (for conversion). In other cases one finds "to put on a new heart" (for repentance, as a way of emphasizing the psychological factors involved) and "to put on a new life" (for conversion, to focus upon the new type of behavior).

Certain features of this series of three terms—*repentance, remorse,* and *conversion*—become even more evident when they are contrasted with *salvation*, which may be described in terms of the following components:

Salvation

1. a bad state   2. outside force or power   3. change of condition

In the term *salvation*, as used in the meaning analyzed here, the focus is not so much upon the bad behavior as the bad condition or state which has resulted from such behavior. The change of condition is, however, only the result of some outside force, for the Biblical view is that one cannot save himself but is only saved by God. At the same time, these components exist in a significant order of temporal priority.

Terms for salvation usually focus upon components 2 and 3, *e.g.*, "to rescue," "to restore," "to make complete again," for the action is always by some external force, and the resulting condition is a complete change from the previous one involving danger and/or incapacity or helplessness.

Hierarchical Relationships Between Meanings of Words

While many sets of words have neatly defined units in related semantic space, the meanings of some words stand in a relationship of inclusion in their semantic areas. For example, the series *walk, skip, hop, crawl, run*, and *dance*, are all included within the area of at least one meaning of *move*. Similarly, *march* and *stroll*, in their central meanings, are included within *walk*, for *march* and *stroll* all share the components of (1) pedal motion, (2) 121212 order of movement of the limbs, and (3) having at least one foot on the ground at any time. *March*, however, differs from *walk* in that *march* implies additionally some externally enforced rhythm, *e.g.*, *The soldiers marched to the tune played by the band* and *The deputies marched the man off to jail*. *Stroll* differs from *walk* in that it specifies slower activity, often accompanied by a shift of pace and even of direction. Of course, *march* cannot be said to be hierarchically subordinate to *walk* in all of its meanings, but in its central meaning it is.[5]

The hierarchical structures of popular taxonomies, *i.e.*, systems of classification used by people generally, are often quite extensive. For example, *animal, mammal, dog*, and *terrier* (as noted above, p. 20) form such a hierarchical structure, with *animal* being the most inclusive term and *terrier* the most restricted term. To say that such a series forms a hierarchical structure is to say that each successive term has all the components of the higher term plus certain other specific, diagnostic features. For example, *mammal* has all the components that *animal* has plus a more specific component, namely, breast-feeding. To this extent the mammals are thus different from salamanders and crocodiles. *Dog*, however, constitutes a still more restricted class, for though it has all the components of *mammal* (and hence also of *animal*), it has certain other features which put it in the class of *canines*, which contrast, for example, with the *felines* (cats) and the *equines* (horses). The term *terrier* also possesses all the dis-

---

[5] It is necessary to point out that many studies of the hierarchical semantic structures have failed precisely because the attempt has been made to structure all the meanings of a term under the meanings of another term. Semantic structure is entirely too complex to be handled in this way. For example, *animal* may have a number of different meanings: (1) *animal*, vs. vegetable and mineral, (2) *animal*, including all animate life (man, birds, fish, amphibians, etc.), and (3) *animal*, including living creatures, exclusive of man, birds, and fish. These three meanings exist in a type of hierarchical arrangement on quite separate levels.

tinctive features (or components) of *animal, mammal,* and *dog,* but in addition has certain other features which distinguish *terrier* from such other types of dogs as *hound, boxer, shepherd, collie,* and *poodle.* In other words, an included term (such as *terrier,* which is included in *dog*) has all of the components of the including term, plus some other or others; this is what is meant by "more specific." The fewer the components (*i.e.,* the fewer restrictions on the coverage of the term), the more general it is in its applicability. A term which is less restricted is therefore more *generic,* while a term which is subject to a great many restrictions has limited applicability and is therefore *specific.* We saw earlier that besides the terms *chair, stool, bench,* and so on, which were specific, there is a generic term which includes only the common component which they all share (*for sitting*) but not the distinctive components which make them contrastive; that term is *seat.* Generic terms, which cover many specific terms, give us an important clue to the existence of semantic *domains, i.e.,* broad categories of things which are conceptually related within the given culture. But it must be emphasized that the only domains relevant to the native speaker, and therefore relevant linguistically, are those which are actually present in the system of the language. We, as analysts of the language with a wider experience of various languages, tend to import into the language external categories, which we may call pseudodomains. (In linguistic terms, the pseudodomains which are imposed by our analysis may be called "etic" categories, while the ones which are found in the language are the "emic" domains.)

Three very important characteristics of such folk classifications must be constantly borne in mind: (1) Folk classifications are often relatively unsystematic, without the neat classifications employed by the specialists (compare, for example, the average English-speaker's classification of plants and animals with those the technically trained botanist or zoologist employs). (2) People may employ the distinctions consistently and meaningfully without understanding all of the componential features which serve to distinguish the different sets of referents. For example, most English-speaking people can name various kinds of dogs without being able to describe systematically what the distinguishing features are. (3) Because there is typically a good bit of redundancy between the various components (*i.e.,* because of the existence of additionally distinctive components to be discussed on p. 77), it is quite plausible that in any given instance different native speakers would emphasize in their own thinking different distinctive components. The important thing is not that all native speakers use the same components in an identical way, but that the resulting distinctions be substantially the same to avoid misunderstanding.

For the Bible translator it is very important to realize that the terminology in the Holy Scriptures is not primarily technical. That is to say, it is not the result of any systematic theological analysis. Therefore, it is most important that the translator not attempt to import into the translation of the Bible technical distinctions known only to systematic theologians or to those who have read into the Bible concepts which come from other systems of thought, *e.g.*, the imposition of Greek canons of thought upon the essentially Semitic viewpoint of the Bible. This approach is particularly important in the selection of terms for human personality and for the cosmological view of ancient times, as represented in the creation accounts. To restructure such statements to fit modern categories is to be guilty of gross insensitivity to the historical setting.

Problem 24

Arrange the following sets of terms in their taxonomic order, and then analyze them componentially in columns so as to show that the generic terms have fewer components and the more specific have more components. If two or more terms belong to the same taxonomic level, show this also.

1. whisper, speak, murmur
2. red, color, scarlet, pink, crimson
3. roast, cook, broil, boil, prepare
4. cat, kitten, animal, bobcat

CONTRAST IN SEMANTIC AREAS AND LEVELS

In dealing with the series *walk, skip, hop, crawl*, etc., it was seen that each word was essentially on the same level; that is, the words occupied related areas on the same semantic level, for above these words were such generic terms as *go* and *move*, and below were such words as *march* and *stroll*. This problem of contrast both in areas and between levels is widespread, and is well illustrated by various series of Biblical terms, *e.g.*, *prayer, meditation, communion*, and *worship*, which are analyzed below in terms of such contexts as "to pray to God," "to meditate on the Word of God," "communion with God," and "to worship God":

prayer	*meditation*	*communion*	*worship*
a. verbal	a. verbal	a. verbal or nonverbal	a. verbal or nonverbal
b. addressed to God	b. not addressed to God	b. addressed to God	b. addressed to God
c. one-way communication	c. internal communication	c. two-way communication	c. one-way communication
d. individual or collective	d. individual	d. individual or collective	d. individual or collective
e. generally a request or petition			

It is, to begin with, the component *religious relationship to God* which defines these terms as belonging to the same set and participating in the same domain.

As will be readily noted, *meditation* differs most radically from the other three terms in not being addressed to God (and accordingly not involving communication between persons), and in being individual, rather than possibly collective. *Communion* differs significantly from *worship* in being a two-way communication, but *prayer* in components (a) through (d) is essentially like *worship* (except for the possibility of worship also being nonverbal). This means that *prayer* differs from *worship* only in one additional component, namely, the feature of request or petition (involving unburdening of the individual's concerns). To this extent, then, it can be said that *prayer* is actually included within *worship*, *i.e.*, hierarchically subordinate to it. And this is, of course, precisely what general experience indicates, for prayer is a part of worship.

There are also a number of supplementary components of all these meanings. For example, *communion* may be highly ecstatic, mystical, or "practical"—the person who seeks communion with God by doing the work of God in the midst of overwhelming human need. *Worship* may also take a number of different forms. *Prayer* may also include the notion of "getting things from God," as some have emphasized. But these features are not the ones which constitute the diagnostic distinctions.

A similar, but structurally distinct, set of contrasts occurs in the series *holy* (The man is holy), *good* (The man is good), *righteous* (a righteous man, in Matthean usage), and *righteous* (a righteous man, in the Pauline sense):

holy	*good*	*righteous* (Matt.)	*righteous* (Paul)
a. dedicated to God	a. ethical behavior	a. ethical behavior	a. a relationship to God
b. ethical behavior	b. conforming to the standard of the society	b. conforming to God's standard	b. right (what it should be)
c. produces awe			c. made possible by God

This series of terms shares certain common components, such as socially approved qualities, religiously appropriate, and characteristics of personality. But the diagnostic components point up some interesting distinctions. In the first place, *righteous*, as found in Matthew, turns out to be hierarchically subordinate to *good*, that is to say, it is a special subclass of *good*, namely, the goodness which is in conformance to the standard established by God. At the same time, *righteous* as used by Paul is quite distinct from *righteous* as used by Matthew, for rather than being ethical behavior, it is essentially a right relationship made possible by God, and thus characteristic of the man who has been "justified," *i.e.*, put into a right relationship with God (cf. Today's English Version).[6]

---

[6] There are certain other features of the componential analysis of *holy, good, righteous* (Matthean) and *righteous* (Pauline) which should be noted: (1) the order of components in *holy* is dictated by essentiality, *i.e.*, "dedicated to God" is more central or essential than "ethical behavior." This is in contrast with the temporal ordering noted among the components of *redeem*. The third component, "produces awe," is not essential in distinguishing *holy* from these other terms, but it is a vital

Problem 25

Compare the componential structures of the following words and meanings:

1. synagogue (Mark 1:21)
   temple (Mark 13:1)
   church (Philemon 2)

2. priest (Luke 1:5)
   scribe (Mark 3:22)
   Levite (Luke 10:32)

3. law (Matt. 11:13)
   (ten) commandments
   tradition (Mark 7:3)

4. king (Luke 1:5)
   emperor (Luke 2:1)
   governor (Luke 2:2)

5. heaven (Luke 2:15)
   heaven (Matt. 5:3)
   heaven (Acts 14:17)

OVERLAPPING IN SEMANTIC AREAS

Until now we have dealt primarily with terms which may be arranged in neat, readily definable compartments, or which are included one within another. A series such as *walk, skip, hop, run*, etc., in the specific meanings analyzed above, could be diagramed as follows in Figure 8:

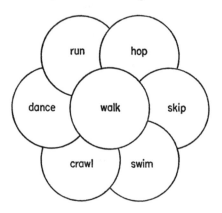

Figure 8

If, however, we consider the relationships of *move* as used in certain contexts to the same specific meanings of *walk, skip, hop, run*, etc., then this meaning of the generic term *move* may be said to include the other meanings in the same way, that certain meanings of *march* and *stroll* are included within *walk*. These sets of inclusions could be diagrammed as follows in Figure 9:

component of *holy* in many other contrastive sets. Similarly, *righteous* in the Pauline sense is analyzed fully here, even though fewer componential contrasts are all that are required to define the essential differences.

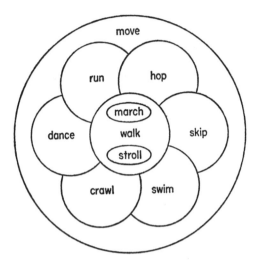

Figure 9

It is necessary to emphasize, however, that we do not include all the meanings of certain terms within others, but only those specific meanings which share certain features of meaning. Now in addition to the patterns of separation or inclusion, there is also a pattern of overlapping. This exists between synonyms, words which share several (but not all) essential components and thus can be used to substitute for one another in some (but not all) contexts without any appreciable difference of meaning in these contexts, *e.g.*, *love* and *like*. Such a relationship may be diagrammatically described, as in Figure 10:

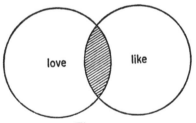

Figure 10

Such a relationship of overlapping may obviously involve many or few of the components of each term. But in either case, if the components which are not shared do not contrast in any specific way, we have synonymy in one degree or another; that is, the fact that essential components are shared and that none contrast permits two terms to be used in some of the same contexts with the same meaning; but the presence of nonshared components, even if they do not contrast, prevents the terms from being used interchangeably in all contexts. If, on the other hand, there is a specific contrast in some one essential component, then we have what may be described as a form of antonymy: *mother* and *father* share all essential components except that of sex, but on that one the contrast is polar, and the two terms are antonyms.

The series *grace, favor, kindness,* and *mercy,* in the context *God shows ... to* exhibit certain patterns of overlapping, as may be noted from the following componential analysis:

grace	*favor*	*kindness*	*mercy*
1. upper to lower	1. upper to lower	1. may or may not be upper to lower	1. upper to lower
2. a benefit	2. a benefit	2. a benefit	2. a bad condition
3. undeserved	3. may or may not be undeserved	3. may or may not involve sympathy	3. alleviation of condition
			4. sympathy

Certain features of this componential analysis require some explanation:

1. The feature of "upper to lower" indicates that the one who shows the grace, favor, etc. is one who is in an "upper" position with respect to the one receiving the benefit of the action. This "upper position" may be defined socially, theologically, or circumstantially.
2. In the case of *grace, favor,* and *kindness* what is done is primarily some sort of benefit, but in the case of *mercy* there are several other factors. Therefore, the component of "alleviation of the condition" has been given, even though it is closely related to "benefit."
3. *Grace* in the theological sense indicates an undeserved benefit, while a *favor* may be deserved or may not be deserved.

There are some contexts in which *kindness,* especially in an intensive expression, "great kindness" may be practically equivalent to *mercy, e.g.,* "he showed him great kindness," or "he showed him mercy." This means that these terms *kindness* and *mercy* overlap to at least a limited extent. *Grace* and *favor,* however, in the meanings described here, do overlap considerably, and this is precisely why a number of translations of the Bible employ *favor* instead of *grace.* At the same time one must recognize that in some contexts *favor* carries certain unfavorable implications, for it may imply favoritism or favor for one person in comparison with another. This is not a basic feature of the word *favor* in the specific frame described here *God shows ... to,* but *favor* does tend to pick up certain connotative (associative) meanings from other combinations and relationships. *Grace,* at the same time, acquires certain other connotative meanings, for in a context speaking of the activity of God it often acquires such a technical religious meaning that it seems to lose much of its real significance. One of the difficulties is that outside of the specific context such as we have analyzed here, *grace* has quite different meanings. Hence, in a context speaking of God it seems to be largely out of place for the average secularized person.

The two Greek terms *agapaō* and *phileō*, both translated "love" in most contexts, have been extensively discussed by exegetes as instances of near synonyms, which are supposed to have certain important distinctions of meaning. Many persons have insisted on marking such a distinction in John 21:15-17, where the two different words are used in the three questions posed by Jesus to Peter after the resurrection. Some individuals have insisted that the very fact that two words exist indicates an inevitable difference of meaning, and the most popular explanation is that *agapaō* refers to divine love while *phileō* indicates merely human love. To prove this type of distinction, however, it would be necessary to find that *agapaō* was used with certain sets of participants, that it occurred in different sorts of semotactic frames from *phileō*. But this is not the case, for both terms are used in speaking of God's love for the Son, the Son's love of the Father, God's love for man, man's love for God, and men's love of one another. There is, therefore, no semotactic frame to distinguish such meanings. If one undertakes to list the features of meaning, they are largely shared components:

agapaō	*phileō*
1. affection for	1. affection for
2. concern for	2. concern for
3. recognition of worth	3. recognition of worth
4. association not implied	4. association

Certain of these components are likely to be challenged by some theologians and therefore require some explanation:

1. The quality of affection in *agapaō* and *phileō* does differ, for *agapaō* can be commanded and *phileō* is never used in the imperative. That is to say, *phileō* seemingly arises out of association and undoubtedly involves a greater degree of sentimental attachment. As some persons have said, one can "love" (*agapaō*) without "liking" (*phileō*), but this is likewise too strong a contrast.
2. The component "loyalty to" would be another way of describing the sentiment of attachment or concern.
3. In both *agapaō* and *phileō* there is inevitably a component of "concern for" the goal of the event, though this concern may express itself in a number of different ways, especially in the contrast between God's love for man and man's love of God.
4. The component of "recognition of worth" must be understood, at least in the case of *agapaō*, as "potential worth," for God is not represented as loving man because of any inherent goodness, but only because of what he can potentially be.
5. The fact that *phileō* does not occur with the imperative, and or-

dinarily at least implies a degree of association, would support the contention that this term does differ from *agapaō* in a feature of association. Certainly, *agapaō* does not imply any necessary association, for one can be expected to love the brethren without having known them intimately or for any length of time.

In view of the fact that these two words do share in such large measure a number of components, they are likely to be synonymous, at least in certain contexts. Certainly there is no clear-cut contextual contrast in John 21:15-17, and moreover, the writer of the Gospel of John frequently exhibits interesting sets of shifts between close synonyms in Greek. For example, in classical Greek *ginōskō* and *oida* are normally contrasted in meaning between "know by experience" and "know intuitively," but in John they are freely substituted. Similarly, *horaō* and *blepō*, two verbs for "seeing," are also substituted for each other without seeming contextual distinctions. As a result, most exegetes have concluded that likewise in the case of *agapaō* and *phileō* in John 21, these terms overlap sufficiently in meaning as to be substituted one for the other in this context without any appreciable difference in meaning.

At the same time, it must be recognized that *agapaō* and *phileō* do differ in certain aspects of their meaning, and it is not without reason that people have tended to think of *agapaō* as divine love (or love in its essentially Christian and religious sense) and *phileō* as human love, or love on a nonreligious plane. This "feeling" about the words is not, however, a part of the basic denotation, or referential significance, but a part of the connotative, or associative, meaning—the meanings which these words have picked up from their associations. Though *agapaō* and *phileō* do occur in similar semotactic frames, the great preponderance of uses of *agapaō* in certain types of contexts does point to the divine element of love. This type of difference in connotation is something which will be treated more fully in Chapter 5.

THE ANALYSIS OF RELATED MEANINGS OF A SINGLE WORD

We have now examined the way in which syntactic and semotactic clues in the context select one from among the several meanings of a given word, and we have analyzed the componential structure of related meanings of different words. Now it is necessary for us to look at the "internal" semantic structure of the different meanings of single words and to identify those semantic components which define the differences between them.[7]

---

[7] Contrasting components can, in some cases, be represented by matrices in which the contrast is marked by positive or negative marking, *e.g.*, + *male* or — *male*. But because many components are not so neatly structured into binary contrasts, such matrices are often clumsy and artificial. The same is even truer of a representation by branching "tree" diagrams, such as those proposed by Katz and Fodor (1963). These almost inevitably involve some forcing of the pattern, the use of excessive *ad hoc* components to fill in gaps, and the arbitrary setting up of hierarchies where no ordering is evident. Since the interrelations of components are often multidimensional, it is best for our purposes to use a simple column

As in the case of related meanings of different words there are three basic types of components:

1. Common components are those which are shared by all the meanings of a word, and which therefore contribute to our feeling that it is one word rather than a set of homonyms. The word *coat*, for instance, has a number of quite different meanings: *The coat has a fur collar*; *The coat matches the trousers*; *The coat of the seed is very tough*; *Certain dogs have a very shaggy coat*; *One coat of paint is enough*, etc. Two of these are garments, one has to do with plant seeds, one with animals, and one with inanimate objects. But they are all united by the common component *covering*. The same component is shared even by the verbal meanings of *coat*, as in: *Coat the metal surfaces with grease*. Obviously, however, since common components are shared by all the meanings of a word, they cannot be used to distinguish the meanings.

2. Diagnostic components are distinctive of one or more meanings, but not of all. Those components which are distinctive of a particular subset of meanings contribute to our intuition that some meanings of a word are "closer" than others. Among the meanings of *coat* mentioned above, for instance, only the first two share the component *garment*.

Other diagnostic components are distinctive of a single meaning, *i.e.*, which no other meaning of the word shares. Since these are the components which are distinctive in the most crucial way, they are the most important in our analysis: they are the ones which enable us to say: This is X, not Y. For instance, the component *part of a living animal* distinguishes one sense of *coat* from all the others. Such a component, which serves by itself to distinguish meanings, may be called centrally distinctive. But there are sometimes several components which are always present in a given meaning of a word, any one of which would suffice to distinguish that meaning, when taken together with the centrally distinctive components. In the basic meaning of *head*, for instance, together with the distinctive component *part of an animate body*, there are several peripheral or additional components: *position*: *top/front*; *function*: *control*; *features*: *eyes, nose*, etc., and so on. Any one of these latter, taken with the distinctive components, specifies that meaning of *head*. Such components are additionally distinctive.

3. Finally, there are purely supplementary or optional components. Some of these give rise to expectations of greater or lesser probability but can be specifically negated without altering the sense of the word: for example, in the expression *Bill hit John*, one automatically assumes that he did it on purpose, and it is necessary to specify *unintentionally* if that is what is intended. Contrariwise, intentionality is impossible in *The ball hit John*, so that it is nonsense to say *The ball hit John intentionally* and tautologous to say *The ball hit John unintentionally*. Other types of supplementary components exist simply by virtue of certain associations of ideas, and these shade off almost imperceptibly into connotative

representation that does not prejudge too many questions and that can more easily be modified as needed.

meanings, which will be studied in the next chapter. Even though these supplementary components are purely optional, and can therefore be specifically excluded, they can give rise to problems if they are overlooked, especially if they are of the sort that lead the receptor to make tacit probabilistic assumptions which are unintended.

It should be said that what is distinctive about a particular meaning may not be one or more components which it possesses exclusively, but rather the particular assortment or configuration of components. This is especially true of sets defined and distinguished by cross-cutting components, *e.g.*, kinship. In most systems of kinship terminology, among the crucial components are such features as *generation from ego* (+1, +2, 0, −1, −2, etc.), *sex* (male or female), *lineality vs. collaterality*, etc. The only feature which distinguishes *father* from *mother* is the sex; but *father* shares *male* with *uncle, grandfather*, etc., and *mother* shares *female* with *aunt*, etc. *Father* and *uncle* are distinguished by *lineal vs. collateral*, but other terms also have these same features. No single component is the exclusive property of a single kinship term, but each term is defined by a unique combination of components.

The techniques for determining the relevant components involve the following steps: (1) isolate and "discard" the universal component(s), since they are not distinctive; (2) isolate the components which occur in one or more but not all of the meanings, *i.e.*, those which are distinctive of subsets of meanings; (3) arrange these components in parallel columns under each meaning, marking as much similarity and difference as is needed; (4) of the remaining components, reject for the moment supplementary components, *i.e.*, those which can be excluded without destroying the meaning, and add to each column those which are necessary to define that meaning; (5) indicate the extent of parallelism or agreement between senses; and (6) determine which components are distinctive, individually or collectively, for each meaning.

These basic techniques can be readily exemplified in an analysis of the components of the four nominal meanings of *chair*, mentioned on p. 58:

1. bought a chair
2. electric chair
3. address the chair
4. the chair of philosophy

The meanings of *chair*, by the application of procedures (1) through (6), may be analyzed as follows:

1	2	3	4
a. manufactured object	a. manufactured object	a. person	a. position
b. for sitting	b. for sitting	b. prominence	b. prominence
c. for resting	c. for execution	c. parliamentary	c. academic

It should be noted that we have not listed all of the possible components of meaning, nor even all of the distinctive ones, which pertain to any of these senses of *chair*. We have listed only those necessary to distinguish these four from each other, not from other words. Sense 1, for instance, has as distinctive components (as we have seen in contrasting *chair* with *stool* and related terms) the components four legs, back, for one person, movable, etc. It is also true that senses 3 and 4 could be distinguished solely on the basic of the difference between parliamentary and academic; but because of the semotactic collocations in which each sense occurs, it is also necessary to specify that 3 is a person and 4 a position.

We can go on to highlight the shared components and the distinctive components by joining the first with lines and marking the latter with asterisks:

1	2	3	4
a. manufactured——a. manufactured		a. person*	a. position*
b. for sitting———b. for sitting		b. prominence——b. prominence	
c. for resting*	c. for execution*	c. parliamentary*	c. academic*

Some of the supplementary components may also parallel some of the distinctive ones. For example, the person designated by sense 3 normally sits in a chair, sense 1. Similarly, the holder of the chair of philosophy may actually occupy a particular chair in the faculty assembly which corresponds to his position or rank. These supplementary components reenforce some of the shared distinctive components, but they are not essential in distinguishing this particular subset of meanings.

In summary, it may be said that the kind of componential analysis which we have been doing is the way we determine the *features* and the *boundaries* which make up the "map" of the conceptual universe; and if we need to know *why* we can substitute certain terms in certain contexts but not in others, we can specify this in terms of the components which the meanings share or do not share. The average person probably does not do this automatically; he simply identifies a particular semantic class in terms of what substitutes can replace them, either at the same level or at a higher hierarchical level.[8] This same notion has been discussed, under the title of "domains," on p. 69.

Problem 26

1. Apply the techniques explained in this section to the following senses of *head*: (1) The hat fits his head; (2) Here is the head of the parade;

---

[8] It is most probable that the human mind, in determining the sense of a word in a particular context, actually proceeds by substituting other terms, at either the same or a higher position in the hierarchical structure of meanings. For example, the substitute for sense 1 might be "piece of furniture." In the terms of the "map" presented on pp. 19-20, the substitute for the name of a "town" may be the name of the "state" in which it is found, to distinguish it from a "town" which has the same name but is in another "state." The componential structures are an analytical approach to what the mind no doubt accomplishes by much more direct paths, but they are recognized by the native speaker as underlying what he does when they are pointed out to him. See also the discussion of domains, p. 69.

(3) He is the head of the firm; (4) I bought a head of cabbage; (5) He was at the head of his class; (6) I will head him off.

   2. Do the same for the following senses of *see*: (1) I see my house from here; (2) I see what you mean; (3) Please see her home.

The same technique of analyzing related meanings of a single term may be applied to certain of the principal meanings of the Greek term *sōma*, often rendered as "body":

    1. the body of people (Matt. 6:25), of animals (James 3:3), and of plants (1 Cor. 15:37-38)—whether dead or alive.
    2. heavenly bodies: stars, planets, sun, and moon (1 Cor. 15:40).
    3. the total person (Rom. 12:1), *i.e.*, "present yourselves."
    4. slaves (Rev. 18:13), where "bodies" are listed as merchandise.
    5. reality (Col. 2:17), where "reality" is contrasted with "shadow."

A componential analysis of this set of meanings would include the following sets of components:

1	2	3	4	5
a. physical	a. physical	a. physical	a. physical	a. abstract quality
b. living or dead	b. nonliving	b. living	b. living	b. existent
c. person, animal, plant	c. celestial	c. person	c. person	c. experienced
d. part	d. whole	d. whole	d. whole	
			e. purchasable	

Certain aspects of these componential features require explanation:

    1. We have not tried to define with complete precision all the componential features. For example, *physical* is to be interpreted in terms of "material," in contrast with the nonmaterial, either spiritual or psychological.
    2. The contrast between part and whole indicates merely that this is the body of a person in meaning 1, while the entire person is intended in meaning 3. Quite naturally the terms *part* and *whole* do not have precisely the same significance in all the contexts.
    3. In the case of meaning 5 we have indicated not only that this is an abstract quality (which would be enough to contrast this meaning with the rest), but also that it implies something existent (parallel to some extent with "living"). This quality is also experienced by people. To this extent this meaning of *soma* differs from "being," which is the abstract quality of existence, but not necessarily experienced.

Not infrequently the problem of analysis of meanings arises from the fact that one is not specific enough as to the context which is being employed. This results in almost endless confusion, for one cannot compare effectively all the meanings of a term with all the meanings of another term, but should restrict himself (at least in the initial stages) to a comparison of those meanings which tend to occur in the same types of contexts.

This problem of context is particularly acute in the case of three different meanings of *redeem*, as used in the Scriptures:

1. redeem (a slave)   2. redeem (Israel)   3. redeem (by Jesus Christ)

In the first context the meaning is the redemption of a slave through the payment of money. The second is the redemption of Israel from Egypt by the mighty act of God. The third refers to the redemption of the believer by Jesus Christ through the atonement.

1. redeem (a slave)	2. redeem (Israel)	3. redeemed (by Jesus Christ)
a. alien control	a. alien control	a. alien control
b. payment of a price	b. by "a mighty act of God"	b. the atonement by Jesus Christ
c. release	c. release	c. release

In this instance it has been necessary to incorporate two common components: (a) alien control and (c) release, for they are part of the essential temporal sequence in the meaning of *redeem*; it is significant to note, as a matter of fact, that such a temporal ordering of components is entirely possible, as is a logical ordering (*e.g.*, cause and effect). Where these three meanings differ is in the second component. For the first meaning there is no doubt as to the meaning, for a price is paid to the person who owns the slave. (Similarly, in the redemption of property a price was paid to the owner.) In the case of the redemption of Israel from Egypt, no price is paid to anyone. Rather, the redemption was accomplished by what is termed "a mighty act of God." The theological problem does arise, however, in the interpretation of the second component of *redeem* in the third sense, namely, the redemption of the sinner by Jesus Christ. Is one to assume that this is based by analogy on the redemption of a slave, in which case Jesus Christ was "paying" God (in propitiation) [9] or he was "paying the devil," a view held by some theologians in the Middle Ages but not seriously defended today. There are, of course, passages which speak of the believer as having been "bought with a price" and as having been "redeemed not with silver or gold but by the precious blood of

---

[9] It should also be noted that in the New Testament Greek *hilaskomai*, translated as "propitiate," or "expiate," is never used with God as the goal. That is to say, sin is expiated but God is not propitiated in the New Testament. It is, of course, true that there is an association of ideas surrounding the Christian sense of *redeem* which includes sense 1, but it is not the critical sense.

Jesus." But the question is whether these passages constitute the basis for the more general use of *redemption* in speaking of the atonement. Most scholars, both Protestant and Roman Catholic, interpret the references to the redemption of the believer by Jesus Christ, not as evidence of any commercial transaction or any *quid pro quo* between Christ and God or between the "two natures of God" (his love and his justice), but as a figure of "the cost," in terms of suffering. They likewise find in the redemption of the people of Israel the basic theological "motif" which provides the understanding for the redemption of the believer by Jesus Christ. The second component, therefore, of the third meaning is equivalent to "the mighty act" of God, as his intervention into history, ràther than being any contractual arrangement by which man is taken out of pawn.

The fact that one and the same word may have such different types of components in various contexts should warn one against the tendency to treat words as "a single set of meanings." One must always choose carefully the particular basic meaning which is intended. This may become even clearer if one contrasts the following meanings of *God* and *gods* in the Bible: (1) *God* in Matthew 5:8, and 9, "they shall see God," and "they shall be called sons of God," and (2) *gods* in Deuteronomy 5:7, "you shall have no other gods before me." Some may argue, of course, that one cannot analyze the meaning of some referent which does not exist, for in strict monotheism the other gods are simply nonexistent. Even in modern "logical analysis" God is sometimes regarded as an irrelevant question. People, however, have many words for things which may not exist or even for things which they may insist do not exist, *e.g.*, *unicorns, ambrosial fluid, Zeus*, and *fairies*, for meaning is not a feature of the referent itself but a feature of the concepts which we have about such a referent. Therefore, quite apart from the reality of any referent we can and must discuss the meanings not in terms of what we may personally think of such a referent but in terms of the ways in which those who use a particular expression conceive of the objects, events, and abstracts referred to.

If we, therefore, carefully compare the meanings of *God* and *gods* (bearing in mind, of course, how the latter differ from such other supernatural entities as demons, devil, and spirits), we may arrive at the following set of componential distinctions:

God	*gods*
Common Components	
1. supernatural	1. supernatural
2. personal	2. personal
3. control over natural phenomena and the actions of men	3. control over natural phenomena and the actions of men
4. holy (in the sense of positive taboo)	4. holy (in the sense of positive taboo) [10]

[10]   Taboo is basically of two types: (1) positive taboo, which means that something is so filled with spirit power that one must beware of approaching too near

Diagnostic Components

1. exclusive supernatural power	1. having supernatural power similar to that shared by other gods
2. moral (expected to act justly) [11]	2. amoral (actions are dependent upon propitiation)
3. unique, to the exclusion of other gods, *i.e.*, monotheism	3. various grades of gods, including possible henotheism,[12] but not a unique god

These distinctions in meaning between *God* and *gods* (a unique singular and a generic plural) are sometimes very difficult to express merely by using a singular in contrast with a plural, especially in languages which may have no definite or indefinite articles. To identify the God of Scriptures in such a way as to imply certain of the contrastive components, some languages use "the true God," "the eternal God," "the only God," "creator God," and "Father God." There are even passages in which there is a measure of ambiguity because the word *Elohim* is plural in form but is used of God as well as of gods; a typical case is Psalm 138:1, in which different versions interpret the word differently. But such cases are relatively rare.

There are, of course, a number of other supplementary features which help to distinguish these different meanings, *e.g.*, *the Father of Jesus Christ*, and *the Creator of the world*, but these are either highly specific features of meaning or are implicit as part of exclusive supernatural powers.

The purpose of this contrast in sets of meanings is, however, not to define the differences by setting up some of the theologically and anthropologically interesting distinctions in meaning, but merely to point out that one and the same term may have quite different sets of meanings in specific contexts. Thus in comparing the meanings of different words one must make certain just which set of meanings is involved. Otherwise, semantic analysis is hopelessly confused.[13]

(the taboo of the Ark of the Covenant), and (2) negative taboo, which means that something is defiled and therefore must not be touched *e.g.* (unclean animals or a corpse).

[11] It should be noted that in the Bible the "holiness" of God differs from *holy* as applied to the gods, in that God possesses a moral quality, for he is expected to act justly quite apart from any propitiation. Note the exclamation of Abraham in Gen. 18:25: "Shall not the Judge of all the earth do right?"

[12] Henotheism means that there is one supreme god over other gods (a belief which is reflected in some passages of the Old Testament), while monotheism means that there is only one God and that other gods simply do not exist.

[13] Perhaps this contrast between the meanings of a single word becomes even more startling when one compares the "meanings" of *Jesus* and *Isa*, the Christian and Muslim name for the same historical personage. In a number of translations employed in the Muslim world some persons have insisted that *Isa* must be used because this is the historical person referred to both in the New Testament and in the Koran. On the other hand, other persons have insisted that some adaptation of *Jesus* must be used since *Isa* is entirely inappropriate. An analysis of the different

The contextual setting of a term often involves a number of extra-linguistic factors. For example, the terms *orthodoxy* and *modernist* have entirely different componential content for different groups. The same person may be denounced as a modernist by one party and be rejected as an obscurantist fundamentalist by another group at the opposite end of the theological spectrum. Such words, therefore, must be defined not in terms of any arbitrary set of standards to which all men are supposed to conform but in terms of the ways in which people who use such terms conceive of the referents.[14] [15]

Problem 27

What are the diagnostic components of the meaning (in the source text) of the following words in Matthew 5: *persecuted* (vs. 10), *blessed* (vss. 3-11), *inherit* (vs. 5)? In each case, do you know any English words of similar meaning that might have been used but were not? What are their diagnostic components?

Problem 28

Compare the translation of Greek *dikaioō* in the RSV, the NEB, and the TEV as noted on page 18:

componential structures of the meanings of these two terms (*i.e.*, the differences in concepts held popularly by Christians and Muslims concerning *Jesus* and *Isa* respectively) will serve to highlight the fact that for what is essentially the same word (or name) there may be such different sets of conceptual values as to override certain historical connections:

Jesus	*Isa*
1. the Son of God	1. a prophet
2. strong emphasis upon the content of his teaching	2. relatively little knowledge of Jesus' teaching
3. worked miracles but repudiated showmanship	3. was a typical wonder-worker
4. died for man's sins	4. was not killed on the cross
5. resurrected from the dead	5. not resurrected from the dead

[14] To overcome the perennial problem of people's twisting and changing the meaning of words (*e.g.*, the Communist use of terms such as *peace, democracy,* and *republic*), some persons want to set up some all-powerful language academy which would rule on all terms once and for all. But this will never work, for words are always subject to reshaping as circumstances and conditions change. In fact, such capacity for growth and change in language is essential to the very nature of language. Therefore, to enjoy the advantage of a living language we must also take the risks of its being perverted. Furthermore, even if it were desirable, so-called language engineering would still be in almost all cases a futile effort, simply because there is no *effective* authority which can impose its will on the way people speak. Cases as diverse as those of the French Academy and the efforts to impose Hindi in India are ample proof of this. Apparent exceptions, as in Israel or Turkey, result from the fact that official efforts happened to coincide with a powerful trend in the social history of the peoples involved, which would no doubt have come to fruition without any official pronouncements.

[15] In trying to analyze the way in which people conceive of referents we cannot, of course, examine the actual neural relationships between symbol and ideas (*i.e.*, we cannot look into people's brains). Rather, we must determine such meanings by the association of words with other words, *i.e.*, by context.

(1) Matthew 12:37: RSV, "for by your words you will be *justified* and by your words you will be condemned"; NEB, "for out of your own mouth you will be *acquitted;* out of your own mouth you will be condemned"; TEV, "for your words will be used to judge you, either to *declare* you *innocent* or to declare you guilty."

(2) Luke 7:29: RSV, "all the people and the tax collectors *justified* God"; NEB, "all the people, including the tax-gatherers, *praised* God"; TEV, "all the people and the tax collectors heard him; they were the ones who had *obeyed* God's *righteous demands.*"

(3) Luke 16:15: RSV, "you are those who *justify* yourselves before men"; NEB, "you are the people who *impress* your fellowmen with your *righteousness*"; TEV, "you are the ones who *make* yourselves *look right* in men's sight."

(4) Romans 3:4: RSV, "that thou mayest be *justified* in thy words"; NEB, "when thou speakest thou shalt be *vindicated*"; TEV, "you must be *shown to be right* when you speak."

(5) Romans 3:24: RSV, "they are *justified* by his grace as a gift"; NEB, "all are *justified* by God's free grace alone"; TEV, "by the free gift of God's grace they are all *put right* with him."

Make a componential analysis of these different meanings.

Problem 29

Make a componential analysis of the different meanings of the following words:

(a) *house*
   (1) "going into the *house*" (Matt. 2:11); (2) "Joseph, of the *house* of David" (Luke 1:27); (3) "thou shalt be saved, and thy *house*" (Acts 16:31).

(b) *soul* (Greek, *psuchē*)
   (1) "[they] have troubled you with words, subverting your *souls*" (Acts 15:24); (2) "You will find rest for your *souls*" (Matt. 11:29); (3) "What shall it profit a man, if he shall gain the whole world, and lose his own *soul*?" (Mark 8:36).

(c) *blood*
   (1) "a woman, which was diseased with an issue of *blood*" (Matt. 9:20); (2) "In him we have redemption through his *blood*" (Eph. 1:7); (3) "And hath made of one *blood* all nations of men" (Acts 17:26).

The difference between diagnostic (or contrastive) and supplementary components is not always easy to determine, especially when different meanings of words do not occupy closely contrastive semantic space. This is well illustrated by some of the problems of definition of the Greek word *baptizō*, "to baptize." This term is used of Jewish ritual washings in Mark 7:4, "washing of cups and jugs and copper bowls" (with some manuscripts having "beds"). It is also used in ancient secular literature in the sense of "to be overwhelmed by something," *e.g.*, by debts, by desire, by misfortune; and related to this is the meaning in the New Testament, "Are you able ... to be baptized with the baptism with which I am baptized?" (Mark 10:38). In a passage such as Acts 2:41, the essential components of Christian baptism are normally regarded to be: (1) the use of liquid (though as to the exact amount there is considerable disagreement), (2) the religious nature of the rite (this is not a secular act of dipping or washing), (3) the name in which the act of baptism is done, and (4) the function of the rite as a symbol of initiation into the Christian community. These are the same essential components of meaning which have continued to be generally recognized by most Christians through the age. There are, however, some supplementary components of the rite which have in some instances competed for priority. For example, some churches have insisted that baptism cannot be valid unless one is actually totally immersed under the surface of the water, though even in the *Didache*, coming from the second century, the possibility of pouring is allowed in cases of necessity. For other persons, baptism must not only be immersion, but immersion three times in order to be in the name of the Father, the Son, and the Holy Spirit. For some Christians the precise form of the verbal formula employed in the rite of baptism is also an essential part, without which the baptism is not efficacious or valid; while for other persons the real issue is whether the individual is a "believer," that is, a person of accountable age (not an infant) who accepts baptism as a believer. In the case of certain churches the giving of a name is such an important part of baptism that the name for the rite has become "to give a name to." [16]

Precisely because there are so many differences of opinion concerning the diagnostic and supplementary features of this term, translators are generally advised to borrow some form of the word *baptism*, usually from the dominant language of the area, so that each church may then be able to define baptism in terms of its own views of the diagnostic and supplementary features. Where an indigenous expression is used, the Bible Societies have insisted that it should not be such as to specify as essential some aspect of the rite which is not regarded as such by other churches in the area. For example, to translate *baptize* as "to immerse" focuses upon one component, which is not regarded as essential by many constituencies. On the other hand, in the Maya language of Yucatán, Mexico,

---

[16] In this discussion of *baptism* we are not attempting to justify or to condemn one or another position with respect to baptism, but only to point out that certain features are almost "universal" in the use of most Christian groups, while certain elements have been supplementary, that is, additional features promoted in one way or another by certain constituencies. Of course, the most extreme form of restructuring of the meaning of baptism takes place among groups such as the Quakers and Salvation Army churches, who in reaction against ritual formalism have "spiritualized" the meaning of baptism and rejected the use of water entirely. The event of baptism among Quakers is, however, an important religious experience, and it marks initiation into the community, but not as a rite conducted by man but as an act of the Spirit of God. Quakers do not hesitate, however, to say that in a passage such as Acts 2:41 water was employed.

the traditional term for baptism is "to enter the water," an expression which would seem to imply immersion, but which was actually first employed by Roman Catholics, later by Presbyterians, and is equally acceptable to Baptists. In some languages the indigenous term means "a religious rite with water," without specifying the amount of water.

THE PROBLEM OF FIGURATIVE MEANINGS

So far we have been dealing almost exclusively with so-called literal meanings. While it does not seem possible to define "literal" with great rigor, it is possible to give a general characterization of the notion. If each term is assumed to have some primary or central meaning, then the term may also have other "literal" meanings which are relatively close to the central one through the sharing of important components; a good example is found in the several senses of *chair* analyzed earlier. On the other hand, a word may have additional meanings assigned to it which are very different in every essential aspect from the primary one; and where the link is not through essential components, such meanings are called "figurative." Though the distinction becomes blurred at the margins, it provides the basis for our intuition that some meanings are actually closer and some more remote.

In terms of the semantic domains discussed earlier (p. 69) and of the hierarchical arrangement of generic and specific terms, it can be said that the higher one has to go in the hierarchy to find a covering generic term for the two senses under consideration, the more figurative the extended sense is. If the two meanings are close in the hierarchical structure, so that a rather low-level term covers them both, they are probably both literal. The higher one goes in the generic hierarchy (*e.g.*, in the realm of English object terms, *thing* is an almost universal cover-term), the less meaningful are the relationships involved, and the more reluctant we are to call the included category a domain. Figurative meanings may in this sense be said not to be in the same domain as the literal meaning of the same term.

It is important for us to consider something of the mechanisms by which the sense of a word can be extended in various directions. If we compare the two meanings of *fox* in *It is a fox* and *He is a fox*, it soon becomes evident that there are practically no shared components:

(It is a) *fox*	(He is a) *fox*
1. animal	1. human being
2. canine	2. cleverly deceptive
3. genus: *Vulpes*	

Though these senses share the component *animate being*, this is so broad that it has little significance. Furthermore, we know as native speakers of English that the link is not of that sort at all; rather it is mediated through a supplementary—and purely conventional—component which claims that the fox is particularly deceptive and clever. Though in actuality this trait is as well developed, if not more so, in the wolf and the jackal, neither of these animals has acquired this arbitrarily assigned supplementary component. But it is precisely this supplementary component which becomes crucial to the extension of meaning into the psychological area.

Because figurative extensions are based upon some supplementary component in the primary meaning which becomes essential in the extended meaning, and because they are often arbitrary and conventional, they are almost always specific to a particular culture and language. In other words, *fox* is assigned the component "deceptively clever" only in Western European culture (note the Reynard stories); in other cultures the same trait is, just as arbitrarily, assigned to the rabbit, or to the spider, or to some other animal. Further evidence of the arbitrariness of such extensions is found in the words *snow* and *ice*: both are equally cold, but the figurative extensions of *snow* have to do with whiteness (*white as snow, snowy laundry*), while those of *ice* have to do with coldness (*cold as ice, icy hands*).

If we compare the two meanings of *flesh* in (1) "a spirit has not *flesh* and bones" (Luke 24:39) and (2) "provoke to jealousy my *flesh*" (meaning "my race") (Rom. 11:14), the componential structures are likewise quite different:

flesh (and bones)	(provoke to jealousy my) *flesh*
1. physical	1. persons
2. part of body of animate being	2. lineage
3. nonbone	
4. dead or alive	

There are actually no specific components in common between these meanings, though if one examines the entire series of meanings of Greek *sarks* "flesh," there are, of course, suggestive links. But this link is again established through certain supplementary components, which do not serve to define contrastively the primary sense (meaning 1): it is the physical part of man which serves as the means of procreation, and people are regarded as biologically linked by such a process.

To summarize: The figurative sense of any term rests on the fact that it has an almost entirely distinct set of components, but that it also has a link to the primary sense through some one component, usually a supplementary one. This supplementary component can be actually relevant to the referent of the primary sense, or only conventionally assigned, but in either case it is not one of the essential, distinctive features by which the primary sense is distinguished from others.

Figurative usage can greatly complicate the analysis of certain phrases. In an expression like "pour out my Spirit upon all flesh" (Acts 2:17), it is evident that once again *flesh* is not being used in its primary sense. In the primary sense, *flesh* refers to a mass object; in its figurative extension, its reference is to a completely different kind of object, namely, people. In the expression "justified by his blood" (Rom. 5:9), *blood*, which normally designates a mass object, actually refers to an event, namely, the atonement. Similarly, when Paul uses the expression "glory in the cross of our Lord Jesus Christ" (Gal. 6:14), he does not mean that he has confidence in the cross as an object, but in the event, the atonement, of which the cross is a symbol. The terms *circumcised* and *uncircumcised* in Galatians 2, though literally object-event words, actually function primarily as object-words, and can more correctly be translated "Jews" and "Gentiles." Their reference is to ethnic groups rather than to the physical operation (or its lack) which typically characterized these groups.

A special case is that of words which are consciously substituted for others which are taboo, either positively or negatively; such words are generally called euphemisms. A typical example is Matthew's use of *heaven* for *God* in the phrase *the kingdom of heaven*, out of deference to the Jews' reluctance to use the name of God.

In some instances, one must deal with special Semitic usages, which may pose certain difficulties. For example, the common phrases *children of* . . . and *sons of* . . . frequently identify persons who are characterized by the term which follows the *of*: thus, *sons of disobedience* (Eph. 2:2) means simply "people who disobey (God)," and *children of wrath* (Eph. 2:3) refers to "persons who will experience the wrath of God" or, better, "those whom God will judge."

Sometimes it is entire phrases which are used in some extended sense, so that it becomes impossible by adding up the meanings of the individual words to determine the meaning of the entire expression. Such expressions are called idioms, and will be dealt with in the next section. Two examples are *the fruit of his loins* (Acts 2:30), which means "his descendants," and *children of the bridechamber* (Mark 2:19), which means "wedding guests," or more precisely, "the groom's friends with whom he celebrates prior to the wedding."

Problems involving the translation of figurative senses are dealt with on page 107.

The Size of Semantic Units

Though for the most part words are selected as the units for semantic analysis, it is also possible to analyze the meanings of subword units. For example, the *re-* [17] in *reupholster, reenter*, and *reconstitute* may be analyzed as meaning "to do again." But one must also deal with units larger than individual words. These are the idioms of the language which cannot be analyzed as consisting of the sum total of the parts, but must be treated as separate entities. For example, one should not treat the Semitic idiom "to close one's bowels" as being endocentric, that is, as deriving its meaning from the sum total of the meanings of the parts. Rather, one must handle this as a semantic unit and analyze its meanings as "lacking in compassion." Similarly, "horn of salvation" must be restructured semantically as "a great savior," and the Hebrew phrase "wind of the

---

[17] This *re-*, meaning "to do again," must be clearly distinguished from the *re-* of such words as *receive, reconcile, restore*, and *respect* and also from the *re-* of *return* and *reform*. Note in this connection the difference between *reform*, meaning "to change," from *re-form*, meaning "to form again."

day" (Gen. 3:8) must be treated as a unit meaning "the evening time," or "the cool part of the day." But the treatment of such idioms is in no sense different from the way in which words are handled, except that in many instances an idiom consists of several different types of components. But this is also true of words such as *sanctifier*, in which object, event, and abstract quality of the goal are all included. Problems in the transfer of idioms are dealt with on page 106.

CHAPTER FIVE

CONNOTATIVE MEANING

The analytical procedures by which we come to understand the message we want to translate involve two quite distinct but closely related aspects of the message: (1) the grammatical and (2) the semantic. In Chapter 3 we considered the nature and analysis of grammatical meaning, and in chapter 4, the referential aspect of the semantics. But we not only understand the reference of words; we also react to them emotionally, sometimes strongly, sometimes weakly, sometimes affirmatively, sometimes negatively. This aspect of the meaning which deals with our emotional reactions to words is called connotative meaning. The fact that such meanings exist has already been made abundantly clear from our brief consideration of the associations of meaning which accompany such Biblical words as *grace* and *favor* (in English) and *agapaō* and *phileō* (in Greek).

The associations surrounding some words sometimes become so strong that we avoid using these words at all: this is what we call verbal taboo. On the one hand, there are negative taboos, with associated feelings of revulsion, or disgust, against such words as the famous four-letter words in English which refer to certain body organs and functions. The fact that the taboo is against the word and not the referent can be seen from the fact that there are quite innocent scientific terms which refer to the same things and which are perfectly acceptable. But the feeling against the words is such that even though everyone knows them, they are not used in polite society, and even many dictionaries refuse to print them. Such words are thought to defile the user.

On the other hand, there are positive taboos, associated with feelings of fear or awe: certain words (often the names of powerful beings) are also regarded as powerful, and the misuse of such words may bring destruction upon the hapless user. A good example is the traditional Jewish avoidance of the name of God, written in Hebrew with the four letters YHWH; another is the existence of a great many euphemisms, in Indo-European languages, for "bear."

Less intense feelings are nevertheless strong enough, in the name of propriety, to cause many to substitute euphemisms such as *washroom, comfort station, lounge, powder room,* and numerous colloquial and baby-talk terms for the word *toilet.* Similar cases are those of *sanitary engineer,* substituted for *garbage man,* and *mortician,* substituted for *undertaker.* The entire complex of euphemisms surrounding death and burial undoubtedly contains a strong ingredient of fear.

The connotations of words may be highly individual. For example, because of some experience in a doctor's office, the word *doctor* may be quite abhorrent to a child. But most such individual connotations are quickly lost, while the socially determined connotations (which are often purely conventional and therefore learned) are acquired by each speaker as part of his language-learning experience.

PRIMARY FACTORS OF CONNOTATIVE MEANING

In order to understand the nature of connotative meaning, it is important to note its three principal sources: (1) the speakers associated with the word, (2) the practical circumstances in which the word is used, and (3) the linguistic setting characteristic of the word. Note that positive and negative taboo apply to all three aspects.

Association with speakers [1]

When words become associated with particular types of speakers, they almost inevitably acquire by this association a connotative meaning closely related to our attitudes toward those speakers. This means, for example, that words used primarily by children or in addressing children get a connotation of being childish speech, and thus are not appropriate for adult usage. Similarly, certain words become associated with specific social classes. In British English much has been made of U and non-U speech, that is, the speech of the upper class in contrast with that of the non-upper classes. An interesting example is that of the use of *napkin*, which is U, as against the use of *serviette* (a French loan word) which is non-U. *Luncheon*, which was originally U, is now non-U, while the reverse process has taken place for *lunch*. It has been shown, both in Great Britain and in the United States (as well as elsewhere), that people in the classes which are socially mobile and ambitious attempt to imitate the speech of the class they hope to enter, but that once they succeed, the upper-class speech has changed also.

Educational levels may also be involved, so that educated persons use what is called "standard speech," while the uneducated tend to use "substandard" pronunciation, words, and grammatical forms. The more extreme instances of educated speech acquire a connotation of pedantry. Note that all such usage levels (standard, substandard, pedantic, etc.) are socially, not linguistically, determined.

Closely related to the differences in educational levels are the connotations derived from technical usage. Expressions such as *habitual criminal* and *recidivist* are almost completely identical in referential meaning, but the latter is markedly technical. Similarly, a nonlinguist will speak about the *sounds* or *letters* of a language, whereas the linguist will speak of *phonemes, phones, graphs, graphemes*, etc. Moreover, the way in which persons employ such terms becomes a mark of their technical ability, so that vocabulary tests are often used by employment bureaus to determine degrees of experience and competence.

Some words acquire special connotations through association with members of one sex: they are considered "women's speech" or "men's speech." There are also regionalisms, such as the speech (in the United

---

[1] For a fuller discussion of the sociological levels of language see p. 127.

States) of the hillbilly. The connotations of words derived from usage by particular religious groups is also of great importance, especially for the Bible translator. For example, expressions such as *the blood, the cross of Jesus Christ*, and *in the heavenlies* mark particular Christian constituencies, just as surely as terms such as *confrontation, dialogue*, and *existential* mark others. The attitude we have toward the people who use a word, whether favorable or unfavorable, becomes our attitude toward that word; that is, it becomes a connotation of that word.

Problem 30

With what kind of people is each of the following words or expressions associated? *bunny, alkaloid, case the joint, it's real cool, ontological, peekaboo, sublapsarian, dogey*. For each one, give a synonymous expression which is not so definitely associated with this group.

Circumstances of usage [2]

Words used by precisely the same persons in different circumstances carry quite different connotations. *Damn* used in church bears a quite different connotation from the same word used in a beer hall, even though uttered by the same person. Moreover, there are certain expressions which are associated with particular language settings, *e.g.*, auction rooms, public markets, police courts, lodges, summer resorts, and academic gatherings, so that almost all speakers tend to adopt several different "styles of language," each with its own distinctive connotations.

An additional factor may be included in the category of circumstances of usage: The nature of the total environment has its effect upon the connotations of words. An interesting experiment was carried out in parts of Africa which were totally different climatically, to see what the connotations of *green* and *blue* might be. In jungle areas, *blue* was the favorite color, and because of its association with the sky and with sunshine it connoted such highly favored meanings as "life," "blessing," etc. In complete contrast, *green*, with its associations with foliage, water, etc., was the favorite color in the desert areas, and carried the highly valued connotations of "life," "blessing," etc.

Problem 31

The following sets of words are in some ways synonymous. Within each set, describe the situation, if any, in which you would feel free to use each term.

    1. policeman, officer, cop, fuzz
    2. thingamagig, gimmick, gadget, throttle, pedal
    3. drunk, inebriated, stoned

Linguistic setting

Words which tend to be juxtaposed, or to co-occur with other words, acquire from them various connotations. For many persons, *green* prob-

---

[2] For a fuller discussion of the situational levels of language, see p. 128.

ably suffers from its occurrence in *green with envy, green at the gills,* a *green worker,* and *green fruit.* From such habitual associations *green* undoubtedly picks up some unfavorable features of emotive meaning.

Sometimes the connotations of words which sound similar but which are in fact quite unrelated may complicate the connotative picture. For example, the expression *rumpus room* gave way in the usage of real-estate advertisers in America to the expression *family room,* probably because *rump* brought in a wrong connotation.

For many persons *sanctification* no longer means "dedication" or "consecration to God," for it has been too closely associated with other expressions such as *second blessing, sinless perfection,* or *sanctimoniousness.* Accordingly, many translations have used *dedication to God* or *consecration,* words which have not acquired the unfavorable connotation of *sanctification.*

One aspect of the total linguistic setting relates to the time dimension. Here the categories are contemporary as against historical (or archaic, or obsolete) on the one hand, and avant-garde (or neologistic) on the other. The emotional reaction will depend upon one's feeling about the past, the present, and the future.

Another aspect of the linguistic setting is that specialized dimension which may be called literary setting. Phrases such as *Uncle Tom* and *Mary's little lamb* are inevitably associated with the literary works in which they are found. In a more restricted context, the phrase *thus saith the Lord* is not merely equivalent to *the Lord says,* but carries with it the connotations of King James language and ecclesiastical intonations. Certainly *once upon a time* no longer means literally "once upon a time." In fact, the connotation is precisely that what is to be told never happened at all: it is a fairy tale.

✳ Levels of Usage

In most languages, even the most "primitive," there is some kind of contrast in what may be called levels of language. One set of labels that has proved generally useful divides this dimension into technical, formal, informal, casual, and intimate language. Even in "primitive" languages one encounters the technical language of the medicine man, the formal language of the chief addressing a gathering, the informal speech of conversations around the evening fire, the casual conversation between "joking relatives," and the intimate speech of home and family. The differences between these levels may be very clearly marked in pronunciation, grammatical forms, and the selection of vocabulary. These levels in turn contribute to the connotations, as they result from the interaction of the three factors mentioned above: speakers, circumstances, and linguistic setting.

The Measurement of Connotative Meanings

Unfortunately, no really adequate method has been found of measuring the connotative values of words. Perhaps the least inadequate developed to date is that suggested by Osgood, Suci, and Tannenbaum. They tested the reactions of a great many persons by using a matrix in which scales from i to io marked off the polar contrasts of pairs of adjectives such as *good-bad, beautiful-ugly, strong-weak, light-dark, high-low, warm-cold,* and so forth. Then each subject was given a list of words to evaluate on all of these scales: words such as *patriotism, love, blood, communism, revolution, woman, mother,* and many more. Each term had to be evaluated on all scales, whether the subject thought it appropriate or not. The evaluations of the subjects were then tabulated and subjected to highly sophisticated statistical analyses by computer so as to draw for each evaluated word a kind of "profile" of its connotations.

One might expect that people's reactions to words might be highly individual, but in fact a high degree of agreement was found, so that in most cases there is a typical "bell curve" of reactions. Of course, when the method is applied in other cultures, it is necessary to make certain substitutions of evaluative scales; but within a given culture, once the scales have been properly selected, there is a high degree of similarity among the reactions of individual subjects.

Approximately sixty persons of American English background were tested as to their responses to the words *woman* and *mother*. Figure 11 shows that *woman* tends to be connotatively rather neutral, but that *mother* is strongly favored.

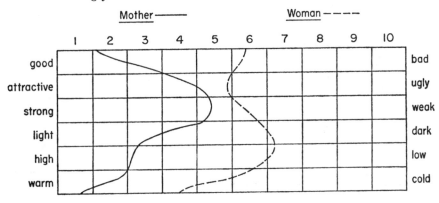

Figure 11

From the standpoint of the Bible translator these differences in the connotative responses to *mother* and *woman* have given rise to real problems in the translation of the Greek term *gunai* (literally "woman") in John 2:4 and 19:26. The King James Version and many others have maintained a literal translation of "woman." But the New English Bible has used "mother." This is not merely because in English "mother" is connotatively more appropriate than "woman," but because in Greek itself *gunai* has a connotatively more favorable value than *woman* does in English. On this basis the translators of the NEB have felt completely justified in shifting the denotative referent in order to provide something which is connotatively closer.

Problem 32

Analyze the connotative values of the following words for yourself in terms of:

1. *Values*: good (G), neutral (N), bad (B).
2. *Level of language*: technical (T), formal (F), informal (I).

	Values G, N, or B	Level T, F, or I
1. communist	— — — — — —	— — — — — —
2. preacher	— — — — — —	— — — — — —
3. justification	— — — — — —	— — — — — —
4. blood	— — — — — —	— — — — — —
5. darling	— — — — — —	— — — — — —
6. native	— — — — — —	— — — — — —
7. primitive	— — — — — —	— — — — — —
8. grace	— — — — — —	— — — — — —
9. father	— — — — — —	— — — — — —
10. Portuguese	— — — — — —	— — — — — —
11. church	— — — — — —	— — — — — —
12. bishopric	— — — — — —	— — — — — —
13. ionosphere	— — — — — —	— — — — — —
14. chief	— — — — — —	— — — — — —
15. confrontation	— — — — — —	— — — — — —
16. pope	— — — — — —	— — — — — —
17. vomit	— — — — — —	— — — — — —
18. ecclesiastical	— — — — — —	— — — — — —
19. democracy	— — — — — —	— — — — — —
20. ecumenical	— — — — — —	— — — — — —
21. holiness	— — — — — —	— — — — — —
22. son	— — — — — —	— — — — — —
23. colonialism	— — — — — —	— — — — — —
24. antelope	— — — — — —	— — — — — —
25. propitiation	— — — — — —	— — — — — —

ASPECTS OF LINGUISTIC MESSAGES WHICH CARRY CONNOTATIVE MEANING

Though traditionally connotative meanings have been associated only with individual words or short phrases (usually idioms), one must recognize that words and idioms are by no means the only units which have connotative values. In fact, all levels of language form may have these associated meanings: (1) pronunciation, (2) words, *i.e.*, semantic units, including both single words and idioms, (3) the discourse (this involves the connotative reaction to the style of the utterance), and (4) the themes of a message.

Pronunciation

The particular types of sounds used in certain forms of speech (*i.e.*, the allophones of the phonemes) may be said to carry connotative meanings. For example, the "Toity-toid and Toid Avenue" dialect of New York, with its special pronunciation of *bird* as *boid*, *girl* as *goil*, and *third* as *toid*, is quite understandable, and after a little practice one can readily "restructure" the sounds. However, these forms do carry certain associative meanings of being substandard. The same is true of many substandard dialect usages.

Words

For the most part connotative meanings are usually discussed merely in terms of the avoidance of vulgarisms and the appropriateness of levels. Rarely is it recognized that there are many more serious consequences of connotative significance. For example, a typical well-indoctrinated Thai Buddhist, who has had no previous acquaintance with the Christian religion, would be likely to interpret the traditional translation of John 3:16 as follows: "God so lusted after this material world that he sent his only Son so that anyone who is gullible enough to believe in him would have the misfortune of keeping on living forever and not dying." These interpretations arise from a number of important differences of viewpoint and association with words:

1. In rendering the Biblical phrase "so loved the world," the Thai translators chose a word for "world" which meant primarily this physical universe, rather than the people in this world. As a result, the term for "love" would then be interpreted connotatively as "lusting after," for to love the material world is something which in the Buddhist world is regarded as wrong; in fact, it is the basis of the all-pervasive delusion, which in turn is the principal cause of evil.
2. The expression "to believe in" represents primarily intellectual agreement, rather than trust or confidence in, and under such circumstances would be interpreted connotatively as a misplaced kind of belief.
3. "Living forever" is in the Buddhist view one of the greatest of tragedies, for this means being trapped in the physical world of delusion and thus never permitted to escape into the eternal bliss of Nirvana, which is the logical and metaphysical opposite to the physical world.

These connotative values associated with the Thai translation of John 3:16 are not merely the result of reactions to the individual Thai words, but also to the message as a whole.

The form of the discourse

The style of a discourse inevitably produces important connotative values, quite apart from the connotations of the words or of the themes which may be treated. The fact that we may be pleased with a style, but quite displeased with the content of a discourse, indicates clearly that there are differences of emotive responses to these two levels of communication. Some speakers may charm their audiences with their flow of language, while providing practically no substance; others may challenge their hearers by the importance of their message, even though the manner in which they communicate the information is quite unappealing. Certain literary farces consist of treating momentous events in trivial language, and trivial events in an elevated style, thus providing clear evidence of the ways in which connotative reactions to form can be separated from connotative reactions to content.

Themes

The fact that people understand thoroughly all the significant details of an account is no guarantee that they will react to the message in the same manner as other people do. For example, the Guaica Indians of southern Venezuela were entirely unmoved by the story of Jesus' trial and death, for they regarded him as a complete coward for not having put up a fight in the Garden of Gethsemane. Anyone who would not fight or attempt to escape was regarded by the Guaica as deserving death. Moreover, the Guaica insist that it is far better to die fighting than to be strung up like a common criminal.

Because any theme is inevitably interpreted in the light of the distinctive set of values maintained by each culture or society, one must expect that events will never be mere events, any more than words are mere words. They are always colored by associations, and evaluated in terms of the emotive reactions of people.

The importance of connotative meanings is much greater than the brevity of this chapter might suggest, for in the effort to attain dynamic equivalence, equivalent emotive responses on the part of the receptors is absolutely crucial. More will be said about this in Chapters 6 and 7.

CHAPTER SIX

TRANSFER

After having completed the processes of analysis, which involve both grammatical and semantic aspects of the text, it is then essential that the results of the analysis be transferred from language A to language B, that is, from the source language to the receptor language. But this must take place in someone's brain, and the translator is the person in whose brain the actual transfer takes place. A number of persons may assist by way of analysis and restructuring, but the transfer itself is the crucial and focal point of the translation process.

PERSONAL PROBLEMS IN TRANSFER

Since the transfer must take place in someone's brain (machines are a long way from effecting adequate transfers), it is inevitable that certain personal problems are likely to distort the process. Unless one is completely objective in his handling of the message, it is easy for misconceptions about the nature of language, the task of the translator, and the ultimate purpose of the translation to skew the results.

The personal problems which confront the average translator are not, of course, the result of any conscious bias against his task or the content of the message. Rather, they are largely unconscious predispositions about translation procedures which tend to color his work and ultimately impair the effectiveness of much that he may honestly be attempting to do. Perhaps some of the more important problems may be stated in terms of the relationships of the translator to the subject matter, the receptor language, the nature of communication, and the procedures which he should use. It should be pointed out that these various personal problems may in some cases be more prevalent among national than among foreign translators, or vice versa.

Too much knowledge of the subject matter

When it is emphasized repeatedly in books and articles on translation that the translator must be complete master of the subject matter, it may seem inconceivable that too much knowledge of the subject matter can be a deterrent to effective translation. In fact, it is actually not the excess of knowledge but the incapacity for imagination which hampers translators at this point. They know so much about the subject that they unconsciously assume the readers will also know what they do, with the result that they frequently translate over the heads of their audience.

Unfortunately most highly trained persons in any field of study tend to discuss the technical phases of their discipline only with their peers. They find it difficult, therefore, to put themselves in the position of people who simply have no knowledge of the technical phases. Since the theologian knows precisely what a verse means, even when it is translated awkwardly, it is no problem to him. If the study of theology tended to stimulate a person's imagination, perhaps he would be more capable of dealing with new and creative situations, but for the most part theological studies concentrate on proving the given truth, rather than on dealing with multiple hypotheses. Accordingly, neither in the area of communication to the uninitiated nor in the handling of the subject matter is there much emphasis upon the creative and imaginative aspects of communcating Christian truth. It is perhaps for these reasons that theologically trained persons have special problems in learning how to translate for a level other than the one on which they habitually operate. In other words, this problem relates more to the amount of specialized training the translator has had than to whether he is a national or a foreigner.

Taking translationese for granted

Under the impact of the wholesale translation of textbooks and other semiliterary materials, a kind of translationese has arisen in many parts of the world. This form of language is often accepted, especially by educated nationals, as the only possible medium for communicating materials which have first been expressed in a foreign language. Since scholars have often had to read a good deal of such material, they come to accept it more and more as a kind of literary standard, not realizing that this banal and artificial form of language fails utterly to do justice to the rich resources of the receptor language.

For the theologically trained national the influence of translationese is likely to be especially strong, for he has probably done most of his advanced study in a foreign language and has read a majority of texts in translation. Being a Christian, he has often felt obliged to repudiate, at least in practice if not in theory, some of the literary developments in his own language. Hence, not being familiar with or expert in the literary use of his own tongue, he falls a ready victim to translationese.

All this is quite understandable, for in some situations the Christian church itself has often taken a hard line against indigenous literature. Moreover, there have been relatively few instances in which Christian colleges and training schools have emphasized the development of creative writing for a general audience. Since most of the encouragement for written communication has been either to a relatively "ingrown" community or has been primarily "propagandistic" or "evangelistic" (depending upon one's viewpoint), little strenuous effort has been put forth to develop outstanding writers and stylists within the Christian community.

Insecurity about one's own language

Without realizing it, some persons have a deep sense of insecurity about their own language. This may express itself in two, almost opposite, tendencies. In the first place, some national writers feel obliged to imitate the forms of other languages which they regard as having more prestige. Hence they borrow wholesale, not only words, idioms, and stylistic devices, but even grammatical forms, for they conclude that these prestigious languages must be right.

In the second place, insecurity in a national about his own language can express itself in an exaggerated confidence, which says: But if English can say it that way, so can we, for our language is not inferior to any. Basically, this is only a superiority reaction to basic insecurity, and the results are as disastrous as those which arise from an inferiority attitude.

A desire to preserve the mystery of language

Some persons, both national and foreign, genuinely fear that if the Scriptures are made fully clear, something of the mystery of religion will be lost. In a sense this is true, if one conceives of "mystery" in a strictly non-Biblical sense, but in the Bible "mystery" identifies something which was not formerly known but which has now been revealed to the initiated. There is a vast difference between (1) the mystery of the Christian faith, e.g., the incarnation, the presence of the Holy Spirit in the world, and the will of God in history, and (2) the confusion which results from people not understanding what is perfectly clear in the Scriptures themselves, i.e., in the original writings. To substitute a sort of false mystery (based on unintelligibility of translation) for the true mystery of Christian faith is a total debasing of religion, and may be merely an excuse for ignorance.

At the same time one reason for not wanting to remove something of the "mystery of words" is derived from the fact that in some instances Christian scholars have a certain professionalism about their task and feel that to make the Bible too clear would be to eliminate their distinctive function as chief expositors and explainers of the message. In fact, when one committee was asked to adopt some translations which were in perfectly clear, understandable language, the reactions of its members were, "But if all the laymen can understand the Bible, what will the preachers have to do?"

Wrong theological presuppositions

Some Christians, both national and foreign, tend to adopt a view of the Scriptures which is more in keeping with the tenets of Islam than with the Biblical view of revelation, for they regard the Bible as being essentially a dictated document, rather than one in which the distinct stylistic features and viewpoints of the individual writers are preserved. This in no way minimizes the doctrine of inspiration, but it does mean that one must look at the words of the Bible as instruments by which the message is communicated and not as ends in themselves. It is essentially for this reason that we can emphasize the basic principle that contextual consistency is more important than verbal consistency, and that in order to preserve the content it is necessary to make certain changes in form.

Ignorance of the nature of translation

Another personal problem is simple ignorance of what translation is all about. Because the average person naïvely thinks that language is words, the common tacit assumption results that translation involves replacing a word in language A with a word in language B. And the more "conscientious" this sort of translator is, the more acute the problem. In other words, the traditional focus of attention in translation was on the word. It was later recognized that this was not a sufficiently large unit, and therefore the focus shifted to the sentence. But again, expert translators and linguists have been able to demonstrate that the individual sentence in turn is not enough. The focus should be on the paragraph, and to some extent on the total discourse. Otherwise, one tends to overlook the transitional phenomena, the connections between sentences, and the ways in which languages structure the discourse in distinctive ways. One of the particularly unfortunate ways of translating the Bible is to proceed verse by verse, for the verse divisions are often quite arbitrary units. Of course, one cannot at one and the same time bear in mind all the components of a paragraph, but every part of the paragraph should be translated with the structure of the whole being carefully considered, since all must fit together to form a unit.

Personnel Involved in Transfer

Transfer must be done by people, and very often by a group of people, usually organized as some kind of committee. Of course, there are some situations in which one individual, unusually gifted in a knowledge of the original languages and skilled in the style of the receptor language, can undertake the task of Bible translating alone. But such one-man translations are increasingly less possible. This means that the actual transfer must take place in a cooperative undertaking, involving primarily two types of situations: (1) cooperation between an expatriate foreigner (the missionary) and the national translator, and (2) cooperation between national translators.

Cooperation between expatriate and national translators

In most instances in which expatriates and national translators collaborate to undertake translation work, it is the expatriate who is the specialist in the source language (Greek, Hebrew, English, French, Spanish, etc.) and the national who is the expert in the receptor language. If these men are to function effectively, however, they must both have a knowledge of both source and receptor languages. If the national translator does not have a knowledge of the source language, he is essentially not a translator, but an informant, or translation helper. The techniques for dealing with this type of situation are not considered in this book, for there are a number of very special problems and difficulties which require highly specialized methods and techniques.

When expatriate and national translators collaborate as a team, it is most important that the problems of translation be discussed not in the source language but in the receptor language. That is to say, the basic difficulties must be raised at the post-transfer point, before the restructuring has been undertaken. If, on the contrary, people attempt to discuss the problems in the source language, there are too many possibilities of slips and distortions taking place when the material has to be transferred into the receptor language.

Cooperation between national translators

The basic structure of committees to undertake the work of translation is discussed in the appendix, but at this point it is important to note the distinctive roles of the "scholar" and the "stylist," for they represent two basic functions which cannot always be easily differentiated. In the past, the tendency has been to have a scholar do the translating and then to ask a stylist, very late in the proceedings, to fix up whatever seemed unduly rough and awkward. But it is very difficult to achieve a good style by reworking a draft which is all but completed. It is preferable to have the stylist involved as early as possible in the enterprise. How early he can be of help depends upon whether or not he has any command of the source language.

Ideally, the stylist has some grasp of the source language but is not a scholar in it. If he does have such an understanding, he can be the primary translator, working from the source text and producing a first draft which is aimed at an appropriate style. In such a situation, the scholar can contribute in a vital way at two points: (1) He can provide the stylist-translator with an analysis of the source text into the quasi-kernel structure *in the source language* at all points where the surface structure is difficult, ambiguous, or otherwise problematic. This gives the stylist crucial guidance in understanding the message, preparatory to transferring it into the receptor language, which he can then do either instinctively on the basis of his native ability, or as the result of training. (2) When the stylist has completed a draft translation, the scholar can then go over it with great care, making sure that it is accurate and bringing to the attention of the stylist errors of various kinds. Experience has shown that it is much easier to achieve the proper combination of accuracy and adequate style in this manner than in the more traditional approach in which the scholar translated and the stylist corrected.

If, on the other hand, the stylist has no knowledge of the source language, the scholar must perforce make the transfer from the quasi-kernel level achieved by his analysis (point X in the diagram, Figure 6, page 33) to an analogous level in the receptor language (point Y in the diagram), in which all statements are as simple as possible and everything as explicit and as unambiguous as possible. The stylist picks up the job at this point and restructures it into a draft of the finished translation, calling the scholar's attention to residual problems of meaning or of awkwardness. In this approach, it is vital that the scholar *not* produce a draft that appears to be finished, for this psychologically inhibits the freedom of the stylist to restructure the text into a really acceptable style.

In either case, it is usually essential that at various points in the collaborative effort of scholars and stylists, someone act as a kind of "go-between" to help each understand the distinctive contributions of the other. This is one of the vital functions of Bible Society Translation Consultants.

It is also important, whichever approach is used, to submit the final draft to a stylist who is not a Christian, or at least who is not familiar with the Bible. This may or may not be the same as the one who does the restructuring. But if the stylist is already too familiar with the Bible, he may too easily accept certain terms or expressions merely because they are traditional, without realizing that they may be rare or awkward.

STAGES OF TRANSFER

In view of the particular manner in which the steps in procedure are outlined in this text, it might seem as though the translator must first analyze all of his material, then make the transfer of the total discourse, and finally restructure it. This is, of course, a mistake, for the steps in procedure followed in the orderly exposition of a technique are not precisely the ones which one employs in the practical application of such a set of procedures. For example, in the actual process of translating, the translator will constantly swing back and forth between the analytical and the restructuring processes by way of the transfer. In split-second fashion the mind is able to shift procedures, and this is all to the good. It is only important that one be aware, insofar as necessary, of precisely what he is doing, and that one not confuse one task with the other.

Not only will a good translator be constantly sweeping back and forth from one aspect of the procedure to another, but he will also inevitably analyze in the direction of what he knows he must do in the restructuring. That is to say, in his analysis he will anticipate what he knows he must confront in the restructuring. For example, if a receptor language employs primarily participial constructions rather than dependent clauses, then automatically the back-transformations will anticipate the types of transfers and restructuring which are required. Similarly, if passives have to be changed to actives under certain conditions he will anticipate this in the steps of analysis.

One must not transfer the message from language A to language B merely in the form of a series of disconnected kernels. Such unrelated simple constructions would make little or no sense. Rather, it is important that one indicate clearly the precise relationship between the kernels. In other words, the transfer is not made at the extreme level of individual kernels, but at the point where they are connected into meaningful series. This means that we must modify slightly our basic diagram, so as to show that after having analyzed the basic components into their simplest relationships within kernels, we "back up" to the point where these kernels are carefully and properly related to each other.

The relations between two kernels may be of three main sorts: (1) temporal, (2) spatial, and (3) logical. The temporal relations arrange the kernels into a time sequence, including the indication of simultaneity and of extended time lapses; and it is in general a good idea to arrange kernels that are related temporally into the absolute time sequence, even though it may not be the actual literary ordering either in the surface structure of the source language or in the final draft translation. The reason for this is that the devices by which different languages permit alteration of the "real time" ordering of events for special effects vary enormously, both in kind and in degree. Few languages permit the involuted reversing of time relations found in the Greek of Mark 6:17-20, which deals with various actions of Herod, John the Baptist, and Herodias in a very complicated way. Temporal relations are especially important in narrative texts, though not necessarily absent from other types.

Spatial relations may be of two kinds: (a) those between objects "out there," *e.g.*, a house, a road, and a clump of trees; and (b) those between the viewer and the objects. In the first kind, one progresses in some kind of order from object to object, or from part to part. The order may be left to right, or top to bottom, or some other. But one does not simply jump helter-skelter from thing to thing. Relations between viewer and object involve questions of proximity or distance (*e.g.*, the "zoom lens" effect achieved when something is first viewed at a distance in a larger setting, and then examined more closely and in detail). It is a universal of narrative and even more of description that one maintains a particular viewpoint until a change is somehow signaled.

Logical relations are of a quite different kind, but there is still a kind of *a priori* ordering between the elements: cause and effect, condition and consequence, purpose and accomplishment, and so on. Again, different languages provide totally different surface structure devices for representing these relations, so that the ordering at point X just before the transfer ought to be as neutral and as unarbitrary as possible.

Semantic Adjustments Made in Transfer

Before discussing the various technical procedures for making semantic adjustments in transfer, it is necessary to mention the theoretical basis for such adjustments in general. This lies in the essential distinction which must be made throughout between the form of a message and its content. If we assume that language is a device for communicating messages, then it follows that language and linguistic forms are means to an end rather than an end in themselves. The content is the conceptual intent of the message, together with the connotative values the source wishes to communicate; it is what the message is about. The form, on the other hand, is the external shape the message takes to effect its passage from the source's mind to the receptor's mind. And it is almost invariably true that for any given content, a language makes available numerous forms which could equally well convey the message.

In transferring the message from one language to another, it is the content which must be preserved at any cost; the form, except in special cases, such as poetry, is largely secondary, since within each language the rules for relating content to form are highly complex, arbitrary, and variable. It is a bit like packing clothing into two different pieces of luggage: the clothes remain the same, but the shape of the suitcases may vary greatly, and hence the way in which the clothes are packed must be different. Of course, if by coincidence it is possible to convey the same content in the receptor language in a form which closely resembles that of the source, so much the better; we preserve the form when we can, but

v. imp.

more often the form has to be transformed precisely in order to preserve the content. An excessive effort to preserve the form inevitably results in a serious loss or distortion of the message.

Obviously in any translation there will be a type of "loss" of semantic content, but the process should be so designed as to keep this to a minimum. The commonest problems of content transfer arise in the following areas: (1) idioms, (2) figurative meanings, (3) shifts in central components of meaning, (4) generic and specific meanings, (5) pleonastic expressions, (6) special formulas, (7) redistribution of semantic components, (8) provision for contextual conditioning. These will be discussed in the following sections.

Idioms   ejemplos

Idioms (see p. 89) are some of the most obvious candidates for semantic adjustment, for the very fact that they are idioms means it is unlikely that the same type of distinctive form will have the same meaning in another language. The adjustments are quite understandably of three types: (a) from idioms to nonidioms, (b) from idioms to idioms, and (c) from nonidioms to idioms.

Frequently idioms are shifted to nonidioms in the process of transfer. For example, "to gird up the loins of the mind" (1 Peter 1:13) may be transferred as "to get ready in one's thinking." And an idiom such as "heap coals of fire on his head" (Rom. 12:20) becomes "make him ashamed."

In certain instances it is possible to match one idiom by another. For example, in Shipibo, "to have a hard heart" (a phrase which if translated literally would mean "to be brave"), is transferred into an idiomatic equivalent, "his ears have no holes." In one African language, the epitome of human wisdom is not "flesh and blood," (in the phrase "flesh and blood have not revealed it unto you"), but "an old man with a single hair." In certain cases some translators have felt that it is essential to indicate in the margin the exact form of the Biblical idiom. This is entirely all right, but in most instances it is really not necessary.

Whereas one inevitably loses many idioms in the process of translation, one also stands to gain a number of idioms. For instance, "faith" may be rendered—as in Tzeltal—as "to hang on to God with the heart," and "peace," as in a number of African languages, is "to sit down in the heart." Such idiomatic renderings do much to make the translation come alive, for it is by means of such distinctive expressions that the message can speak meaningfully to people in terms of their own lives and behavior.[1]

---

[1] It is not without interest to note that many persons who readily agree to the addition of idioms, *i.e.*, changes from nonidioms, are nevertheless reluctant to permit any changes from idioms to nonidioms. But one cannot have his cake and eat it too. What one must give up in order to communicate effectively can, however, be compensated for, at least in part, by the introduction of fitting idioms. One of the difficulties is that too often translators are not sufficiently sensitive to the possibilities of idiomatic expressions, and hence the end result is a weakening of the figurative force of the translation, since they do not compensate for loss of certain idioms by the introduction of others.

Problem 33

1. Give the meaning of the following idioms in nonidiomatic form: *they lifted up their voices* (Luke 17:13); *flesh and blood* has not revealed this (Matt. 16:17); *your hardness of heart* (Mark 10:5); *his countenance fell* (Mark 10:22); *the heaven was shut up* (Luke 4:25); he *set his face* to go to Jerusalem (Luke 9:51); men's *love will grow cold* (Matt. 24:12); *fill up ... the measure* of your fathers (Matt. 23:32).
2. In the language in which you are working, how many of these can be rendered by idioms? What are they?

Figurative meanings of individual words

As in the case of idioms, there are three situations in which figurative expressions (see pp. 87-89) are involved in the transfer process: (a) shifts from figurative to nonfigurative usage, *e.g.*, "possess the gate" is changed to "possess the city"; "my flesh" is changed to "my race"; "taste death" becomes "die"; (b) shifts from one type of figurative expression to another figurative expression, *e.g.*, "heart" changed to "liver" (as in a number of African languages); "praise the Lord with the tongue" changed to "praise the Lord with the lips"; (c) nonfigurative expressions changed to figurative ones, *e.g.*, "to trust" rendered as "to lean on."

Problem 34

1. Replace the words which are used in their figurative senses with equivalent literal expressions in English: *bear fruit* that befits repentance (Matt. 3:8); the *lost sheep* of the house of Israel (Matt. 15:24); the *wages* of sin (Rom. 6:23); who *devour* widows' houses (Mark 12:40).

Shifts in central components of meaning

Undoubtedly it is in the shifts of central components of meaning that one becomes involved in some of the most dangerous types of modifications. Nevertheless, in many instances such changes are obligatory. For example, the Biblical term "holy," as used in speaking of God, has as a very central element in many contexts the moral quality of God, not merely his inviolate unapproachableness. But in some languages, it is necessary to shift to a term which means primarily "taboo." Nevertheless, by means of careful contextual conditioning, the translator can gradually build into this indigenous term something of the values which became associated with the corresponding Hebrew term.

Of course, in many instances shifts of components involve only a shift from a literal or etymological meaning to one which is functionally more relevant. For example, the Greek word "devil" etymologically means "slanderer," but this literal translation may mean nothing in another language. Rather, an expression such as "chief of the demons" will be much more meaningful and accurate. In such a situation, there is actually no shift from central meanings, but only a shift from "etymological" meanings.

Some translators, however, have unwittingly made shifts which have thoroughly distorted the original concept. In some languages, "Holy Spirit" means little more than a "white ghost," for "holy" has been equated with cleanness or whiteness, and *Spirit* is more readily understood in such a context as "ghost" rather than as the "Spirit of God." An even worse situation was encountered in a language in which "holy" was rendered as "that which makes taboo" and "spirit" meant primarily an evil or malicious spirit. It was quite understandable that the people in this area were very reluctant to receive "a tabooing demon," especially when the possession of such a demon ruled out any sexual relations with one's spouse.

Problem 35

In the language in which you are working, describe the central components of the term or terms which you are considering for: *holy, demon, spirit, soul.* What are the pros and cons of each one? For each possibility, what would you have to do to invest it with the Biblical meaning?

Generic and specific meanings

Some of the most common shifts in meaning found in the transfer process are modifications which involve specific and generic meanings. Such shifts may, of course, go in either direction, from generic to specific, or from specific to generic. In some languages, for example, there may be no general term for demons, so one has to choose the name for that particular class of demonic spirits which most closely approximate the Biblical counterparts. In the process, however, there is a shift from a more generic term in the Greek to a more specific term in the receptor language. Similarly, one may not have a general word for brother, and hence may have to use more specific words designating either "younger brother" or "older brother."

On the other hand, one often goes from specific to generic. For instance, some languages cannot speak of "the brethren," a generic use of "brothers," but must use a word meaning "relative." Terms such as *denarii* may be translated as "pieces of money" in some contexts (in which the actual value is not important), and the more technical term "parable" may have to be translated as "story" in some languages.

Pleonastic expressions

There are a number of phrases which seem quite awkward and unnecessarily repetitious when transferred into a receptor language. For example, in Job 33:2, "the tongue in my mouth speaks" is rather ludicrous in some languages, for where else can one have a tongue than in one's mouth? A phrase such as "spoke by the mouth of the prophets" (Luke 1:70) may also seem pleonastic, for in some languages one does not speak "by another's mouth" but only "causes someone else to speak." "For his name's sake" (3 John 7) may in some contexts be better rendered as "for his sake"; and "answering, said" may be more appropriately translated as "answered." A phrase such as "fruit trees bearing fruit in which is their seed after its kind" can be rendered literally, even though, of course, it means only "all kinds of fruit trees," but such a literal rendering may sound more like some technical botanical distinction whereby peaches and pomegranates are to be included but cashews and bananas are to be ruled out. In the original there was no such intention of classifying fruit trees into various groups, but only the contrast of grain-bearing plants (in which the seeds have no fleshy covering) to fruit-bearing plants. If one insists upon the full, literal form, the original contrast is likely to be lost and another substituted in its place.

Formulas

The epistolary formulas, e.g., Romans 1:1-7, 1 Corinthians 1:1-3, and Ephesians 1:1-2, are troublesome elements for the translator, for they inevitably require some sort of modification in the process of transfer. Otherwise, there is very little meaning, especially if people do not understand the use of the third person for the first person. But certain other formulaic expressions may also need to be altered, e.g., "blessing I will bless thee" (Heb. 6:14), must become in some languages, "I will surely bless you." A phrase such as "an eye for an eye and a tooth for a tooth" (Matt. 5:38) may need to be expanded or modified in some languages. Otherwise, the emphasis is on revenge rather than on justice or retribution.

Redistribution of semantic components

The redistribution of semantic components is of two principal types (a) analytical, i.e., "expansion" or distribution of the components over a number of different words, and (b) synthetic, grouping of several semantic components into a single term. The analytic process is well illustrated by such expansions as "one who will receive" for heir, "to put into a right relationship" for justify, "God's people" for saints, and "caught having sexual relations with a man not her husband" for taken in adultery. So-called "descriptives" are also examples of the analytic tendency, e.g., "charms with holy words in them" for phylacteries, "not eating in order to worship" for fast.

In contrast with the analytical process, one also encounters instances of the very opposite tendency, i.e., combining into single words what may have been a phrase in the source language. For example, "brothers and sisters" may be reduced to a single term meaning "siblings." Or as in Moré (a language of the Upper Volta), "got up early before daybreak and went out to an uninhabited place" (Mark 1:35) is appropriately translated by a single word.

Provision of contextual conditioning

When there are distinct differences between the cultural forms or functions of Biblical referents and the corresponding receptor-language parallels, it may be necessary to provide a certain amount of contextual conditioning. In many instances such conditioning can be provided in the text itself. For example, when certain completely unknown terms are borrowed, one may find it very useful to add so-called "classifiers," *e.g.*, "animals called camels," "precious stone ruby," "city Jerusalem," and "rite of baptism." In other instances one may find it important to employ a descriptive phrase so as to provide some basis for comprehending the significance of the original. In translating "firmament," for example, one may wish to use "dome of the sky," or "vault in the sky," rather than merely "vault," for otherwise one will not understand that this is a description of a celestial phenomenon.

In some cases the text of Scriptures does not adequately identify the object involved, especially if the sets of semantic components are not mutually reinforcing. For example, in Mark 1:12, it is possible that people will understand "the Spirit drove him into the wilderness" as being the activity of a demon rather than of the Holy Spirit. In the Greek New Testament the term *pneuma*, "spirit," without qualifier usually designates the Holy Spirit. In many languages, however, the general term for "spirit" by itself may designate evil spirits. In such languages, it is best in all passages in which the Greek uses simple *pneuma* for the Holy Spirit to use whatever specific expression has been adopted to refer to the Holy Spirit. In most cases this involves the use of some qualifier, which provides the required contextual conditioning.

The provision of cultural conditioning always implies the entire problem of the extent to which certain adjustments can and should be made in the transfer. Basically, alterations are not employed unless (1) the text is likely to be misunderstood by the receptors, (2) the text is likely to have no meaning to the receptors, or (3) the resulting translation is so "overloaded" that it will constitute too much of a problem for the average reader to figure it out. But even within the range of these three types of expressions, there are certain specific problems relating to the historical significance of the event and the importance of the religious symbolism involved. For example, in translating John 15 it is not necessary that the people know about grapevines or that they understand the precise methods of cultivating and pruning such plants. One can often use a generic term which will designate almost any kind of plant having similar types of growth and requiring pruning in order to produce better. In this context the grapevine as such does not seem to have any special symbolic value. On the other hand, in the cursing of the fig tree (Mark 11:12-14) and the fertilizing of the fig tree (Luke 13:6-9), some scholars believe that specific reference must be made to the fig tree, since this has the symbolic value of identifying the fruitfulness of the Jewish national life. However, in the passage concerning gathering "grapes from thorns" or "figs from thistles" (Matt. 7:16), it is not necessary to identify these specific Biblical plants, for there are almost always close functional, if not formal, parallels in other lands. Moreover, the use of these plants in this saying is merely for the sake of analogy, and there seems to be no important symbolism attached to them. At the same time, of course, a translator can, if he so wishes, attempt to identify the specific plants by means of some marginal notation, but this may seem more pedantic than useful.

There are situations, however, in which culturally strange objects must be retained because of their symbolic values. For example, one cannot dispense with a term for sheep or lambs, for these animals figure so largely in the entire sacrificial system. Moreover, there are important analogies employed in the New Testament, *e.g.*, Jesus Christ as the Lamb of God. Similarly, though crucifixion may not be known in the local culture, the use of some expression for "cross" and "crucifixion" is essential, though it may be necessary to provide some fuller explanation in a glossary or marginal note.

In certain cases there is no way to provide such conditioning within the context, for a completely different cultural function may be involved. For example, in West Africa "casting branches in front of one" is a way of insulting an approaching chief or ruler. But one cannot change the account in Matthew 21:8 to accommodate an entirely different local West African practice, namely, the sweeping of the path before an approaching dignitary. At the same time, if the Biblical account is not to be misunderstood, one must add some sort of explanatory note.

Explanatory notes are largely of two types: (1) those which are related to specific historical situations, in which the explanation normally needs to appear on the same page as the episode described, and (2) those which are more general in character and can thus often be placed in a glossary (*e.g.*, explanations of Pharisees, Sadducees, Herodians, Levites, etc.) or treated in some type of Table of Weights and Measures (*e.g.*, denarii, shekel, talent, etc.).

It must be further emphasized that one is not free to make in the text any and all kinds of explanatory additions and/or expansions. There is a very definite limit as to what is proper translation in this difficult area: one may make explicit in the text only what is *linguistically* implicit in the immediate context of the problematic passage. This imposes a dual constraint: one may not simply add interesting cultural information which is not actually present in the meanings of the terms used in the passage, and one may not add information derived from other parts of the Bible, much less from extra-Biblical sources, such as tradition. When one attempts to make too much explicit, one falls into eisegesis rather than exegesis. For example, some have wanted to put into the first person references in John's Gospel to "the disciple whom Jesus loved" (13:23, 21:20, etc.) as well as specific references to John the son of Zebedee. But these identifications are extra-Biblical, and should not be read back into the text. Again, some have wanted to translate the notion of *redemption* in its Christian, New Testament sense in such a way as to make explicit in every instance the paying of a price by the death of Jesus Christ. But most scholars are agreed that the primary allusion in this use of the term is not to the redemption of a slave by the payment of a price but to the rescue of Israel by a mighty act of God. Finally, some have insisted on using for *inheritance* an expression which made explicit the notion of someone's dying and leaving property to another by a will. But this is a serious misreading of the Greek term, which denotes a possession promised or due to someone. Death is only one of the ways by which people could come into such a possession.

Errors of translation involving making explicit too much or the wrong notions are not restricted to one segment of the theological spectrum. One finds them, on the one hand, in such a conservative effort as the *Amplified Bible*, and, on the other, in the *New Testament Wordbook of Kittel*, which James Barr has so cogently criticized in *The Semantics of Biblical Language*. Further discussion of the difference between linguistic and cultural translation will be found on p. 134.

STRUCTURAL ADJUSTMENTS

As with the transfer of semantic content, one endeavors to keep the structural form if it is possible, but in most cases it is not. The attempt to preserve structural form usually results in either complete unintelligibility, or in awkwardness. There is nothing sacrosanct about such features of structure as sentence length and phrase structure patterns, and too often the effort to reflect the source in these formal aspects results in badly overloading the communication and thus making it very hard for the reader to understand.

The structural adjustments affect the entire range of linguistic structure, from the discourse to the sounds, and they may most conveniently be classified in terms of various levels: (1) discourse, (2) sentence, (3) word, and (4) sounds. The adjustments being discussed in this outline of factors in the procedure of transfer are all "obligatory." This does not mean that such changes are obligatory in all languages, but when they are necessary to guarantee intelligibility or to avoid awkwardness, they need to be regarded as minimal adjustments, which constitute the basis for still further adjustments that are required or expedient in the process of restructuring.

Discourse structure. [2]

The problems of the discourse are very extensive, and only a few can be noted here, but these should be sufficient to indicate something of the range of difficulties which must be taken into consideration. Further aspects of this very complex issue will be discussed in Chapter 7.

One of the most common problems of adjustment in discourse is the handling of direct and indirect discourse. Some languages show decided preference for one or another form, and accordingly, one must make the necessary changes, many of which involve not one sentence but a whole series of sentences. In some cases, the pressures for direct discourse are so great that almost any verb of speaking has to be turned into direct discourse. For example, instead of saying, "They glorified God," one must translate, "They said, 'God is wonderful.'"

The problems of discourse structure frequently involve distinctive uses of pronominal forms. This is especially true of the use of the third person

---

[2] The types of changes discussed here under "discourse structure" can, of course, also be treated as a part of the sentence structure, since all the changes are actually parts of sentences. However, the factors which lead to such changes are those which concern primarily the suprasentence level, from the paragraph to the total discourse.

pronouns when referring to the first person. Hence, "Paul ... to the church" becomes "I, Paul, write to the church." Also the phrase "Son of man" in discourses by Jesus must be modified to read "I who am the Son of man," since in some languages such a third person reference could not be to Jesus.[3]

An even more important problem of the discourse structure is the way in which the receptor language handles the identification of participants, whether by nouns, pronouns, and/or substitute reference. Once a person has been introduced into a discourse, languages differ considerably in the ways in which they may continue to refer to him. In some languages there is actually a fourth person, *i.e.*, the next third person introduced into an account.

Sequence of tenses may also pose certain problems. For example, in some languages only the initial verb of a paragraph indicates the temporal setting, and all the dependent verbs use a "neutral tense." In other languages, one can begin with a historical tense, but then in narration one regularly shifts to the present in order to present the story in a more lively manner. Whatever the pattern of the receptor language may be, it is essential that the proper adjustments be made, or the discourse will sound badly organized and even contradictory.

Sentence structure

There are numerous features of the sentence structure which must be adjusted in the process of transfer from one language to another. Some of the most important of these are the following: (a) word and phrase order, (b) double negatives, (c) singular and plural agreement, (d) active and passive structures, (e) coordination and subordination, (f) apposition, (g) ellipsis, and (h) specification of relationship.

Word and phrase order: While English and Greek permit attributives both before and after a head word (the word which is modified), some languages have a "decided preference for," or may require that most attributives precede the word they modify. In other languages, most attributives must follow. Moreover, the basic order of Subject-Verb-Object may be altered in a number of ways, *e.g.*, Subject-Object-Verb, Verb-Object-Subject, or Verb-Subject-Object. Whatever the basic patterns of word order are in the receptor language, one should adjust to these in the transfer process. Whenever a language has an obligatory order, the situation is somewhat easier than when there are a number of optional patterns, for though the different choices may appear to be substantially identical, there are usually certain subtle distinctions which are only mastered by long association with and close study of a language.

Double negatives: These are especially confusing, for in some languages

---

[3] Some persons have argued that Jesus did not actually speak of himself as "the Son of man," but that this is a wrong attribution made to him by his disciples. Regardless of what position one might take with respect to such a reinterpretation of the data, it is evident that the Gospel writers themselves made this identification, and it is their text which we are translating rather than any presumed underlying original.

they add up to a positive, while in other languages they constitute an emphatic negative expression. In some cases one form of double negative is actually negative, while another form is positive. All of these subtle differences must be carefully noted by the translator.

— *Gender, class, and number concord*: While some languages, *e.g.*, the Indo-European ones and the typical Bantu class-prefix languages, adhere to strict rules of gender, class, and number concord, some languages pay very little attention to such distinctions, *e.g.*, Chinese. In Quechua, a term may occur in the plural form at the beginning of a paragraph but any later references to the same term normally do not have the plural suffix. To keep attaching plural suffixes regularly to every occurrence of a plural word seems awkward and childish in Quechua.

In some languages the problems of plural and singular become especially acute in a phrase such as "the two shall be one," for if the language requires plural concord on predicate attributives, such as "one," a literal rendering of this Biblical phrase may be meaningless, even as it is in so many Bantu languages, for "one" cannot occur with a plural prefix. Accordingly, one must often transform this expression into "the two shall be just like one."

— *Active and passive constructions*: The problems of active and passive constructions also figure largely in the problems of transfer. This is especially true in languages which may have no passive at all, or which may have a decided preference for the active. In such cases passives must be changed into actives or pseudo-actives, *e.g.*, *They received punishment*. But some languages, *e.g.*, Nilotic languages, have almost an opposite tendency, namely, employing a high percentage of expressions in the passive. There is no difficulty in transferring a passive with agent—*e.g.*, "Jesus was baptized by John" becomes "John baptized Jesus,"—but where the agent is not mentioned one must supply such an agent from the context. In most cases this is quite easy, but there are some passages in which some persons understand a general agent, when actually a specific agent is implied. This is particularly true in the so-called "passives of divine avoidance," a Semitic type of avoidance of the divine name. This means, for example, that in a sentence such as, "Judge not that you be not judged," the real agent of the second event is God, *i.e.*, "Judge not so that God will not judge you." Similarly, in the Beatitudes the agent of the passive expressions, *e.g.*, "be comforted," "be called the sons of God," and "be filled," is in all instances God.

— *Coordination and subordination*: Transfer normally involves a number of shifts in coordinate and subordinate patterns. For example, the phrase "grace and apostleship" (Rom. 1:5) is better rendered as a subordinate construction in many languages, *e.g.*, "the privilege of being an apostle." On the other hand, "baptism of repentance" is a subordinate type of construction, but it is semantically equivalent to a coordinate construction, "repent and be baptized." Similarly, in the translation of clause structures, what may be coordinate in one language, *e.g.*, "He went and found it," may correspond to a subordinate construction in another language, "Having gone, he found it." And conversely, what in Greek is expressed as subordinate, *i.e.*, hypotactic, turns out to be paratactic, or coordinate, in many other languages, *e.g.*, "John's disciples and the Pharisees were keeping a fast; then some people came to him and said."

— *Apposition*: An apposition such as "Paul, a servant of Jesus Christ" can always be readily changed into a dependent expression, *e.g.*, "Paul, who is a servant of Jesus Christ." What is more difficult is to spot those subtle forms of apposition which are formally disguised, *e.g.*, "God and Father of our Lord Jesus Christ." To translate "God and Father" literally in some languages is to imply that these are two different persons. Therefore, one must render this phrase as "God, the Father. . .," or "God, who is the Father. . . ." Similarly, "the land of Judea" is a form of apposition, and in some languages one must translate "the land called Judea."

— *Ellipsis*: All languages employ ellipsis, but the patterns of ellipsis are usually quite diverse in different languages. "He is greater than I" must be rendered in some languages as "He is greater than I am great," while in other languages the equivalent is "He is great, I am not." Such ellipses as these pose few problems, but there are some which may escape one's notice. For example, "The sabbath was made for man, not man for the sabbath" (Mark 2:27) must in many languages be translated as two paratactically combined positive-negative sentences: "The sabbath was made for the sake of helping people; people were not made for the sake of honoring the sabbath." Here, the ellipsis is of two types: (1) the absence of the verb in the second clause of the English model, and (2) an ellipsis in the phrases "for the sake of the man" and "for the sake of the sabbath," for in these two instances the events which may contribute to the benefit of man and the sabbath are quite different. It is for this reason that the implied terms, "helping" and "honoring," must be added.

Specification of relationship: There is much in any communication which is taken for granted, for the original participants in the communication are aware of a good deal of information which does not require explicit statement in the particular form of a message. For example, "lord of the sabbath" (Mark 2:28) involves a very complex relationship, since "lord" implies not only an individual but one who controls or commands (see Chapter 3). In the NEB this relationship is made more explicit by the phrase, "sovereign even over the sabbath," but in some languages one must make the relationship even more specific, *e.g.*, "commands what men should do on the sabbath." In Mark 6:16 Herod is quoted as saying, "John, whom I beheaded." This seems to be a perfectly clear relationship among the subject, the verb, and the goal of the action; but in reality, as shown by verse 27, Herod did not himself behead John but ordered a soldier to do it. In many languages it is obligatory to make clear this causative relationship, and therefore the relationship between the participants and the action must be made more specific, *e.g.*, "John, whom I ordered a soldier to behead."

Word structure

The relationships of word structure to the problems of transfer are of two principal types: (1) the grammatical classes of words which may be used and (2) the so-called morphological categories which are associated with the various classes. The adjustments in word classes are most often changes from nouns to verbs (when the nouns express events) and shifts between nouns and pronouns, depending upon the syntactical requirements of the language in specifying the participants. There are languages, however, which use nounlike words to correspond to Greek conjunctions. For example, in Maya, "and," "in order to," and "because of" are all translated by "possessed" nouns. "John and Peter" is literally "John his-withness Peter." In some languages there are very few prepositions indicating spatial relationships. In such cases, one cannot say, "Jesus arose from the dead," but rather, "Jesus got up and left the dead," for such a language simply does not employ a preposition "from" but rather a verb indicating an event of movement.

There are numerous subtle problems of morphological categories which can only be touched upon: (a) aspects, (b) tenses, (c) inclusive and exclusive first person plural, (d) the distinction between persons who are dead or alive, and (e) honorifics.

Aspects: In Hebrew and in the nonfinite tenses of Greek, there are certain aspectual features of the verbal patterns, *i.e.*, completive vs. incompletive and punctiliar vs. durative (or continuative), but many languages have a number of subtle differences of aspect, *e.g.*, seen and unseen participant, durative and repetitive, beginning (inceptive) and ending, seen, quoted, and legendary. In the Guaica language of Venezuela, for example, each complete sentence must end with one of the aspectual particles which indicates whether the described was seen by the speaker, was heard from reliable persons, or is purely legendary or imaginary. The implications of this for the Bible translator should be immediately evident.

Tenses: Whereas in most Indo-European languages we are accustomed to three basic tenses: past, present, and future, with several tenses of relative time, *e.g.*, pluperfect, future perfect, and past perfect, in some languages there are a number of temporal gradations, *e.g.*, past time of a few minutes ago, past of earlier today, past time of yesterday or recent weeks, past time of a month to a year, and past time of legendary events. A similar, but not so extensive, series sometimes occurs for future tense forms. Such distinctions naturally require the translator to introduce a good deal of information which is not explicit in the Biblical text. Moreover, he must make certain rather extensive adjustments in the case of Mark's use of *euthus*, "immediately," for generally this transitional adverb does not mark something which happened shortly after a preceding event, but only something which constituted the next vital phase of the continuing account.

Inclusive vs. exclusive first person plural: The problems of inclusive-exclusive first person reference are very extensive. It is, of course, not too difficult to decide whether to use the inclusive or the exclusive in such a passage as "Do you not care if we perish?" (Mark 4:38), for the inclusive would seem to be the only expression which would really make sense. It is, however, much more difficult to decide in the case of the Pauline

Epistles just when Paul is speaking for himself or for his colleagues and when he is presuming that his audience shares with him the spiritual experiences he describes. For example, in Colossians 1:1-12 the "we" forms are essentially exclusive, but at verse 13 Paul evidently shifts viewpoints and includes his audience, and in verse 21 there is another shift back to the I-you or the we-you distinction. In Ephesians the problem is somewhat more acute. Verses 3-10 of chapter 1 seem to be distinctly inclusive, in that the writer is assuming in his audience the same type of experience which he has had, but in verses 11 and 12 there is no such certainty, for verse 13 introduces a contrast between the "we" and the "you." In general, translators have tended to favor the inclusive forms when there is real obscurity, for the exclusive would seem to imply too great a barrier between the writer and his audience.

Dead and alive: Some languages mark continually the differences between persons who are dead (or have died) and those who are still alive. What is one to do, however, in speaking of the risen Christ? To use an affix meaning "still alive" would imply that he did not die, but rather only fainted. On the other hand, what is one to do in the case of Lazarus, who was not only raised from the dead, but who died later? In most instances languages with this type of distinction resolve the situation by using the "dead" affix in speaking of Christ, for he did not die again, but they use the "alive" affix in speaking of Lazarus, for he was destined to die again.

Honorifics: The various patterns of honorific language constitute some of the most difficult of all problems for the translator. These, however, are not restricted merely to matters of grammatical categories; they involve lexical usage (the choice of words), complexity of grammatical expression, and word forms. A number of languages with such honorific structures define three major levels: (1) speaking up (as to royalty or deity), (2) speaking down (as to servants or persons of inferior status), and (3) speaking to peers (those on the same level). It is obviously quite impossible to deal here with all the types of problems or special situations. For example, in Balinese, Isaiah is spoken to and about with honorific forms, because of his princely lineage, but Amos is not addressed or spoken of with such terms because he had no such high social rank. But there are two other problems which are even more complex than the intricacies of form and arrangement: (1) the viewpoint of the original participants vs. the viewpoint of the writer (and the church), and (2) the attitudes of present-day readers.

In a language with honorific distinctions it is quite unnatural that the Pharisees should be represented as addressing Jesus with honorific terminology, even though he was regarded by some as a rabbi, for he was a young man and had not been educated in the rabbinic tradition. On the other hand, in an honorific-using society, Jesus is likely to have addressed the prestigious Pharisees with honorifics, for most of them would have been relatively well-to-do, since only the rich could afford to keep the ritual observances. But by the time the Gospel writers composed their accounts, Jesus would not be regarded by the writers or by the church as anything less than divine, and hence deserving of such recognition by all.

The same is even more true of church members today, for they would regard it almost as blasphemy to have Jesus addressed in words which seemed to degrade his deity, even though such words might be used by his enemies. Accordingly, it is not merely a matter of trying to reconstruct what might have been the sociolinguistic patterns of language usage in Jesus' day. Rather, one must look at such events through the eyes of the Gospel writers and of the early church, and with the perspective of the present-day believers.

Corresponding sounds

In the recasting of borrowed words, including proper names especially, one normally attempts to follow the phonological structure of the receptor language. This may mean, for example, that *Mark* may become *Maliko* and *Peter* may become *Petelo*. There are, however, two principles which tend to alter a systematic adjustment to the phonological patterns of the receptor language: (1) the prestige of the orthography of a dominant language and (2) the problems of accidental correspondences.

Perhaps the problems involved in the adjustments of forms of proper names are as complex and as fraught with emotional overtones as anything else in the Scriptures, for their very arbitrariness (this is due to the differences between languages) leads to much emotional identification and attachment. It is, however, quite impossible to deal here with all the myriad difficulties which may be encountered, not merely when languages already have one or more existing traditions of transliteration (these problems are especially difficult when Roman Catholic and Protestant translators attempt to resolve differences, since the traditions are usually based on very different principles and go back to quite different bases), but also when languages are being newly reduced to writing. Nevertheless, it is important to point out that the adjustments cannot be mechanical or automatic. For example, in many of the Indian languages of Latin America the people insist that the forms of common proper names must be like Spanish or Portuguese. Despite the difficulties the people may encounter in pronouncing the strange letters or combinations of letters, they feel that names are only "right" and "correct" when they are written in the forms of the culturally dominant language. The same is true in many situations in Africa where French, English, and Portuguese tend to dominate.

But even when there is due regard for the phonological structures and even for the prestigious, dominant languages of the area, one may have to make certain further adjustments if the forms of a name or borrowed word accidentally resembles another word in the receptor language. For example, a systematic transliteration of *Messiah* in one language of West Africa turned out to be identical with an indigenous expression meaning "death's hand." Quite obviously, it was necessary to make an adjustment in order to avoid a wrong association.

In conclusion, let us remind ourselves of the priorities in the process of transfer:

1. At all costs, the content of the message must be transferred with

as little loss or distortion as possible. It is the referential, conceptual burden of the message that has the highest priority.

2. It is very important to convey as well as possible the connotation, the emotional flavor and impact, of the message. This is harder to describe than the first, and even harder to accomplish, but it is very important.

3. If, in transferring from one language to another the content and connotation of the message, one can also carry over something of the form, one should do so. But under no circumstances should the form be given priority over the other aspects of the message.

CHAPTER SEVEN

RESTRUCTURING

In restructuring the message after having transferred it from the source language to the receptor language, it is essential that one consider the problems from three perspectives: (1) the varieties of language or of styles which may be desirable, (2) the essential components and characteristics of these various styles, and (3) the techniques which may be employed in producing the type of style desired.

VARIETIES OF LANGUAGE

Though we have emphasized the enormous variability between different languages, it must not be thought that each particular language is perfectly homogeneous. Rather, within any given language there are a greater or lesser number of varieties of language. In an overview of the problem, one ought to mention that a language varies in terms of time (older vs. newer forms, archaisms, neologisms, etc.), geography (dialects), socio-economic classes or castes, circumstances of use, oral or written usage, types of discourse, and literary genres. Various ones of these dimensions of variation will be discussed in this chapter, insofar as they are relevant to restructuring in translation.

From the standpoint of the translator the problems involved in the diverse varieties of language differ greatly, depending upon the literary status of the language in question. This means that he must consider at least three quite different types of situations: (1) languages with long literary traditions and a relatively well-defined literary style, (2) languages which have been reduced to writing within the last generation or so and which have acquired, even in this relatively short period, certain types of "accepted" and even "hallowed" usages, and (3) languages which are only now being reduced to writing by the translator. At the same time it is important to realize that for situations 2 and 3, there is always the likelihood of a relatively extensive oral literary tradition, which will significantly influence anything which is put into written form in the language.

LEVEL OF LANGUAGE FOR SOCIETIES WITH A LITERARY TRADITION

Within the Christian community of any language group having a relatively long literary tradition (*e.g.*, three or four hundred years), there are a number of special features which must be carefully considered in determining precisely what style or level of language one should follow in the production of a translation. But if we are to understand the problems involved, we must consider the levels and types of style from a somewhat more scientific orientation than is usually employed. For one thing, this means distinguishing clearly between the oral and the written language, and between the consumer and the producer language. Certain of these differences can be well illustrated by the following diagram, Figure 12:

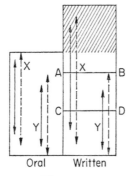

Figure 12

In Figure 12, X and Y represent two typical speakers, one on the so-called higher language level and the other on the lower language level. This does not mean that the actual forms of language used by these persons are intrinsically inferior or superior, or that one is more complex or intricate than the other. It only means that speaker X uses such forms as are employed by those who carry on the affairs of the language community, while Y uses forms which are typical of those who do not enjoy such "leadership" privileges. Generally such differences may be described in terms of educational levels, but as in most large urbanized and industrialized societies, these levels are also correlatable with socioeconomic advantages and status.

The solid lines in each instance represent the producer language, that is to say, the type of language which the person X or Y is able to produce, whether in speaking or writing. The broken lines represent the corresponding "consumer" language, that is to say, the range of language which these same persons are able to understand. It should be noted that in each instance, the spread or range of the consumer language is greater than that of the producer language. In other words, one is generally able to hear or read more than he can say or write.

It should also be noted that the total range of the X is in each instance greater than Y, for he is in a position socially and educationally to have wider linguistic contacts, and thus acquires a wider range of both production and consumption. It is important to realize, however, that speaker X does not usually understand the total range of Y. That is to say, there are certain substandard forms which he probably can neither understand nor use correctly.

The extension of the written language above the oral language represents the fact that the written language has a literary accretion coming from its historical traditions. It extends on the upper limits, for it is generally that form of written language which the upper-class person, such as X, will study in school.

In general both X and Y will have a slightly greater range in the written form than in the spoken form of language. This is true for Y if Y is reasonably familiar with the written language, at least in those forms which he constantly meets in his work and commercial contacts, and to a limited extent in his recreation, though reading plays a more limited role in the recreation of the typical person at level Y. On the other hand, for some persons in the Y category, the range of the written language is considerably less than the oral range. This is especially true if the language in question has a difficult orthographic system, *e.g.*, Chinese, or a wide discrepancy between the oral and written forms, *e.g.*, Arabic.

One of the most interesting elements in the relationship between the usage of X and Y is the area of overlap, represented by the lines A-B and C-D. In every language one finds that people such as X will not write for general publication or circulation anything which dips below the standard suggested by the line C-D. Such persons may, of course, employ substandard forms in writing to close friends and family, but in general for anything aimed at an "unknown" audience, a relatively fixed set of "rules" is followed. At the same time, persons represented by Y do not wish to receive any general communication which is below the line C-D. In fact, if persons in class X employ substandard forms in writing to or for persons of class Y, the latter are quite understandably offended, and usually refuse to accept such communications, for the use of such substandard forms is regarded as a kind of paternalism.

There are, of course, a number of publications which employ substandard forms extensively, but these publications are generally read not by the people of class Y but by persons of class X. It is the educated classes which enjoy "dialect" stories or substandard argot.

If one is to communicate with persons of class Y, it is obvious that they must be addressed in a level of style which is above C-D, but it must also be below the A-B line. That is to say, it must be in the "common language" of overlap between the usage of X and Y. This means that its lower limit must be the line of standard vs. substandard forms, and the upper limit must be the consumer level of class Y. This common area of language is actually where most people communicate most of the time, whether in an oral or in a written medium.

The diagram employed in Figure 12 is not, however, adequate, since it does not reveal the historical perspective, and in all languages with a literary heritage there are many documents which reflect earlier stages of language. This is especially true of the Bible, which so often reflects long-established literary associations and well-entrenched stylistic usages. We must accordingly modify the diagram of Figure 12, in order to provide some historical view, as in Figure 13.

Several features of this diagram should be noted:

    1. The historical depth has been indicated only for the written language, since the oral language, though it was spoken in the past, exerts no such continuing influence upon the present.[1]

---

[1] It is altogether possible that with the advent of recording we shall experience

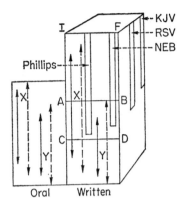

Figure 13

2. We have also added a dimension of "informal-to-formal": (I to F), going from left to right, and thus are able to plot such divergent translations as the NEB and Phillips, which are both on a relatively high stylistic level but differ essentially in the degree of informality. The NEB is, however, somewhat higher in its literary style (as will be seen very clearly from some of the problems discussed later in this chapter).

3. The King James Version is listed at the extreme of the historical dimension, even though, of course, it was preceded by others. However, it is the only translation from the early period that exerts a significant continuing influence.

4. The RSV represents a somewhat middle position between the King James Version and contemporary usage. As far as vocabulary usage is concerned, however, it is not on such a high literary level as the NEB. On the other hand, the NEB is stylistically much simpler in sentence structure, so that in some measure these two factors produce an average which makes the RSV and the NEB somewhat parallel. It is, of course, quite impossible to represent all the finer grades of contrast in a diagram of this type.

5. Phillips' translation may be said to dip a little further than the NEB into the language of overlap between the upper and lower languages.

6. To avoid overburdening an already complex diagram, the bar which represents each version is in reality a composite of all linguistic features of that version, including both grammatical structure and vocabulary. But different versions may be at different levels in terms of structure and vocabulary.

quite a different role for the oral language, but anything which is likely to be preserved over any long period of time is also likely to be relatively close to acceptable written style.

LEVEL OF LANGUAGE FOR SOCIETIES WITH A
RESTRICTED LITERARY TRADITION

The Bible translator is often faced with problems involving the level of language to be used in a translation being prepared for people having a language with a relatively short literary history. This is true for some 200 different languages with Bibles or New Testaments less than one hundred years old. In such cases there is no heavy literary superstructure which dictates just what should or should not be employed. However, even in such languages there are different levels of language, and there are certain problems of traditional usage, as represented not only in the speech of the older generation, but also in the type of translations which have been published in earlier times, many of which are extremely literal. Some of these aspects of the situation may be illustrated in Figure 14:

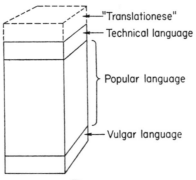

Figure 14

Within the basic structure of the language there are always at least three fundamental levels: (1) the language of the specialists, *e.g.*, the medicine man, the priest, the "professional" storyteller, (2) the language of the common people in their daily activities (*i.e.*, the popular language), and (3) the vulgar language, known by all but not used in those circumstances in which it seems inappropriate (vulgar language is a universal phenomenon).

In many languages which have been reduced to writing within the last two or three generations there is usually a kind of "literary" capstone, consisting largely of a form of translationese, which has been superimposed upon the language, and which may be regarded by many literate persons in the language as the only appropriate form in which to write the language. If the Bible has been produced in this relatively artificial form of language, its religious authority tends to be extended to the area of language, with the result that many people regard this form of language not only as proper and correct, but also as indispensable for any religious communication.

In these situations there is also a historical dimension, for often such languages are in process of rapid change. The generational spread (the differences between older and younger people) in such languages becomes a problem and constitutes certain serious difficulties for the translator, especially in those instances in which the authority of the church may be in the hands of the older generation, while the more educated and capable persons belong to the newer, younger generation. However, for a translation to have any future value it cannot be translated into the language of a dying generation, but must use the speech of the oncoming generation, which will soon be carrying on the affairs of the language community.

In languages without long literary traditions, one should attempt to produce a translation in the "popular" form of language, which represents the usage between the technical levels at the top and the vulgar speech at the bottom. The artificial forms of translationese should certainly be rejected as not representing the true genius of the language, and speech which is only used by the older generation should be largely rejected. However, in these situations one is generally able to employ a relatively wider range of the total resources of the language than in the case of "common language translations," in which usage must be restricted primarily to the specific area of overlap.

THE LEVEL OF LANGUAGE FOR SOCIETIES IN WHICH THE LANGUAGE IS ONLY NOW BEING REDUCED TO WRITING

At the present time some 500 languages are in the process of being reduced to writing and are being given the Scriptures and other published materials for the first time. These situations are very similar to those described in the preceding paragraphs, except for the fact that there is no existing translationese tradition, and one need not be concerned with the influence of this semihallowed form of language. This means that there are no artificial limits to the use of the total resources of the language.

But whereas in case of languages with long literary traditions one is faced with the problems of socioeconomic and educational "dialects," in the case of languages only now being reduced to writing, the problems are not those of vertical (sociological) dialects but of horizontal, or geographical, ones. Without the normalizing influence of a national educational program, local geographical dialects quite naturally proliferate, and one is confronted with certain very serious difficulties.

DIMENSIONS OF VARIATION IN LANGUAGE

We have diagrammed in a composite way a number of factors which are relevant to the production of a satisfactory style in the receptor language. It is now time to examine the more important of these dimensions at some length. We will, therefore, consider in order (1) the contrast between oral and written usage; (2) various sociological factors; (3) levels of style which reflect circumstances of usage and relations between speaker and hearer; and (4) geographical dialects.

ORAL AND WRITTEN STYLE

As has been suggested at several points in the preceding discussion, there are certain important distinctions between oral and written style, and this is in some measure true of all languages, even for those in which writing may have been only recently introduced. One usually finds, for example, that the written style is "better organized." This means that written style exhibits greater syntactic regularity (fewer grammatical mistakes or "abnormalities"), fewer anacoloutha (sentences which begin with one structure and end with another), and a more systematic treatment of the various points or topics of the discourse. In other words, both on the syntactic and on the discourse levels written style is more effectively organized.

In addition to being better organized, the written style is often more complexly organized. It often has more subordination, rather than coordination. It usually employs more transitional features, to show the relationships of sentences and clauses to each other, and may use a number of subtle rhetorical devices, such as chiasmus. In terms of vocabulary, there is generally greater variety in written than in spoken communication. Moreover, one often encounters greater semantic condensation, so that more information is carried per unit of length; or stated in a different form, there are fewer words in proportion to the number of concepts expressed. On the other hand, while in their oral form many languages exhibit an abundant use of sound symbolism, written communications in these same languages tend to use such expressions much less. Perhaps this is due in part to such expressions seeming to be inappropriate to formal discourse, but it may also be that these linguistic forms are more difficult to represent in traditional orthography. In various styles of poetry a great deal may be made of sound symbolism, but often this is on a much more subtle level of sophistication than in oral language.

One of the conspicuous differences between oral and written communications is the attempt in writing to compensate for the loss of intonational features, which contribute so much to the forcefulness and subtleness of oral language. Not being able to signal the emotional setting of the discourse by means of intonational "gestures," the writer must rely more on "value" words to provide hints as to how he interprets the events or objects he describes.

A number of suggestions have been made as to why written language tends to differ from oral language in these various ways, but perhaps the most important factors are: (1) the apparent greater importance attached to written communication, since it potentially reaches a larger audience and has a more lasting character, thus demanding greater care, (2) the fact that greater time is required to produce a written message, thus enabling the encoder to give more careful attention to the structure of the communication, and (3) the possibility of correcting a written message before dispatching it, thus rendering the writer more accountable for the form of his communication.

It is worthy of notice that oral language when used at either a formal or a technical level (in a formal speech or sermon, or in a paper delivered to a scholarly society) is much more like written language than more casual forms of speech. This is no doubt in part a reflection of the greater seriousness of situation and subject matter, but it results from the greater effort at prior preparation on the part of the speaker, who plans his discourse more thoroughly than is the case with conversational speech. It is also true that in such formal situations, the communication is much more largely one-way than in conversation, and in this respect also it resembles written language and must conform to the same constraints.

Though in all languages the oral and written styles tend to differ, in some languages there is a very marked difference, due to the special literary history of the language. In fact, in some instances the written language may almost be a "foreign language," as in the case of written Arabic, which differs so markedly from the colloquial form of speech that a child must go to school for several years before being able to read standard written Arabic with ease. In the principal European languages the contrasts between written and spoken forms of language have always been much less marked, except in the Middle Ages, when Latin might be said to represent a "written" form of some of the spoken Romance languages. One well-known linguist has compared this relationship to that between a person and a dog being walked on a long elastic leash. The dog (written language) can get quite far from the man (oral language), but the leash imposes limits, and the elasticity of the leash forces the dog to return to the man from time to time.

The Bible translator who is working in a language with a great disparity between the written and the spoken forms must avoid usages which will stamp the message as completely unworthy; that is, he must not employ language used only in the comic strip or in vulgar writing. On the other hand, he cannot afford to use a form of language known only by the literary elite, unless, of course, he is aiming to produce a translation only for such a select group. On the whole, he does best to use a form of "common language," which represents a satisfactory overlap, based on consumer language.[2]

SOCIOLOGICAL LEVELS OF LANGUAGE

We have already seen (pp. 92-93) that we tend to evaluate various forms of language in terms of our evaluation of the kinds of people who use them, and that linguistic usage reflects certain sociological facts. Among the factors that affect linguistic variation are: (1) age, (2) sex, (3) educational level, (4) occupation, (5) social class or caste, and (6) religious affiliation.

Young people in almost all societies tend to speak differently from their elders, and this difference contributes greatly to the "generation gap" about which so much is said these days. Young people tend readily to adopt new forms of speech, including slang, which is almost a badge of belonging in their age group; they tend to reject anything which sounds linguistically "old-fashioned."

It is also an observable fact that women and men differ in their speech, and not only in terms of the traditional interests of each sex. In some

---

[2] For an analysis of these problems see Dr. William L. Wonderly, *Bible Translations for Popular Use.*

languages, these differences are highly formalized, while in others they are informally applied; but they are present in all societies.

The other dimensions, even religion, are not really independent of one another in their workings; they tend to go together. Two major factors can be assigned in explanation of this fact that people who are alike in one or more of these dimensions speak alike. The first factor is the simple matter of density of communication: people who are alike are for this very reason brought together more than people who are different, and for purposes of effective communication there is an unconscious process of homogenization to make their speech more and more alike. The second conscious factor is that recognized differences in speech can easily become badges of belonging, a mark of pride in one's group. Working against this, especially among members of the more ambitious and socially insecure groups, is the opposite tendency to imitate the speech of the more secure and privileged class to which the speaker aspires. In any case, the levels of language represented in the diagrams, at least in their vertical dimension, largely reflect these sociological factors, as well as the situational ones to be discussed next.

✗ SITUATIONAL LEVELS OF LANGUAGE

The situational factors which help to define levels of language relate to the occasion and circumstances of the speech event and to the relationships between speakers. They are thus in a way an individualized reflection of the more general sociological factors just discussed. But the terms we will use to identify these levels themselves are largely situational: technical, formal, informal, casual, and intimate. Technical language is that which is used in professional discourse between specialists. It is characterized by its complicated vocabulary and heavy grammatical constructions, and is intended for a very restricted audience and for certain special situations. Formal language, on the other hand, may deal with equally complex subjects, but the audience is generally a wider one, and hence one cannot afford to use terminology known only to the specialist. Moreover, the grammatical structures need to be more readily comprehensible. In general, formal language is used in speaking on an important subject and to an audience that one does not know. When, however, one is well acquainted with his audience and is under no constraint to appear profound, he will usually employ a more informal style—more fitting to serious discussions between friends. On the other hand, he may come down a notch lower in the scale of formality and employ casual speech, the language of close friends and associates, who need not be addressed in complete sentences or with completely standard grammatical forms. The same person may also employ intimate speech in the home with members of his family. "The language of lovers," in which only a word may speak volumes, is one example of intimate speech.

These levels of speech are in a sense analogous to clothes, for one and the same person may wear quite different sets of clothes, depending upon his roles and circumstances. For example, the medical doctor wears his typical white uniform in his technical capacity, white tie and tails for formal occasions, a business suit for informal contacts, sport shirt and slacks for casual wear, a dressing gown for the least formal situation. Similarly, the same message may be dressed up in a variety of words and phrases, representing quite distinct levels of language.

In translating the Bible one must recognize certain quite different styles and attempt to produce something which will be a satisfactory dynamic equivalent. Lyric poetry should sound like poetry and not like an essay; letters should read like letters and not like some technical treatise on theology. Some of the most conspicuous differences in style of translating can be found in a comparison of the New English Bible and Phillips' translation. For example, in Acts 8:20 the NEB reads, in typical "university English," "you and your money . . . may you come to a bad end," whereas Phillips translates, "To hell with you and your money," which is really an excellent equivalent of the Greek term *apollumi*. In Bible translating perhaps the greatest distortion in style comes in the rendering of the Epistles, for so often instead of producing letters the translator becomes so hopelessly entangled in technical theological language that the results sound more like a legal document than a letter. The first part of Romans appears in some languages to sound something like the following: "I, Paul, a slave of said master Jesus Christ, have been specifically called and summoned by God to be sent for a particular purpose and have been commissioned to that end, appointed to serve as a preacher of what is commonly known as the Good News, a message disclosed and published prior to final pronouncement in the Scriptures, widely known as the Old Testament." Of course, no one translates quite so badly as this, but the heavy, involved, and ponderous style of some translations is equally out of place and poorly designed to represent something of the "spontaneous fullness" with which Paul speaks.

GEOGRAPHICAL DIALECTS

The problems of geographical dialects are extremely complicated and could be treated adequately only in a volume dedicated exclusively to this subject. However, for the average Bible translator the statement of certain fundamental principles may be useful.

In the first place, it is hopeless to try to bring together those dialects which are linguistically too far apart. If, for example, languages differ by more than 15 percent in their basic vocabulary (the central core of vocabulary which tends to be the most conservative), it is almost impossible to bring such dialects together, for they represent a linguistic separation, in glottochronological terms, of more than 700 years. Moreover, if more than 15 percent of the basic vocabulary is different, then often fully 30 percent of the nonbasic vocabulary is diverse. However, the problems of vocabulary are not the most crucial issues. Far more important are the grammatical features of tense, aspects, pronominal reference, etc. If there are a number of completely contradictory features (*e.g.*, a tense form which is present in one dialect and past in another, or a pronoun which is second person in one dialect and third person in another), it is not advisable to try to "bridge" the dialect gap.

In order to analyze the linguistic diversity between dialects, it is
very advisable to have the help of a qualified linguist, for only he can
judge the diversity of factors and the "communication load" they carry.
However, linguistic features are not the only factors which must be
considered. In fact, the "cultural elements" may be even more important, for it is not so much the extent to which people of dialect A can
understand people of dialect B, but the extent to which they are willing
to do so. In some instances peoples of quite different dialects have
overcome seemingly insuperable linguistic difficulties, while in other instances peoples with only minor differences between dialects have refused
to adjust to the speech of a neighboring group.

The ability of people of different dialects to converse freely together
is, of course, a useful rough criterion of dialect proximity, but one must
also determine something of the linguistic experience of the persons involved, for it may be that through frequent contacts they have practically
learned each another's dialects. Moreover, ability to understand the oral
form of a strange dialect is often much easier than to read materials
published in the same dialect, for decoding of oral speech is done in relatively large units, while the decoding of written language, especially for the
new literate, must be taken in smaller units and in strict sequence.
Perhaps the most satisfactory rough calculation of mutual intelligibility
can be determined by judging the extent of intelligibility between two
women who have had no previous contacts with their corresponding
dialects. If they can understand each other with relative ease, then the
dialects should be "combinable." But the range of intelligibility must
involve much more than so-called market talk. If such women can understand each other with relative ease on a wide range of subjects, it is
presumable that a single translation can "cover" the dialect differences.
Otherwise, one must give very careful consideration to some other
type of solution.

Unfortunately, it often happens that translators have attempted to
solve the problems of geographical dialects by a kind of "democratic
method," by which they select certain words and forms from one dialect,
other words and forms from a second dialect, and so on, until presumably
all the dialects have been democratically represented. Such a procedure
results in a hopeless mélange, a kind of language that no one speaks and
all persons unanimously reject.

The only practical and satisfactory solution to the problems of dialects
is (1) to accept one dialect as being the culturally more important and
the linguistically more central form of speech and to translate exclusively
in this dialect, with the hope that it will eventually supersede other
dialects, or (2) to employ forms which have the widest possible distribution among the various dialects and which are at the same time
acceptable to speakers of the principal dialect, even though such forms
may not always be preferred. In the first instance, one is only concerned
with having those forms which are most appropriate to the one dialect
that is chosen. In the second instance, one does not violate the usage of
such a principal dialect, but will often use alternatives, which may not be

quite so well known or so widely used in the principal dialect, but which are more widely known in the neighboring dialects.

Very frequently one must supplement these approaches with a plan for publishing primarily in the principal dialect, while putting out some additional materials in some of the so-called dependent, or lesser, dialects. This means that people can be encouraged to learn to read in their own dialect (which is so much easier for them), and can then be introduced more satisfactorily to materials published in the larger, dominant dialect.

TYPES OF DISCOURSE

Before describing the various general types of discourse, it will be useful to examine some of the universals of discourse. Anyone can distinguish, in any language he knows well, between a well-constructed discourse, a badly constructed discourse, and a random collection of sentences, though he can seldom pinpoint the reasons for his intuitive judgment. But regardless of the type of discourse, a well-constructed discourse in any language will respect a variety of constraints designed to give the discourse structure. It is these constraints which we call universals of discourse. There are at least eight of these, two relative to the discourse as a whole, three to the events in the discourse, two to the objects in the discourse, and one to the author. Though each of these will be taken up in more detail later (p. 152), they will be briefly named here.

Those relating to the discourse as a whole are (1) the various ways, often formulaic, of marking the beginning and end of the discourse and (2) the means of marking transitions between the major internal divisions of the whole discourse.

Those which have to do mainly or largely with events are (3) temporal relations, which can be marked by tense and concord of tenses, separate particles, and various temporal modifiers, among other things; (4) spatial relations; and (5) logical relations, such as cause and effect. For a discussion of these factors in a different context, see p. 112. When we come to consider the relations of events to other elements within single kernels, we find that the relevant categories are the semotactic classes already discussed (pp. 58-63), as well as features of the events themselves, such as intransitive, transitive, and ditransitive (predicates with double goals).

Factors having to do largely or entirely with objects include (6) the identification of all participants in a discourse, keeping straight the successive references to a particular one and keeping distinct references to different ones, and (7) the various devices used for highlighting or backgrounding various elements, for bringing them into or out of focus, and for emphasis. These involve in all languages complex use of nouns and nominal expressions, and substitute terms such as pronouns, as well as pointers to previous reference (*e.g., the* in English, as opposed to *a*). Among the pronouns and similar substitute terms in all languages, there are at least three kinds of participation in the speech event, and they are marked by the first, second, and third persons (some languages have a fourth person, but it is a specialized kind of third person, not a really distinct one). One also frequently finds abstracts used in the identification of participants, either purely descriptively, or actually in contrasting one participant with another. And all languages have means for expressing degrees of comparison, though the methods are not all the same.

Finally, the factor which relates to the author is (8) author involvement, *e.g.*, his attitude and viewpoint, which are reflected in the choice of terms and constructions, as well as the choice of levels and rate of speech, intonation, and many other features of the message.

It should be said at this point that when we call these features of discourse "universals," we are by no means suggesting that all languages make use of the same formal devices, such as grammatical categories and constructions, to express them. In fact, it is rarely the case even within a single language that a given device has only one function and a given function is served by a single device. Rather, there is a complicated total structure, involving all of these factors, together with the concordance of semotactic classes, and this whole does the job. It is this complexity which gives language its marvelous flexibility, so that anything which can be said in one language can be said in another. The essential differences between languages are thus not in what can be said, but in what are permissible and/or probable combinations, and especially in what categories are marked obligatorily (*e.g.*, number in count nouns in English) and what are purely optional.

We may now turn from discourse universals to the different types of discourse and the features which differentiate them from one another. When we have completed this overall characterization, we will discuss in more detail the components of style. The discourse types may be compared with the overall shape and size of a building, while the style is a matter of texture of the exterior, amount and type of color, landscaping, and interior decor.

We may begin by following the traditional distinction between prose and poetic language (note that we say "poetic language" rather than "poetry," which is a major subclass of poetic language). Prose, in turn, comprises three major types: (1) narrative, (2) description, and (3) argument. Narrative is structured principally around one or more chains of related events. Description is based in large part on spatial relations between objects and parts of objects, and also makes great use of abstracts; the perspective is a given point of view (or successive points of view) rather than a sequence in time. Finally, argument is based on logical relations, mainly of two sorts, (a) the "because ... therefore" kind and (b) the "if so ... then" kind.

Poetic language is used in poetry and song, in proverbs, epigrams, aphorisms, and so on. Its principal trait is a multilevel parallelism: (a) in sound, as in rhyme, alliteration, assonance, rhythm, intonational contours, etc.; (b) in morphological and syntactic patterns, as when successive lines show similar or identical grammatical structure; (c) in lexical choices; and especially, perhaps, (d) in semantic structures. It seems to be a frequent if not universal feature of poetic language that there are at least two levels of meaning throughout a given work: there will be first the literal meaning, what the poem is about on the surface—say, the spring of the year—and then one or more extensions or plays on meaning. If the play is on another quite distinct literal meaning, we have a pun. Otherwise, we may have a conventional second level, as when a poem which seems to be about spring turns out to be really about resurrection (it is conventional because, at least in Western poetry, spring is a recognized symbol of resurrection); or it may, as in many works of T. S. Eliot or e. e. cummings, be a highly individual second meaning which requires a key other than general cultural knowledge to understand. Though figures of speech are found in prose, it is a mark of poetic language that figures of speech are used more abundantly and more imaginatively than in prose. The poet, as we have already observed, sees extensions of meaning and associations which others have not yet seen, but which they can see under the skilful tutelage of the poet.

A partly overlapping way of describing poetic language is to say that it is characterized by unity, novelty, complexity, compression, and simplicity. Unity involves such things as consistency of theme and imagery and overall structure. Novelty means that the poet tends to use fresh expressions and collocations rather than clichés. Complexity is certainly seen in the multilayered parallelism we have just discussed, with further complications in the interplay between levels. Compression means that poetic language is generally very dense and economical, with very little redundancy. Simplicity is seen primarily in grammatical structure, because it seems to be a fact that much poetic language is in kernel or near-kernel form. No doubt this is in compensation for the novelty, complexity, and compression, which tend to make the work difficult to understand.

One of the special problems confronted by translators is that such a high percentage of any Biblical text combines various types of discourse. For example, so-called exposition is largely a combination of argument and description; and conversation may be narrative, argument, and description. Poetry may involve narration (epic poetry) or argument (in the sense of being didactic).

Languages, however, differ not only in the discourse types but also in the functional significance of such types. For example, in classical Greek the epic poem was the accepted way to describe a momentous historical event, but in the modern Western world this is no longer the accepted way. The most effective translations of Homer's *Iliad* and *Odyssey* are now in prose, not in poetry, for poetic translations seem rather unnatural and even, at times, "silly," but as prose, translations of Homer can be full of life, vigor, and punch (*cf.* Rieu's translations). On the other hand, in India the poetic form is still much appreciated in many of the languages, and one of the very popular accounts of the life of Christ has been done in Malayalam verse by a skilled poet.

THE COMPONENTS OF STYLE

Before discussing in more detail the components of style, it may be useful to specify that it is style we are concerned with, not exegesis. The two questions are quite independent. Exegesis is wrong, entirely apart from any stylistic considerations, if it (1) misinterprets the point of the original, or (2) adds information from some nontextual source, and especially from some other cultural milieu. Compare, for instance, the following passages from the TEV and from Phillips:

	TEV	Phillips
Matt. 7:12	"this is the meaning of the Law of Moses and the teaching of the prophets"	"this is the essence of all true religion"
Luke 13:11	"a woman . . . who had an evil spirit in her that had kept her sick for eighteen years"	"a woman who for eighteen years had been ill from some psychological cause"
Luke 22:3	"then Satan went into Judas"	"then a diabolical plan came into the mind of Judas"

There is nothing wrong with the style of these passages in Phillips, but they show the introduction of cultural ideas which are at least absent, if not foreign, to the culture of the text.

We may then contrast a linguistic translation, which is legitimate, and a cultural translation or adaptation, which is not. This is because we believe in the significance of the historical events and situations just as they occurred. It is the job of the pastor and teacher, not of the translator, to make the cultural adaptation. This is also one of the major differences between an exegetical commentary and a homiletical or devotional commentary. See also page 110 for a related discussion.

Every feature of language, from the total structure of the discourse to the sounds of the individual words, is included in the components of style. However, merely to list the features of style is not so important as trying to determine how they function, in terms of efficiency of communication and impact. But before classifying stylistic components, it is important to determine just how one can recognize such stylistic features. To do this most effectively one can compare the way in which different translations have rendered certain specific passages.

Comparison of Luke 15:11-24 in the Revised Standard Version and the New English Bible:

The Revised Standard Version

[11] And he said, "There was a man who had two sons; [12] and the younger of them said to his father, 'Father, give me the share of property that falls to me.' And he divided his living between them. [13] Not many days later, the younger son gathered all he had and took his journey into a far country, and there he squandered his property in loose living. [14] And when he had spent everything, a great famine arose in that country, and he began to be in want. [15] So he went and joined himself to one of the citizens of that country, who sent him into his fields to feed swine. [16] And he would gladly have fed on the pods that the swine ate; and no one gave him anything. [17] But when he came to

himself he said, 'How many of my father's hired servants have bread enough and to spare, but I perish here with hunger! [18] I will arise and go to my father, and I will say to him, "Father, I have sinned against heaven and before you; [19] I am no longer worthy to be called your son; treat me as one of your hired servants."' [20] And he arose and came to his father. But while he was yet at a distance, his father saw him and had compassion, and ran and embraced him and kissed him. [21] And the son said to him, 'Father, I have sinned against heaven and before you; I am no longer worthy to be called your son.' [22] But the father said to his servants, 'Bring quickly the best robe, and put it on him; and put a ring on his hand, and shoes on his feet; [23] and bring the fatted calf and kill it, and let us eat and make merry; [24] for this my son was dead, and is alive again; he was lost, and is found.' And they began to make merry. . . .''

The New English Bible

[11] Again he said: 'There was once a man who had two sons; [12] and the younger said to his father, "Father, give me my share of the property." So he divided his estate between them. [13] A few days later the younger son turned the whole of his share into cash and left home for a distant country, where he squandered it in reckless living. [14] He had spent it all, when a severe famine fell upon that country and he began to feel the pinch. [15] So he went and attached himself to one of the local landowners, who sent him on to his farm to mind the pigs. [16] He would have been glad to fill his belly with the pods that the pigs were eating; and no one gave him anything. [17] Then he came to his senses and said, "How many of my father's paid servants have more food than they can eat, and here am I, starving to death! [18] I will set off and go to my father, and say to him, 'Father, I have sinned, against God and against you; [19] I am no longer fit to be called your son; treat me as one of your paid servants.' " [20] So he set out for his father's house. But while he was still a long way off his father saw him, and his heart went out to him. He ran to meet him, flung his arms round him, and kissed him. [21] The son said, "Father, I have sinned, against God and against you; I am no longer fit to be called your son." [22] But the father said to his servants, "Quick! fetch a robe, my best one, and put it on him; put a ring on his finger and shoes on his feet. [23] Bring the fatted calf and kill it, and let us have a feast to celebrate the day. [24] For this son of mine was dead and has come back to life; he was lost and is found." And the festivities began. . . .''

In order to highlight the differences between the forms of these two translations, it is useful to list the more important contrasts in parallel columns (repeated items are listed only once):

	RSV	NEB
Luke 15:11	1. And he said	1. Again he said
	2. There was a man	2. There was once a man

15:12	3.	younger of them	3.	the younger
	4.	the share of property that falls to me	4.	my share of the property
	5.	And he divided	5.	So he divided
	6.	his living	6.	his estate
15:13	7.	Not many days later	7.	A few days later
	8.	gathered all he had	8.	turned the whole of his share into cash
	9.	took his journey	9.	left home
	10.	far country	10.	distant country
	11.	there	11.	where
	12.	his property	12.	it
	13.	loose living	13.	reckless living
15:14	14.	when he ... spent..., a great famine	14.	He ... spent..., when a severe famine
	15.	spent everything	15.	spent it all
	16.	great famine	16.	severe famine
	17.	a great famine arose	17.	a severe famine fell upon
	18.	to be in want	18.	to feel the pinch
15:15	19.	joined himself to	19.	attached himself to
	20.	one of the citizens of that country	20.	one of the local landowners
	21.	into his fields	21.	on to his farm
	22.	to feed swine	22.	to mind the pigs
15:16	23.	have fed on the pods	23.	to fill his belly with the pods
	24.	that the swine ate	24.	that the pigs were eating
15:17	25.	came to himself	25.	came to his senses
	26.	hired servants	26.	paid servants
	27.	have bread enough and to spare	27.	have more food than they can eat
	28.	I perish here with hunger!	28.	here am I, starving to death!
15:18	29.	I will arise and go	29.	I will set off and go
	30.	sinned against heaven and before you	30.	sinned, against God and against you
15:19	31.	I am no longer worthy	31.	I am no longer fit
15:20	32.	And he arose	32.	So he set out
	33.	came to his father	33.	for his father's house
	34.	yet at a distance	34.	still a long way off
	35.	had compassion	35.	his heart went out to him
	36.	embraced him	36.	flung his arms round him
15:21	37.	And the son said	37.	The son said

15:22	38. Bring quickly the best robe	38. Quick! fetch a robe, my best one
	39. put a ring on his hand	39. put a ring on his finger
15:23	40. let us eat and make merry	40. let us have a feast to celebrate the day
15:24	41. this my son	41. this son of mine
	42. is alive again	42. has come back to life
	43. they began to make merry	43. the festivities began

Several features of the above sets of contrasts require some comment and explanation, and in each instance it is important to indicate the type of stylistic (or interpretive) problem which is involved:

1. The Greek text reads literally "and he said," but this expression is used frequently by Luke as a marker of discourse transition, that is, to signal the shifts from one story or account to another. Accordingly, the NEB is thoroughly justified in introducing an equivalent marker in English. Stylistic feature: Discourse-transition marker.

2. The use of "once" in the NEB suggests the discourse type, *i.e.*, the fact that this is a parable, rather than the account of a particular person and his two sons. In Greek this is clearly marked by the indefinite pronoun *tis*, "some," "any," "a." Stylistic feature: Discourse-type marker.

3. Though the phrase "younger of them" is a literal rendering of the Greek text, the closer natural equivalent is "younger," since with comparatives, "of them" is pleonastic in English. Stylistic feature: Elimination of pleonasm.

4. Though the phrase "that falls to me" is a literal rendering of the original, the NEB has avoided a phrase which is semotactically unnatural. Stylistic feature: Semotactic appropriateness.

5. The use of "so" in place of the literal translation "and" is used to mark the intradiscourse transition. This is a perfectly legitimate translation of the Greek conjunction *kai*. Stylistic feature: Intradiscourse transition.

6. Though "living" is a literal rendering of Greek *bios*, it is misleading in present-day English, for "living" would refer to "income" and not to one's entire estate. The NEB rendering is basically not a matter of style but of correctness in rendering, based on the principle of dynamic equivalence and not on the principle of formal correspondence.

7. The phrase "not many" is semantically more complex than the positive expression "few." Stylistic feature: Semantic simplicity (and therefore easier decodability).

8. The NEB is a more idiomatic rendering and is fully justified by Koine usage. Moreover, it results in a much more understandable account. This is not so much a matter of style as of interpretation.

9. The phrase "took his journey" is semotactically obsolescent. One may "take a trip" or "go on a journey" or even "take a journey," but not "take his journey." Stylistic feature: semotactic appropriateness.

10. The collocation "distant country" seems semotactically more natural than "far country." Stylistic feature: Semotactic appropriateness.

11. The NEB "where" results in subordination, and thus greater linkage of clauses. Stylistic feature: Subordination of clauses.

12. The NEB "it" is a necessary reference to "cash" in the earlier part of the verse. Stylistic feature: Pronominal reference.

13. The phrase "loose living" implies immorality, but this element in the story does not come out until one hears the accusation of the elder brother. The NEB "reckless" seems a much better rendering of the Greek *asōtōs*. This is essentially a matter of interpretation.

14. The RSV construction, "when he ... spent ...,, a great famine arose...," suggests that the first action took place with anticipation of what was to follow. The NEB, however, makes the second clause the dependent clause to emphasize the unexpectedness of the famine. The Greek sentence would normally be translated as in the RSV, since the "spending" is a dependent participle. However, it is by no means necessary to treat all Greek participles in this rather mechanical fashion. Therefore, the NEB rendering can be justified as a much more effective and semantically appropriate means of showing relationships between clauses. Stylistic feature: Inter-clause markers.

15. The phrase "spent it all" seems to suggest something more final and conclusive than "spent everything." Stylistic feature: Connotative effectiveness.

16. The adjective "great" normally suggests something valuable or important, and is not so semotactically appropriate with "famine." Stylistic feature: Semotactic appropriateness.

17. Normally so-called natural calamities are said to "fall"; they do not "arise." Stylistic feature: Semotactic appropriateness.

18. The phrase "to be in want" is obsolescent, but "to feel the pinch" is rather weak. This suggests to many Britishers rising income taxes rather than being completely out of money. Stylistic feature: Contemporary usage (but misleading).

19. The expression "joined to" suggests a meeting of equals or an association, while "attached to" shows dependency relationship. Perhaps a better rendering would be "went to work for." Stylistic feature: Semotactic appropriateness.

20. The phrase "citizen of that country" seems to place the expression in a political, rather than a commercial, context. Therefore, the NEB has attempted a semotactically more appropriate equivalent. Stylistic feature: Semotactic appropriateness.

21. The phrase "into his fields" suggests a more temporary arrangement. Thus "on to his farm" seems semotactically more applicable. Stylistic feature: Semotactic appropriateness.

22. The phrase "to feed swine" is relatively obsolescent, while "to mind pigs," though perhaps appropriate in England, is not used in all other places in the English-speaking world. Stylistic feature: Contemporary usage.

23. The verb "fed" suggests primarily the action of animals, not of a person, but "to fill his belly" is for many people connotatively inappropriate. It is a literal translation of the Greek, but in Greek the term *koilia*, "belly," does not have the same connotative significance that its literal equivalent has in English. Stylistic feature: Connotative equivalence (in this instance, a lack of).

24. The verb phrase "were eating" provides a livelier narrative equivalence in tense. Stylistic feature: Tense equivalence.

25. The phrase "to come to oneself" is less well known than "to come to his senses." For some persons "to come to himself" may be interpreted as "he came to," *i.e.*, recovered from a fainting spell. Stylistic feature: Equivalence of idiom.

26. The word "hired" is somewhat more obsolescent than "paid," in this type of context. Stylistic feature: Contemporary usage.

27. The phrase "bread enough and to spare" is obsolescent. Stylistic feature: Contemporary style.

28. The expression "perish . . . with hunger" is a case of translationese. On the other hand, the order "here am I" is quite unnatural, at least for many English speakers, even for this type of exclamatory context. Stylistic features: Unusual word order (for an unusual effect) and contemporary usage.

29. The phrase "I will arise and go" is strictly "Biblical." The NEB equivalent is more contemporary. Stylistic feature: Contemporary usage.

30. The phrase "sinned against heaven" is very likely not to be understood as it was actually meant by Luke. Therefore, the NEB translates this Greek expression in terms of dynamic equivalence, rather than formal correspondence. This is not a matter of style but of appropriate referent.

31. The adjective "worthy" sounds somewhat out of keeping with the context; for though it is denotatively equivalent to "fit," it carries a somewhat more elegant connotative significance. Stylistic feature: Connotative equivalence.

32. The verb "arose" is semotactically obsolescent. Stylistic feature: Semotactic appropriateness.

33. The RSV rendering suggests that he had arrived where his father was, but the next phrase shows that he was still "far off." The NEB avoids this pitfall by translating "set out for his father's house," and in this way renders the Greek preposition *pros* quite effectively while avoiding the awkwardness which the RSV introduces. Stylistic feature: Narrative progression.

34. The rendering "yet at a distance" is obsolescent. Stylistic feature: Contemporary usage.

35. The phrase "had compassion" is rather stilted for this type of event.

"His heart went out to him" is a much better present-day equivalent of the Greek term *splanknizō* and carries much more connotative significance. Stylistic feature: Idiomatic equivalence.

36. The verb "embraced" seems not only somewhat stilted, but to many people it carries a rather heavy sexual connotation. Stylistic feature: Connotative appropriateness in word choice.

37. The conjunction "and" in the RSV is a case of translationese. The narrative structure suggests in English an abrupt transition. Stylistic feature: Intradiscourse transition.

38. The NEB rendering "Quick! fetch a robe, my best one" is an attempt to provide something which is connotatively more appropriate. Stylistic feature: Connotative appropriateness in syntactic structure.

39. The rendering "ring on his hand" is simply a case of translationese, a literal rendering of the Greek. The NEB corrects this obvious error. Stylistic feature: Semotactic appropriateness.

40. The rendering "eat and make merry" is obsolescent. Stylistic feature: Contemporary usage.

44. The unnatural word order of "this my son" is shifted to natural word order. Stylistic feature: Natural word order.

42. The phrase "is alive again" seems rather strange, in contrast with "has come back to life." Stylistic feature: Contemporary usage.

43. "To make merry" is quite obsolescent. Stylistic feature: Contemporary usage.

In contrast with this passage from Luke 15, one finds that the differences between the RSV, NEB, and TEV in Hebrews 1:1-4 provide quite a number of other stylistic features:

The Revised Standard Version

[1] In many and various ways God spoke of old to our fathers by the prophets; [2] but in these last days he has spoken to us by a Son, whom he appointed the heir of all things, through whom also he created the world. [3] He reflects the glory of God and bears the very stamp of his nature, upholding the universe by his word of power. When he had made purification for sins, he sat down at the right hand of the Majesty on high, [4] having become as much superior to angels as the name he has obtained is more excellent than theirs.

The New English Bible

[1] When in former times God spoke to our forefathers, he spoke in fragmentary and varied fashion through the prophets. [2] But in this the final age he has spoken to us in the Son whom he has made heir to the whole universe, and through whom he created all orders of existence: [3] the Son who is the effulgence of God's splendour and the stamp of God's very being, and sustains the universe by his word of power. When he had brought about the purgation of sins, he took his seat at the right

hand of Majesty on high, ⁴ raised as far above the angels, as the title he has inherited is superior to theirs.

Today's English Version

¹ In the past God spoke to our ancestors many times and in many ways through the prophets, ² but in these last days he has spoken to us through his Son. He is the one through whom God created the universe, the one whom God has chosen to possess all things at the end. ³ He shines with the brightness of God's glory; he is the exact likeness of God's own being, and sustains the universe with his powerful word. After he had made men clean from their sins, he sat down in heaven at the right side of God, the Supreme Power.

⁴ The Son was made greater than the angels, just as the name that God gave him is greater than theirs.

The following sets of contrasts in these three translations should be noted:

1. RSV: in many and various ways
   NEB: in fragmentary and varied fashion
   TEV: many times and in many ways
2. RSV: of old
   NEB: in former times
   TEV: in the past
3. RSV: to our fathers
   NEB. to our forefathers
   TEV: to our ancestors
4. RSV: by the prophets
   NEB: through the prophets
   TEV: through the prophets
6. RSV: by a Son
   NEB: in the Son
   TEV: through his Son
7. RSV: whom he appointed the heir of all things
   NEB: whom he has made heir to the whole universe
   TEV: He is the one whom God has chosen to possess all things at the end
8. RSV: through whom also he created the world
   NEB: through whom he created all orders of existence
   TEV: through whom God created the universe
9. RSV: he reflects the glory of God
   NEB: the Son who is the effulgence of God's splendour
   TEV: he shines with the brightness of God's own glory
10. RSV: bears the very stamp of his nature
    NEB: the stamp of God's very being
    TEV: he is the exact likeness of God's own being

11. RSV: upholding the universe by his word of power
    NEB: sustains the universe by his word of power
    TEV: sustains the universe by his powerful word
12. RSV: when he made purification for sins
    NEB: when he brought about purgation of sins
    TEV: after he had made men clean from their sins
13. RSV: he sat down at the right hand of the Majesty on high
    NEB: he took his seat at the right hand of Majesty on high
    TEV: he sat down in heaven at the right side of God, the Supreme
    Power
14. RSV: having become as much superior to angels
    NEB: raised as far above angels
    TEV: the Son was made greater than the angels
15. RSV: as the name he has obtained is more excellent than theirs
    NEB: as the title he has inherited is superior to theirs
    TEV: just as the name that God gave him is greater than theirs

These detailed contrasts in phraseology by no means cover the entire range of contrasts in these translations. It will also be necessary to discuss some of the more extensive formal contrasts of paragraph, sentence, and clause structures, but these differences, noted in the parallel listings, do provide some rather effective illustrations of significant stylistic contrasts.

1. Quite apart from some differences of interpretation which lie behind the diversities in these renderings, it is still quite evident that basic differences in the principles governing the choice of vocabulary levels account for such usages as "fragmentary," "varied," and "fashion," in contrast with "many," "various," and "ways." Stylistic feature: Vocabulary level (common or uncommon).
2. The phrase "of old" is decidedly obsolescent, while "in former times" is rather "academic." The rendering "in the past" is quite ordinary and natural. Stylistic features: Contemporary usage and level of language (formal vs. informal).
3. The usage of "fathers" is obsolescent (and translationese), while "forefathers" is rather technical. "Ancestors" is more normal (at least for American English). Stylistic features: Contemporary usage and level of language.
4. The preposition "through" is much more normal for expressing secondary agency. Stylistic feature: Semotactic appropriateness.
5. The NEB rendering is primarily dictated by exegetical concerns, for though the RSV and the TEV can have this meaning, the phrase "these last days" is not so explicit. However, the rendering "this the final age" is on the level of technical language. Stylistic feature: Level of language.
6. The rendering "by a Son" is merely translationese, a more or less literal rendering. If the word "Son" is to be capitalized, it can refer only to Jesus Christ, and therefore it should be "the," not "a." The NEB employs "the," but renders the Greek preposition

literally, evidently for certain exegetical reasons. The TEV has justifiably employed "through," since this is the normal way of indicating agency (and in this passage agency is certainly the principal meaning of the relationship). Stylistic feature: Semotactic appropriateness.

7. The TEV makes for easier understanding by introducing a new sentence at this point. In addition it has not used the word "heir," not only because it is less widely known, but also because it can be misleading, by implying, as it does, that the original owner must die before the heir can come into possession of the property. Stylistic features: Syntactic simplification, language level, and avoidance of connotative inappropriateness.

8. Though the principal lexical differences in this series are due primarily to differences of interpretation, there is nevertheless a resulting difference in level of style, for "all orders of existence" is a much more difficult lexical unit than "world" or "universe." Stylistic feature: Level of lexical usage.

9. The use of a term such as "effulgence" is likewise typical of the lexical high level of academic or technical style. The other differences are largely due to differences of interpretation. Stylistic feature: Level of lexical usage.

10. The term "stamp" is very little used in the meaning which it is supposed to have in this context. Accordingly, the TEV has made a substitute. The use of "very" with a noun is likewise a relatively rare combination. Stylistic features: Use of central vs. peripheral meanings and semotactic frequency.

11. The structure "his word of power" is typical of so-called Semitic Greek (the construct case in Hebrew). The more natural expression in English is to take a term such as "power" and put it into a corresponding adjectival construction. Stylistic feature: Natural grammatical construction.

12. The term "purification" is very seldom used with "sins," except in certain traditional religious contexts. The word "purgation" is even less used in such a context and is understood, if it is known at all, by most persons as applying to "purgation of gastrointestinal wastes." Stylistic feature: Semotactic appropriateness.

13. The phrases "the Majesty on high" or "Majesty on high" are primarily translationese, and are little understood. The TEV has accordingly attempted to make sense out of this title. Stylistic feature: Meaningfulness.

14. The principal differences in this series results from the diverse syntactic treatments, including of course the fact that in the TEV this clause occurs in a different paragraph. Stylistic feature: Intradiscourse transition.

15. The three levels of vocabulary in these three translations are clearly illustrated by the key words in these three renderings:

RSV	name	obtained	excellent
NEB	title	inherited	superior
TEV	name	gave	greater

The term "inherited" is avoided in the TEV because of the awkward associations of this term, for it seems to imply that an original owner must die before another person can possess the inheritance. Stylistic features: Lexical level and semotactic appropriateness.

In addition, however, to these essentially lexical contrasts there are certain very important differences in overall syntactic structure. In the RSV and the NEB these four verses are three sentences, while in the TEV they are five. (Stylistic feature: Sentence length.) In the RSV the shift from God to the Son, as the subject of the discourse, is not marked (the use of "He" is stylistically quite misleading). In the NEB this shift is marked by a relatively rare device of apposition (following a colon), while in the TEV the shift is much more clearly indicated by beginning a new sentence and introducing it with "the Son of God," thus linking the previous subject of the action with the subject which is to follow. This transition between participants is much more in keeping with normal English discourse usage. (Stylistic feature: Designation of participants.) Since the subject matter of verse 4 is more closely related to the contents of what follows than to what precedes, the TEV has combined this with the following verses and made a paragraph break between verses 3 and 4. (Stylistic feature: Intradiscourse break.)

As can be readily seen in a number of contexts one of the very significant differences between the RSV, the NEB, and the TEV is the level of vocabulary. This may be more fully illustrated by the following selected series of terms used in various contexts in Hebrews:

Hebrews	RSV	NEB	TEV
1:1	ways	fashion	ways
1:3	reflects	effulgence	shines with the brightness
1:3	purification	purgation	make clean
1:6	worship	homage	worship
1:14	ministering	ministrant	who serve
2:4	various	manifold	many kinds of
3:3	counted worthy	deemed worthy	is worthy
3:13	deceitfulness	wiles	deceived
5:4	take	arrogate	choose
6:18	unchangeable	irrevocable	cannot change
7:18	weakness	impotent	weak
7:28	weakness	frailty	imperfect
7:28	came later	supersede	came later
9:5	mercy seat	place of expiation	place where sins are forgiven
9:16	one who has made (a will)	testator	man who made (the will)

10:29	outraged	affront	treats as a cheap thing
11:4	receive approval	attest	won approval
11:26	abuse	stigma	scorn
11:33	mouths of lions	ravening lions	mouths of lions
11:35	refusing to accept	disdain	refusing to accept
12:15	bitterness	noxious	bitter
12:19	voice	oracular voice	voice
12:22	innumerable	myriads	thousands
12:22	festal gathering	concourse	joyful gathering
13:17	submit	defer	follow . . . orders

✵ CLASSIFICATION OF FEATURES OF STYLE

In the above passages selected from Luke and Hebrews a number of different features of style have been noted; discourse-transition marker, discourse-type marker, elimination of pleonasm, semotactic appropriateness, intradiscourse transition, semantic simplicity, pronominal reference, subordination of clauses, connotative equivalence, length of sentences, etc. These are, of course, only a few of the formal and lexical features of language which combine to produce certain styles.

The analyst of style must, however, do more than list stylistic features. He must also endeavor to describe the significance of such features. In a sense, this is somewhat easier when one can compare different translations of the same text. However, in doing this one finds that often more than one perspective is valid for judging stylistic features. For example, "elimination of pleonasm" describes a particular process, while "semotactic appropriateness" describes a resulting situation. Furthermore, any expression which is more natural may be said to illustrate greater semotactic appropriateness. In the preceding description of the features of style we have endeavored, however, to name the feature primarily in terms of its function, rather than merely to identify some stylistic device or form.

This functional approach to style is dictated by our concern to understand something of the purposes of style. Primarily, these purposes (or functions) can be divided into two categories: (1) those which serve to increase efficiency and (2) those which are designed for special effects, that is to say, those which enhance interest, increase impact, or embellish the form of the message. Of course, there are a number of grades between what might be considered these two principal functions, but for the most part the role of stylistic features can be best understood in terms of these two principal purposes. The features themselves are most readily divided between (1) formal and (2) lexical. The formal features are the arrangements of the words, while the lexical features are the words or lexical units (the idioms).

This combination of factors, *i.e.*, roles and features, produces a two-way split, with four resulting types, as in Figure 15.

Figure 15 provides us with four basic feature-function classes: (A) those formal features designed primarily for the sake of efficiency, that is, those arrangements of words which provide the greatest ease of decoding

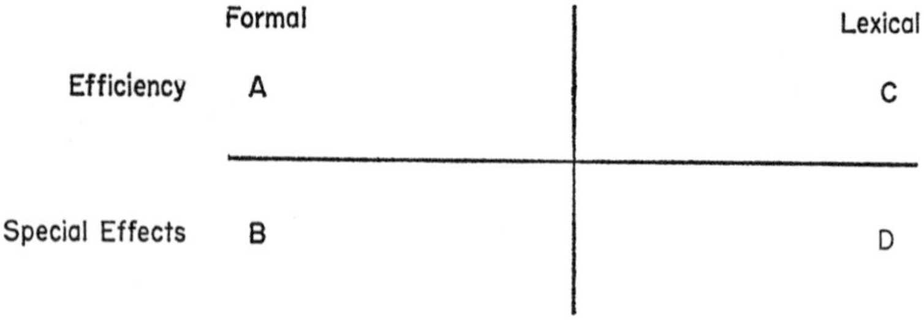

	Formal		Lexical
Efficiency	A		C
Special Effects	B		D

Figure 15

for the least amount of energy expended, (B) the formal features effective for enhancing interest, creating impact, and embellishing the message, (C) the lexical features (the choices of words) most effective in facilitating comprehension, and (D) those lexical features which provide the special effects, similar to what can be done by means of the corresponding formal features. It is on this basis that we classify the various stylistic features (including those noted in the inductive approach to the passages in Luke 15 and Hebrews 1), in order to see such features in terms of their principal functions.

Formal features designed for efficiency

It is impossible to deal with all the formal features which are designed primarily for the sake of efficiency (*i.e.*, for the greatest ease of decoding for the least amount of effort), but the following list is illustrative of some of the major types:

1. *Simple discourse structure.* The discourse that is easiest to comprehend is one in which there is only one series of events and only one participant (or set of participants).
2. *Discourse-type markers.* It is most important that in any discourse the reader know what type of account to expect, *e.g.*, parable, proverb, poem, description, or conversation.
3. *Discourse-transition markers.* When the account shifts from one episode or section to another, it is most helpful to have such transitions clearly marked. (Section headings are one means of helping in this respect).
4. *Intersentence markers.* If the connections between sentences can be marked, by such terms as "moreover," "therefore," "according," "in this way," etc., the reader can comprehend the relationships more easily.
5. *Marking of relationship between clauses.* The marking of the meaningful connection between clauses, by such conjunctions as "or," "but," "when," "because," "for," "while," etc., is important in increasing the efficiency of understanding.
6. *Parallel subject–predicate constructions.* When juxtaposed clauses have completely parallel subject-predicate constructions, the efficiency of comprehension is increased.

7. *Short sentences.* In general, shorter sentences are easier to understand than longer ones, especially if the structures are essentially simple and parallel with preceding and following sentences.

8. *Overt marking of participants.* Each language has its own system of identifying participants in a discourse and of referring to such participants in subsequent clauses. In many contexts, however, it is possible to leave some participants unmarked, *i.e.*, not specifically indicated in each clause. Nevertheless, the more clearly one marks such participants, the easier it is for the reader to understand.

9. *Sentences with simple structures.* The difficulty of a sentence is not merely a matter of length, but of structural complexity and so-called "depth," *i.e.*, the number of dependent relationships. For example, the sentence, "John made him appoint Bill leader of the troop," has only nine words, but three kernel utterances, while the sentence, "Jane and Bill have always gotten along so well," also has nine words, but is basically much simpler.

10. *Potential terminals in a sentence.* A sentence containing a number of potential stopping places is much easier to comprehend than one in which the temporary memory has to retain a good deal of information before some final expression completes the utterance. Compare, for example, the following sentences: (1) "He paid the man who came yesterday to fix the furnace which had broken down at least two weeks before our guests came from California," and (2) "The man who came yesterday to fix our furnace which had broken down at least two weeks before our guests came from California was paid."

11. *Clauses in sequence.* Basically the contrast between inclusion and sequence is a matter of depth of structure, but it is one of the very common elements in stylistic structure. For example, compare the included clause structure: "The fellow, whom I dislike so intensely, is nevertheless always coming to see us," with the sequential clause structure: "I dislike this fellow so intensely. Nevertheless, he is always coming to see us."

12. *Fit between semantic categories and grammatical classes.* Though other classes are also involved, it would seem that both statistically and stylistically the most important pairing here is that between events and verbs: the text in which events are expressed by verbs rather than nouns is usually both more efficient and more vivid than the one which has many events expressed by nouns.

Though all of the above feaures are very important for the sake of efficiency, any attempt to employ them exclusively would result in a text which would be very insipid and dull. It is for that reason that good style must also have certain features for special effects.

Formal features designed for special effects

Though it is impossible to treat anything like all of the principal formal features designed for special effects, some of the more common of these features include the following:

1. *Complex discourse structures.* In order to treat highly complex actions with several layers of events and participants, the style may reflect the circumstances by being complexly structured in a parallel manner.

2. *Lack of discourse-type markers.* When he does not have discourse-type markers, the reader is left to discover for himself, often after some time and perhaps with considerable surprise, just what kind of account he is reading, *e.g.*, history, legend, or fantasy.

3. *Lack of transition markers.* Abrupt shifts from one episode to another provide a sense of rapid movement and intense activity, and as such may be useful in creating impact.

4. *Paratactic constructions.* The meaningful relationship between clauses and sentences can often be effectively left to the reader to surmise (note, for example, Hemingway's frequent use of parataxis).

5. *Nonparallel constructions.* Nonparallel constructions, *e.g.*, chiasmus, may provide relief from stylistic monotony and help to "modulate" the account.

6. *Long and structurally complex sentences.* Well-constructed long sentences may be effectively used to describe highly complex events or relationships. (But they are perhaps more often employed to gain a reputation for being clever in so-called scholarly writing).

7. *Failure to mark participants.* The purposeful failure to mark participants may result in making the reader "guess" and in this way becoming involved in a pleasant linguistic detective game.

8. *Discrepancy between semantic and grammatical classes.* Some languages, such as Greek and English, make frequent use of a shift of class, as when events are expressed by nouns. The effect, at least in English, is to achieve a rather cold, impersonal style, which is much used in certain kinds of scientific or scholarly writing.

9. *Nonparallel semantic structures.* The use of antithesis in meaning may be an interesting and effective device for producing special effects.

10. *Formal confusion.* Some modern writers have introduced calculated formal confusion in order to suggest by the style something of the confusion and "absurdity" of the action or the responses of the participants.

11. *Sound effects.* The use of assonance, alliteration, rhyme, and onomatopoeic effects may all be useful in creating special effects.

12. *Rhythm.* Any elaborate or rigid systems of rhythm are likely to require certain uncommon combinations or orders of words, and thus to decrease efficiency of understanding. However, rhythmic features of poetry are highly valued for their special effects, and the avoidance of jerkiness is essential to good, readable prose.

Lexical features designed for efficiency

1. *Well-known words.* Familiar words are obviously easier to comprehend than those which are not well known.
2. *High-frequency words.* One might assume that well-known words would automatically all be high-frequency words. That is not, however, always the case. For example, *headache* and *knee* are not high-frequency words, but they are quite well known by any user of English. On the other hand, words such as *matter* and *object* are relatively frequent, but they are not always easy to comprehend.
3. *Familiar combinations of words.* The problems of comprehension are not merely ones of word familiarity or word frequency, but of combinations. That is to say, well-known combinations are more readily understood than rare and unusual ones.
4. *Combinations of words which have "semantically agreeable" parts.* In order to produce a new message one inevitably uses some new combinations of words. However, if such combinations are to be readily understood, the componential structures of the respective words need to "agree." For example, words such as *strange, good, fine, valuable,* and *swell* go frequently with *idea,* and as such are readily understood. Words such as *disconcerting, baffling, philosophical, metaphysical,* or *intriguing* are much less frequent with *idea,* but they seem to fit. On the other hand, words such as *purple, cast-iron, horizontal,* and *fat* do not seem to "agree" with *idea,* for the components of these words have few links with the components of *idea.* Nevertheless, just such attributives as these are used in figurative language for the sake of special effects.
5. *Present-day rather than obsolescent or archaic words.* Many words have a historical connotative dimension, *i.e.,* they become associated with certain historical periods. For special effects obsolescent or archaic words may be useful, but present-day words are best for easy comprehension.
6. *Specific vs. generic terms.* As long as they are within a domain of general cultural interest, very specific terms are easier to understand than more generic ones. But if one is dealing with a highly specialized domain, such as a rather abstruse scientific discipline, generic terms are easier than specific terms.
7. *Central meaning of words.* The problems of word frequency have often been treated naïvely by persons who have assumed that in every occurrence of a word one is dealing with essentially the same significance. This is by no means the case. Therefore, the use of a familiar word, but in an unfamiliar meaning, produces no gain in ease of comprehension. In fact, this is likely to produce misunderstanding, or to increase considerably the burden of figuring out just what is meant.
8. *Words appropriate to the constituency.* In all the considerations noted above—*e.g.,* familiarity, frequency, and present-day usage—one can only evaluate word usage in terms of the particular con-

stituency to which a translation is directed. This is supplementary to all the preceding considerations, but it has seemed necessary to list separately this factor of appropriateness for the constituency in order to emphasize the importance of such a consideration.

Lexical features designed for special effects

As in the case of formal features designed for special effects, these lexical features for special effects are almost the converse of those which are so important for the sake of efficiency.

1. *Little-known words.* Unfamiliar words carry special impact and may help to create "atmosphere."
2. *Infrequent words.* Infrequent words, especially of a technical nature, may suggest the importance or the academic "dignity" of a theme.
3. *Specific vs. generic terms.* Here terms at both ends of the scale can be used to special effect. Highly specific terms, which are very low in the taxonomic hierarchy, can give a very vivid effect when the terms are in the more general cultural domain, or a very technical effect when they are in more specialized domains. Generic terms, on the other hand, can give a diffuse or a pompous effect, because they are more abstract and harder to define than specific terms.
4. *Unusual combinations of words.* New and striking combinations of words make a writing fresh and give the impression that the ideas are also new and important.
5. *Contrasting words.* Words which seemingly clash, but which on closer examination are found to suggest unrecognized relationships (so characteristic of the figurative language of good poetry), may be much appreciated.
6. *Dated words.* The use of obsolescent or archaic words may add "color" and "setting" to an account.
7. *Peripheral and figurative meanings.* The use of familiar terms in rare meanings adds a dimension of novelty and curiosity to the style.
8. *Puns.* Plays on words can be especially intriguing, particularly if they are both subtle and symbolic.
9. *Calculated avoidance.* Euphemistic expressions may suggest a number of subtle psychological moods.

As has been suggested, good style consists primarily in a proper combination of factors designed for efficiency and for special effects. However, in preparing something for certain special groups or levels, it is obvious that one may wish to have more of one type than of another. For example, in preparing materials for new literates, one should concentrate on A and C (see Figure 16), with primary consideration being given to A. Moreover, in preparing materials for children or for those who have acquired only a limited use of the language, one must make even greater restrictions in C than in the case of materials being prepared for newly literate adults. In producing a common-language translation one must also sacrifice many features of B and D in order to concentrate on A and C. On the other hand, in a translation for the more educated constituencies and especially in the more rhetorically elaborate portions of the Bible, one must inevitably do everything possible to employ in the receptor languages features from B and D which will be functionally equivalent to what occurs in the Biblical text.

Problem 36

1. For each of the following words; (a) without consulting a dictionary or talking with others, put each word into a sentence applicable to everyday life (not a quotation from the Bible); (b) evaluate each word as literary (L) or common (C), and explain your evaluation:

1. fashion	6. manifold	11. impotent	16. affront	21. oracular
2. effulgence	7. deem	12. frailty	17. attest	22. myriads
3. purgation	8. wiles	13. supersede	18. stigma	23. concourse
4. homage	9. arrogate	14. expiation	19. disdain	24. defer
5. ministrant	10. irrevocable	15. testator	20. noxious	25. ravening

2. After completing the first part of this problem, compare the renderings of these terms in the context of Hebrews:

Hebrews	NEB	RSV	TEV
1:1	fashion	ways	ways
1:3	effulgence	reflects	shines with the brightness
1:3	purgation	purification	make clean
1:6	homage	worship	worship
1:14	ministrant	ministering	who serve
2:4	manifold	various	many kinds of
3:3	deemed worthy	counted worthy	is worthy
3:13	wiles	deceitfulness	deceived
5:4	arrogate	take	choose
6:18	irrevocable	unchangeable	cannot change
7:18	impotent	weakness	weak
7:28	frailty	weakness	imperfect
7:28	supersede	came later	came later
9:5	place of expiation	mercy seat	place where sins are forgiven
9:16	testator	one who has made (a will)	man who made (the will)
10:29	affront	outraged	treats as a cheap thing
11:4	attest	receive approval	won approval
11:26	stigma	abuse	scorn
11:33	ravening lions	mouths of lions	mouths of lions
11:35	disdain	refusing to accept	refusing to accept
12:15	noxious	bitterness	bitter
12:19	oracular voice	voice	voice

12:22	myriads	innumerable	thousands
12:22	concourse	festal gathering	joyful gathering
13:17	defer	submit	follow ... orders

DISCOURSE STRUCTURE

Though the fact of discourse structure has been mentioned several times, we have not actually discussed the components and characteristics of such structures, since in this treatment of the theory and practice of translating it is not possible to deal satisfactorily with this very extensive and increasingly more important phase of language structure, and accordingly, of translation.

In the past linguists have tended to regard the sentence as the upper limit of what is formally structured in language. But increasingly it has become evident that speakers of a language do not put their sentences together in a purely haphazard or random fashion. In fact, the relationships between sentences are quite elaborately structured, and the features of such structures are important, not merely for understanding the message but also for comprehending the nature of such structuring.

It must be recognized, of course, that in the same way that sentences may be well or awkwardly formed (while all being grammatically correct), so paragraphs and larger units may also be well or awkwardly formed, while also conforming to some of the larger units of structure. It may be that not all persons always employ all the elements of discourse structure which are available to them. Moreover, they are not under the same kind of compulsion to do so, as they are in the case of the sentence structure. Nevertheless, all languages do have certain important features which can be used, and which in "effective" communications are used, to mark the units larger than sentences.

We have already seen (p. 131) that the universals of discourse are:

1. the marking of the beginning and end of the discourse
2. the marking of major internal transitions
3. the marking of temporal relations between events
4. the marking of spatial relations between events and objects
5. the marking of logical relations between events
6. the identification of participants
7. highlighting, focus, emphasis, etc.
8. author involvement

We will now discuss these in more detail.

1. *Markers for the beginning and the end of discourse.* Introductory expressions such as "once upon a time" or "there was once a man" show clearly that one is beginning a story. The end may be indicated by some such trite expression as "they lived happily ever after" or "and that's how the chipmunk got his stripes." The end of a discourse may, however, be more subtly suggested by such phrases as:

How else could one account for such behavior that night?

Now we know, and now we can all wait.
And a kiss wiped away her tears.
But, as I have said, it all happened so very long ago that hardly
anyone remembers about it any more.

2. *Markers for internal transitions*. There are many common, traditional
means of introducing new paragraphs in English, such as:

On the other hand, however. . .
Then all of a sudden. . .
In contrast with all this. . .

But one also finds many standard devices which are more subtly designed:

When finally all the people had left. . .
When he woke up the next morning. . .
Now everything was changed. . .

3. *Markers of temporal relationships*. Temporal relationships are marked
in a number of ways: (1) by temporal conjunctions, *e.g.*, "when," "after,"
"while"; (2) temporal phrases, *e.g.*, "the next morning," "all that day,"
"sometime next year"; (3) relative tenses, *e.g.*, future perfect and past
perfect; (4) sequence of tenses, *e.g.*, "He said he came," vs. "He said he
was coming"; (5) order of events, with the assumption that unless otherwise marked the linguistic order is also the historical order.

4. *Markers of spatial relationships*. The principal markers of spatial
relationships are (1) special particles, *e.g.*, prepositions such as "in, on,
at, by, around, through, with, over, under"; (2) expressions of distance:
"long way off," "ten miles long," "a day's trip"; (3) event words of
motion, *e.g.*, "went," "came," "left," "removed," "shoved," "cut down,"
which imply a direction of motion.

5. *Markers of logical relationships*. Logical relationships may be
marked in a number of ways: (1) by so-called sentence adverbs as conjunctions, *e.g.*, "moreover," "therefore," "nevertheless," "accordingly";
(2) by conjunctions introducing dependent clauses, *e.g.*, "if," "although,"
"because"; (3) by forms of the verbs, *e.g.*, participles indicating dependency on other event words; (4) by lexical units which state logical relationships, *e.g.*, "these were his reasons," "he concluded," "he argued that,"
"he discovered the cause of his trouble."

6. *Markers of successive references to the same subjects*. All languages
have techniques for referring to the same subject, whether participant,
event, or abstract, at different points in an account and without necessarily repeating the same name or formal designation. The principal
means for doing this consist of (1) pronominal references, *e.g.*, "he,"
"she," "they," "who"; (2) deictic (pointing) references, *e.g.*, "this,"
"that"; and (3) synonyms, *e.g.*, "dog . . . animal . . . pet . . . puppy"
(as successive references to the same object). Events may also be referred
to by successive references, *e.g.*, "He drove furiously . . . his speed . . . the
way he handled the car . . . he went faster and faster."

7. *The foregrounding and backgrounding of successive series of partici-*

pants and events. In any complex account not all the sets of participants and events are of equal importance. Therefore, some of these are set in the foreground (the center of the linguistic stage), while others are put into the background. One may find several different layers of such participants and events, with intricate signals by which the receiver of the message is clued in on what is to be understood as primary, secondary, tertiary, etc. For narrative, it is possible to distinguish at least three distinct degrees or levels of complexity of structure:

    a. one or more participants, linked to a single chain of events
    b. more than one participant, linked to two or more chains of events which may be going on simultaneously, with one in focus or front-stage, and the other(s) back-stage
    c. use of flashback and/or anticipation which substantially changes the surface structure order from the chronological order

    8. *Author involvement.* The involvement of the author is of two principal types: (1) autobiographical (either real or fictional) by the use of first person pronominal forms or (2) judgmental, through the use of value terms for or against persons or events, *e.g., he had an attractive manner; His action was fully justified; Her behavior was inexcusable;* and *This was an ugly scene.*

    The basic techniques required to analyze the discourse structure of any passage consist primarily of: (1) back-transformation of the surface structures to kernel or near-kernel structures, (2) separation of the various degrees of foregrounding and backgrounding into primary, secondary, or tertiary structures (this information is usually clear from the way in which the language keeps the principal subjects in focus), (3) reduction of near-kernels to their most essential features, (4) analysis of the extent of parallelism and contrast between successive sets of primary structures, (5) diagrammatic lining up of the chains of participants and events, and (6) treatment of nonprimary sets as dependent, "included" structures with their own internal relationships.

    Though it is not possible here to deal with all the details of method and procedure in discourse analysis, the following material from Ephesians 1:3-10 may prove illustrative of what can be done. In the "outline" of this passage only the "skeleton" of the major kernel expressions has been given, based in considerable measure on the translation and interpretation employed in the Today's English Version:

1. we thank	God					
2.	God	blessed	us			
3.	God	chose	us			
4.			we	. . .be holy. . .		
5.	God	loved	us			
6.	God	destined	us			through Christ
7. we praise	God's	grace				
8.	God	gave	us			in. . .Son
9.	God	set	us	free		in Christ

10.	God	forgave	our sins		in Christ
11.	God	gave	us grace		
12.	God	revealed to us			
13.	God	plans			by Christ
14.	God	unites all			with Christ as head

Though these particular verses of Ephesians are perhaps some of the most complexly organized in the entire New Testament, nevertheless it is instructive to discover just how much organization there is, and how subtly this organization has been structured.

Kernel 1 introduces the passage, and kernel 7 echoes this about halfway through the passage. Otherwise the initial concept might have been lost. It is interesting to note also that at the very end of this long sentence in Greek, namely, at the end of verse 14, this same introductory refrain is taken up again, *i.e.*, "to the praise of his glory," which is structurally equivalent to "we praise God" in kernel 7. Accordingly, within the framework of an initial expression of thankfulness and two expressions of praise, the sequence of events in the discourse structure of argument is presented.

Kernel 2 takes up the goal of kernel 1 and makes it the subject of a long series of events through kernel 14 (with the exception of kernel 4, which is actually on a secondary level, and kernel 7, which is an echo of kernel 1). Note that "we," "us," or "our" mark the person goals of the kernels 2-3, 5-6, and 8-12.

In the Greek text "Christ" or "the Beloved" is introduced each time by the preposition *en*, literally "in," except for kernel 6, in which the preposition is *dia*, "through." Kernel 11 is actually only a reinforcement of kernel 8, and kernel 12 is an anticipation of kernels 13 and 14. Kernel 5 is dependent upon kernel 6 or kernel 4, depending upon the way in which one wishes to divide the Greek text.

Some exegetes insist that *en* with "Christ," "Son," or any other designation of the second person of the Trinity can only mean "in Christ" in a very special Pauline sense. The principal difficulty with such a rendering is that it simply does not make much sense, if any, in English. Such an expression has no meaning at all outside this type of Biblical context, and then only after long, detailed explanation. Even in the more than four hundred years that this expression has been used in the English language, Christian preachers and scholars have been quite incapable of making it really meaningful.

The real semantic problem, of course, is that one can speak of a spirit being in an object, but not of an object being in a spirit. Nor do we speak of one person being in another. Another aspect of this problem must also be considered, for "in Christ" may in some instances represent the relationship of objects to each other, *i.e.*, "We are in Christ" (often translated in modern English as "united with," or "in union with"), but in many other contexts it is apparently not the relationship of objects to objects but of Christ as object or participant (in the transformational sense of the word) with an event. It is precisely for this reason that even in this passage various translators have translated *en* as "by means of" or "by."

However, quite apart from arguments with respect to the meaning of Greek *en* with "Christ" (and for the purposes of this particular analysis of discourse structure such exegetical distinctions are not essential) it is important to note that there is a very considerable and largely unsuspected degree of parallelism of structure. The problem for the translator is to make sure that in his restructuring of such a passage in another language he pays close attention to the means of identifying successive references to the same persons, *e.g.*, "God," "Christ," and "us," without ambiguity and without tediousness, and also to ways of subordinating certain actions to other actions, *e.g.*, 4 to 3; 5 to 6; 13 as the result of 12; and 14 as an explanation of 13.

It should be evident, therefore, that one must not translate this passage a clause at a time. The entire passage must be dealt with as a unit and its essential structure analyzed, transferred, and then restructured, so that it will preserve something of the same grandeur it has in the original Greek text.

Problem 37

In the following passage (Mark 6:16-18, RSV), formulate the kernels, and arrange them in chronological order:

> But when Herod heard of it he said, "John, whom I beheaded, has been raised." For Herod had sent and seized John, and bound him in prison for the sake of Herodias, his brother Philip's wife; because he had married her. For John said to Herod, "It is not lawful for you to have your brother's wife."

What grammatical or other linguistic devices are used in the RSV surface structure to make intelligible such a large-scale reversal of chronological order? Compare the devices used in the TEV version of this passage.

Problem 38

In the following passage (Luke 8:28-29, RSV), state the kernels and arrange them in chronological order; then determine what order they should have in the receptor language in which you are working and what devices are to be used to mark such sequences effectively.

> When he saw Jesus, he cried out and fell down before him, and said with a loud voice, "What have you to do with me, Jesus, Son of the Most High God? I beseech you, do not torment me." For he had commanded the unclean spirit to come out of the man. (For many a time it had seized him; he was kept under guard, and bound with chains and fetters, but he broke the bonds and was driven by the demon into the desert.)

Problem 39

In the following passage (Rom. 6:7-10, RSV), formulate the kernels, and specify as precisely and as fully as necessary the logical relations between them:

For he who has died is freed from sin. But if we have died with Christ, we believe that we shall also live with him. For we know that Christ being raised from the dead will never die again; death no longer has dominion over him. The death he died he died to sin, once for all, but the life he lives he lives to God.

Problem 40

By using a map of the New Testament world, determine to what extent there is a discernible order in the citing of place names in Acts 2:9-11, (RSV):

Parthians and Medes and Elamites and residents of Mesopotamia, Judea and Cappadocia, Pontus and Asia, Phrygia and Pamphylia, Egypt and the parts of Libya belonging to Cyrene, and visitors from Rome, ... Cretans and Arabians.

Problem 41

Apply the relevant procedures outlined on p. 154 to the following passages (RSV or KJV): Mark 6:45-52 (historical narrative), Luke 10:30-35 (narrative parable), Rev. 1:12-16 (description), Eph. 4:11-14 (argument).

PRODUCING AN APPROPRIATE STYLE

It is one thing to analyze the components of style and often quite a different thing to work out the means by which a satisfactory style can be produced. In the case of languages with long literary traditions, one can usually obtain the help of a professional stylist, either to translate the first draft, on which theologically trained persons can then proceed to make the necessary corrections, or to try to "fix up" translations which theologically trained persons have produced.

If a stylist is to be employed either for the initial work or for later revision of the manuscript, it is important that he have certain very essential qualifications: (1) he must be a good writer, (2) he should not have too much acquaintance with the traditional forms of the Scriptures, (3) he should be sympathetic with the message of the Scriptures (though not necessarily a "believer"), and (4) in general he should work as a special consultant or assessor, and not as a member of a committee.

Being a good writer must mean much more than his having turned in a couple of publishable articles for a church paper. If at all possible a stylist should be a professional writer. It is not even enough that he be an editor or a corrector of other people's writing. He should have creative writing abilities himself, for in the process of providing stylistic help for a translation he must do more than spot awkward sentences; he must be able to provide the creative assistance which is so essential.

If the stylist knows the Bible too well, he is likely to be deceived by his very familiarity with the text and thus let many things slip past which really do not make sense. At the same time, of course, he must be essentially sympathetic with the Christian message, or he will not have sufficient empathy to be creative toward the form.

Though committees are sometimes organized to include a "stylist," such a person is usually not a top-flight specialist in style but only someone who seems to be much more competent than perhaps the rest of the committee. The really first-rate stylist usually does not survive as a member of a committee, for his job is an aesthetic type of contribution, and aesthetics is something many theologically trained persons simply do not understand. Since the stylist reacts primarily to aesthetic and artistic standards (many of which cannot be easily defined or explained), rather than to theological arguments based on original texts, he is usually ill equipped to defend his suggestions against the onslaught of those who claim to know just what the original means. The fact that what the committee is rendering may not make sense to the common man or that, if it is intelligible, it is painfully awkward, seems not to be too important to many theologically trained people translating the Bible. Accordingly, it is probably better for the stylist to do his work alone, in circumstances in which he can be far more creative.

If the stylist is really good (and if he is not good, he is not needed), it is usually found that about 50 percent of his suggestions can be accepted without modification, another 30 percent of his recommendations will lead to still further changes, and 20 percent will need to be rejected, since they may reflect an inadequate understanding of the meaning of the original message. In considering a competent stylist's suggestions the Editorial Committee should be prepared to accept all stylistic recommendations unless there are strong exegetical reasons for rejecting them. This means that an Editorial Committee must learn to respect the stylist's contribution, for a committee is usually very poorly prepared to produce anything with a really good style. Legal documents and treaties, which are famous for their lack of good style, can of course be written by committees, but good style does not result from group discussion.

When the languages in question do not have an adequate literary tradition, the problems of producing a good style are much greater, for generally two quite different processes are involved: (1) the analysis of the oral literature in the receptor language, and (2) the training of stylists among those who speak the receptor language as a mother tongue. To understand something about the style of oral literature in a language, it is essential to make thorough studies of the literary forms of legends, myths, and stories from candidly recorded texts. That is to say, recordings should be made when the speaker is unaware of the fact that a recording is being made. Otherwise he will almost inevitably introduce a number of artificialities into the material. The translator who comes to the receptor language as a foreign language must also "soak up" the language by saturating himself in hearing and speaking the language. And to do this, he will need a number of years. Even with all the formal analysis of texts which he might be able to undertake, there is simply no substitute for the millions and billions of words a person should listen to and speak, if he is to build up a "feeling" for the semotactic appropriateness of certain combinations. The average person can quite well master the syntactic structure of a language in four or five years, but it is the rare individual who masters the semotactic structure of a foreign language in less than twenty years, especially if he begins this process after he has become an adult.

The necessity for the expatriate to have an adequate mastery of the stylistic form of a language is (1) that he may provide valid alternatives to those with whom he is working, (2) that he may not skew the translation by his own way of speaking and using the language (thus imposing, even in very subtle ways, his own "will" upon the committee), and (3) that he may really be a creative person on the team, rather than merely the "expert on the Greek."

Training Stylists for Languages Lacking a Literary Tradition

Many persons have insisted that stylists, like any other artists, are born, not made, and in very large measure this is true. However, even persons with artistic talent need to have their capacities developed, and even those persons who seemingly have limited abilities can improve their output immensely through careful and consistent practice under guidance.

Perhaps the most important aspect of training is the selection of those who may potentially have ability and to whom it is advisable to provide instruction. For the most part such persons should have (1) good oral ability in the language, (2) creative imagination, *i.e.*, the capacity to put words together, (3) some evidence of ability to write their own language reasonably well, (4) pride in their own language, (5) knowledge of the oral literature, *i.e.*, of the legends, myths, etc., or a keen desire to study them, and (6) willingness to listen to and carefully consider suggestions made by others. Without these minimal qualifications it is unlikely that a person will really succeed in doing quality work as a stylist, regardless of how much help he may be given in trying to learn how to write and to edit.

The selection of potentially qualified persons is, however, only the beginning. They must also be carefully guided through a relatively long and carefully worked-out series of steps in learning how to write. The principal steps in this procedure include: (1) expansion techniques, (2) selectivity techniques, (3) structuring techniques, (4) writing for different levels of audience, (5) writing for different degrees of impact, (6) writing for differences of response, (7) adaptation of articles and stories, (8) learning to respond to orally given alternatives, (9) diagnosing problems in written texts, and (10) providing stylistically satisfactory corrections of written materials.

1. *Expansion techniques.* Perhaps one of the most serious problems to overcome in the completely "new writer" is his tendency to be unbearably brief. For example, people who are unaccustomed to writing in their own language may describe a trip in only four or five short sentences, *e.g.*, "I left for home when school was out. We had trouble because the river was flooded. I arrived safely. My brother was sick. Nothing happened on my return to school."

Faced with this type of writing some teachers of composition give up in despair. However, it is possible to build on even this type of poor beginning by asking the student to take any one of the sentences, particularly one which sounds as though it had some potentialities, *e.g.*, the trouble crossing the river, and to expand it into a fuller description. Often it will be expanded into about five or six more short sentences. But each of these sentences can be used as a topic, and further expansion can be introduced. In fact, each sentence in each successive series can be used for still further expansion until the writer has gotten the point of how an account can be given in rather full detail.

2. *Selection techniques*. Expanding a story into a number of short episodes is, of course, not "writing," and so one must also teach selection. This means that the student must then be taught just how he is to select from a long series of sentences those which are the most significant. Significance can be defined in terms of making this account as distinctive as possible in terms of content (*i.e.*, as different as possible from any other such trip) and as interesting as possible for the audience in question.

3. *Structuring the account*. Even when expansion and selection have been carried out, the series of sentences may be monotonously similar and without any meaningful linkage. At this point one can often ask the student to imitate in writing the way good storytellers in his village would put such information together. At this point, the student should practice telling the story aloud to someone who has never heard it before. As he does this, the teacher makes notes on how he links the sentences together, how certain facts are highlighted and others left less important, and how the linguistic order in which the events are given is altered in order to make them "stand out."

With these important "hints" as to the way in which discourse may be structured, the teacher can then call attention to the techniques, discuss them with the student, and see to what extent these can be applied in writing. But it is essential that the student learn how to do this in his own language rather than memorizing what books on writing and rhetoric say.

It is assumed that anyone who has the potentiality of a translator will know at least one other language, one which can serve as a "source language" for him. This means that he can then read some well-written stories in the source language and see how they are put together, in terms of linkage between sentences and organization of the account.

One might argue that someone who is so pitifully inadequate in writing his own language as to have such difficulties in the stages of expansion and selection should never be selected to become a "stylist" in the first place. However, there are some exceptionally bright persons who seem to have all kinds of potential, but who nevertheless for lack of experience seem to "freeze" when they are asked to put anything into written form. One should, therefore, be prepared with the necessary techniques in order to overcome some of these initial obstacles, and by the processes of expansion, selection, and structuring guide potentially capable individuals over these early obstacles.

4. *Writing for different levels*. Once the student has grasped the idea of expanding, selecting, and structuring (using, when necessary, the

oral literature as a model), he must then be helped to learn how to manipulate his language, that is, to handle the tools of language in a conscious way. The first step in this procedure is learning to write the same account for different people, *e.g.*, for an old man, for a child, and for a school friend. In each instance it is important that the "audience" be as specific as possible; for one must learn to visualize the person for whom one is writing, for only then can he anticipate "feedback"—the questions that such a person will want to ask and the objections which such an individual is likely to raise.

(5) *Writing for differences of impact.* After one has learned to understand some of the features which go into writing for different types of people, it is then important to learn to write to the same person with quite different force. For example, one may wish to write an account in such a way as to make it seem quite insignificant, or on the other hand, to describe the very same event in such a way as to make it seem extremely important. The facts may be precisely the same, but the way in which they are arranged, the mood words which are used to suggest the writer's reactions to the experience, are all part of the stylistic resources of a language, and only a conscious knowledge of how they can be used will make one capable of judging whether a particular rendering in a translation is appropriate.

(6) *Writing for differences of response.* In a sense, making something seem important or insignificant is one form of writing for response, but in this sixth step we are suggesting something more specific, namely, writing an account first so that people will be very happy about, sympathetic with, or pleased by something, and then turning around and rewriting the same account in such a way that people will be angry about what happened and deeply disturbed.

This type of writing is often called "slanted" writing, and it is precisely this. This does not mean that we are encouraging the training of potential Bible translators as propagandists, so that they can write about something that is black and make it seem lily white. That is not our purpose. Rather, we are concerned that people learn something about the total resources of a language and discover those features of their own language which influence people favorably or unfavorably. Here is precisely where one teaches the concept of connotative meanings. By learning how to use language, one also learns how to react to language, and to sense the appropriate and the inappropriate use of terms. Moreover, one can do far more teaching about style by teaching people how to use their own language than by giving them rules to memorize and articles to analyze. Furthermore, one does not learn how to write in one's own language merely by studying the models of a foreign language.

7. *Adaptation of articles and stories.* Rather than beginning with translation it is much better to begin with adaptation. In a sense adaptation is much harder, for it requires so much more overall control and many more cultural insights. Moreover, one must also be more creative in good adaptation. But if one can make good adaptations of material, he can almost always be a good translator. Moreover, in adaptations the student

is much more likely to apply in a conscious way some of the basic concepts he has learned about style.

8. *Responding to alternatives.* Learning to respond to alternatives which are given in oral form is the first basic step in learning how to "edit." For this step the teacher needs to be able to suggest valid alternatives which can be evaluated and then the basis for the judgment discussed. At first, however, the ear must be trained, for sounds come before letters and hearing before reading. In fact, the student should learn to read everything aloud and in this way to judge certain aspects of the style from the "sounds" of the words. The range of alternatives to which the student's ear must be trained should include a number of basic features, *e.g.,* word order, tense sequence, semotactic appropriateness, complex structures, pronominal reference, and ambiguous grammatical and lexical usages.

9. *Diagnosing problems in written texts.* The student must now be given texts in which some of the sentences are poorly written, and he must be shown how to find the problems and to diagnose what seems to be wrong. At this stage he does not necessarily have to suggest a correction, but the recognition and analysis should be directed toward this end. It may even be enough at the beginning stages to have the student underline the various words, phrases, or sentences which seem to be awkward or difficult.

10. *Providing stylistically acceptable alternatives.* Finally, the student is in a position where he can and should be able to provide satisfactory alternatives, for little by little he has been able to build up a sensitivity to the stylistic resources of his language; and now that he has learned how to control these for his own writing, he can more easily find the mistakes in materials prepared by others. At this point he should be well qualified to make a significant contribution to the stylistic problems of a translation into his mother tongue.

CHAPTER EIGHT

TESTING THE TRANSLATION

Once the process of restructuring has been completed, the next essential step is the testing of the translation. This should cover the entire range of possible problems: accuracy of rendering, intelligibility, stylistic equivalence, etc. But to do this one must focus attention not upon the extent of verbal correspondence but upon the amount of dynamic equivalence. This means that testing the translation does not consist in merely comparing texts to see the extent of verbal consistency or conformity (translators can be consistently wrong as well as consistently right), but in determining how the potential receptors of a translation react to it. In a sense this is something like market research, in which the response of the public to the product is tested, for regardless of how theoretically good a product might be or how seemingly well it is displayed, if people do not respond favorably to it, then it is not going to be accepted. This does not mean, of course, that a translation is to be judged merely on the extent to which the people like the contents. Some people may object strongly to the themes and the concepts which are communicated, but there should not be anything in the translation itself which is stylistically awkward, structurally burdensome, linguistically unnatural, and semantically misleading or incomprehensible, unless, of course, the message in the source language has these characteristics (the task of the translator is to produce the closest natural equivalent, not to edit or to rewrite). But to judge these qualities one must look to the potential users.

The Problem of Overall Length

As has already been intimated at several points in the preceding chapters, there is a tendency for all good translations to be somewhat longer than the originals. This does not mean, of course, that all long translations are necessarily good. It only means that in the process of transfer from one linguistic and cultural structure to another, it is almost inevitable that the resulting translation will turn out to be longer.

This tendency to greater length is due essentially to the fact that one wishes to state everything that is in the original communication but is also obliged to make explicit in the receptor language what could very well remain implicit in the source-language text, since the original receivers of this communication presumably had all the necessary background to understand the contents of the message. Moreover, there seems to be a relatively fixed tendency for languages to be approximately 50 percent redundant, not only in the sounds which are used but also in the flow of lexical information. From all the evidence we have it is also assumed that most languages have approximately the same rate of flow of information for corresponding types of style and levels of usage. Hence, if one is obliged to be somewhat more explicit in the receptor language than in the source language, the translation will inevitably tend to be longer.

One can, however, describe much more precisely the basis for the fact that good translations tend to be somewhat longer than the original text. In the first place, it may be said that each message which is communicated has two basic dimensions, length (l) and difficulty (d). In the original communication which takes place within the source language, any well-constructed message is designed to fit the channel capacity of the receptors. This relationship may be indicated by Figure 16:

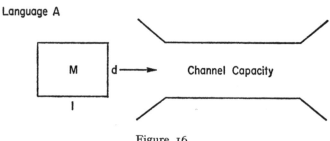

Figure 16

In Figure 16, the message (M), which has the two basic dimensions of length (l) and difficulty (d), is designed to pass through the channel capacity of the original receptors. Of course, a communicator may fail to estimate accurately the channel capacity of his audience, but this was not true of the Biblical writers, for they were not engaged in idle speculations nor were they trying to be obscure. Rather, they had urgent messages which they were intensely concerned to communicate, and hence they undoubtedly did structure their messages with the channel capacity of the receptors in mind. In the case of the Pauline Letters, one must remember that in so many instances these communications were sent to groups of people who had heard Paul on many occasions. They were undoubtedly familiar with many of his ideas, and they understood many of the allusions which are difficult for us to grasp, for we just do not have the background to appreciate all that was involved.

If, however, one translates a message literally from the source to the receptor language, and in doing so employs a message with the same dimensions of length, almost inevitably the dimension of difficulty will be appreciably greater. But the problem becomes really acute because the average channel capacity of the receptors in the second language is much less than that of the original receptors. This is certainly true if the languages belong to quite different linguistic families and particularly true if the cultures are quite different. This type of situation may be diagrammed as in Figure 17.

Since in the case of a literal translation the dimension of difficulty is greater, while the channel capacity is less, the only possible solution is to "draw out" the message, that is, to build in redundancy, as suggested in Figure 18.

Language B

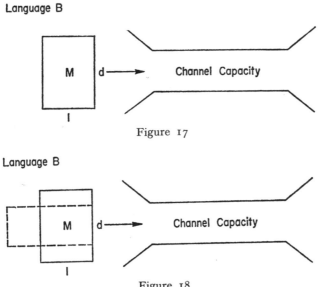

Figure 17

Language B

Figure 18

In the process of building in redundancy one does not add any information not implicit in the original message. One is only raising such information from an implicit to an explicit level. There are some so-called translations which do, however, introduce "new information." The Amplified Translation and the Expanded Translation, for example, add information not implicit in the original, and as such cannot be said to come within the scope of this definition of legimate redundancy, which may be required in order to make a translation dynamically equivalent in the sense that it fits the channel capacity of the present receptors to approximately the same extent as the original communication fit the channel capacity of the original receptors.

When this problem of calculated and justifiable redundancy in translation was being explained to a group of Africans in the Cameroun, one of the men insisted that he understood exactly what was meant, for as he said, "That is just what a python does when he kills an animal he cannot swallow. He coils his body around the animal, crushes it, and thus squeezes it out long and thin. Then he can swallow it. The meat and the bones are all there. They are just in a different form." This is precisely what the translator does with an "unswallowable" linguistic portion of text. He analyzes its components, builds in proper redundancy by making explicit what is implicit in the original, and then produces something the readers in the receptor language will be able to understand.

TYPES OF EXPANSIONS

Since expansions constitute the major elements in the testing of dynamic equivalence, it may be useful to point out those particular types of expansions which occur most commonly, for in this process not only will it be more evident what kinds of expansions are often obligatory but also which kinds of expansions are not necessary or legitimate.

The expansions may perhaps be most conveniently divided between syntactic (or formal) expansions and lexical (or semantic) ones.

Syntactic expansions

The most common expansions required by the syntactic structure of the receptor languages include: (a) identification of the participants in events, (b) identification of objects or events with abstracts, (c) more explicit indication of relationals, and (d) filling out of ellipses, which may involve any type of syntactic structure.

It is obvious that in order to identify participants unambiguously one must often introduce nouns in place of pronouns, but this is regarded here as a substitution rather than a syntactic expansion. What is involved at this point is something more complex. For example, in reading the clause, "I am the resurrection and the life" (John 11:25), a person may completely miss the point unless the subject of the "resurrection" is clearly identified, for "resurrection" is not a transform of an intransitive verb but of a causative one. That is to say, "I am the resurrection and the life" means "I am the one who causes people to rise again and to live." Unless the subject of these two events of "rising" and "living" is clearly identified, the reader may assume that this is only a reference to the fact that Jesus himself would rise from the dead and live. In fact, this is precisely the way in which most English-speaking people understand this passage.

There is, however, another type of participant which should be clearly marked in translation: the source of direct statements. For example, in many languages a more or less literal translation of Mark 1:2, "As it is written in Isaiah the prophet, Behold I send my messenger. . .," suggests that it is Isaiah who is sending his messenger. Of course, this misunderstanding can be corrected by explanation, but there is no need for this type of explanation when the relationship of the source to the direct quotation can and should be made perfectly clear in the translation itself, either by introducing a phrase such as, "Isaiah, speaking as a prophet on behalf of God," or ,"as Isaiah the prophet wrote, 'God says, Listen, I am sending my messenger. . .' "

The identification of objects and events with abstracts may be a very simple matter, as in the case of "know the truth," which may be expanded to read, "know the true word" or "know the true message" (as in some languages). On the other hand, such expansions may also be relatively complex, as in Luke 1:17, where "turn... the disobedient to the wisdom of the just" may require considerable expansion, e.g., "to change the disobedient persons so that they will act wisely as the just people do."

Not infrequently, the relationals of one language require greater specification in another language. For example, "Be angry but do not sin" (Eph. 4:26) can be interpreted as two quite independent imperatives, both of which are valid and which may be only very remotely related to one another. To do justice to the rendering of this type of Semitic expression, one must make the relationships somewhat more explicit. For example, a possible translation of this sentence would be: "Even if you do get angry, you must not sin."

The fourth class of syntactic expansions consist in filling out ellipses. These problems, however, have been treated in considerable detail at the end of Chapter 6, and further examples need not be given at this point.

Lexical expansions

The most common lexical expansions consist of (a) classifiers, (b) descriptive substitutes, and (c) semantic restructuring. Classifiers are relatively common and can be used whenever a borrowed word needs some semantic redundancy attached to it, so that the reader will be able to understand at least something about its form and/or function, *e.g.*, "city Jerusalem," "cloth linen," and "sect Pharisees."

Descriptive substitutes are almost always longer than the corresponding originals, for they require several different lexical items to describe the form and/or function of the object or event in question. For example, a synagogue may be described as "the worship-house of the Jews."

Some expressions, however, are so semantically condensed in the source-language text that they often require considerable expansion in the receptor language. For example, "I am a jealous God" (Exod. 20:5) can be badly misunderstood if translated literally, for it may only suggest that God acts like some jilted lover or that he has a mean, possessive disposition. More often than not, a literal rendering introduces quite unwarranted sexual connotations. Accordingly, in some languages this sentence must be semantically restructured by expansion to read, "I am a God who demands that my people love no one else other than me."

LEXICAL EXPANSIONS IN MARGINAL HELPS

In making explicit what is fully implicit in the original translation, one can often insert material in the text itself without imposing undue strains upon the process of translation. On the other hand, information indispensable to the understanding of the message is often not specifically implicit in the passage itself. Such information may only be part of the general cultural background shared by the participants in the source language. This type of information cannot be legitimately introduced into the text of a translation, but should be placed in marginal helps, either in the form of glossaries, where information about recurring terms is gathered together in summary fashion, or in marginal notes on the page where the difficulty in understanding occurs. For example, among some of the tribes in South America gambling is not known nor are there any devices for "selecting by lot." Accordingly, in order for readers to comprehend the significance of certain accounts in the Scriptures, some supplementary information must be given in marginal notes. Similarly, a custom such as levirate marriage may be not only unknown but even abhorrent, and under such circumstances one must make some explanation, or certain of the passages of Scripture will be severely distorted in meaning.

TYPES OF REDUCTIONS

It would be quite wrong to suggest that in every instance, that is, in all types of contexts and in all types of style, one inevitably encounters the need for expansion. There are quite naturally some expressions which are reduced in the process of transfer from one language to another. Such reductions are primarily (1) simplification of doublets, *e.g.*, "answering, he said," becomes "he answered"; (2) reduction of repetitions, *e.g.*, "verily, verily," must in some languages be reduced to one "verily," for repetition does not convey the same meaning that it does in Greek; (3) omission of specification of participants, *e.g.*, the overabundant use of "God" as subject of so many sentences in the first chapter of Genesis (in some languages certain of these occurrences of "God" must be eliminated in order to avoid syntactic confusion); (4) loss of conjunctions, when hypotactic structures are reduced to paratactic ones; (5) reduction of formulas, *e.g.*, "for his names 'sake" may be changed to "for his sake"; (6) more extensive ellipsis than may be typical of the Greek or Hebrew; that is to say, while some languages require expansion of possible ellipsis, some languages prefer more extensive ellipsis than occurs in the source-language texts; and (7) the simplification of highly repetitious style, often associated with stateliness of form and importance of the theme, *e.g.*, the first chapter of Genesis. While in Hebrew such repetitions and pleonasms may have a valued liturgical significance, a close formal parallel in another language may seem awkwardly heavy.

These types of reductions are not so numerous as the expansions, nor are they so frequent. And as a result they are not so important structurally. However, it is just as important to employ the proper reductions as it is to introduce the proper expansions, for both expansions and reductions are based on the same fundamental principles of reproducing the closest natural equivalent.

TESTING PROCEDURES

It is impossible to set up a single series of tests for all translations, for the constituencies whose opinions are needed differ so greatly in cultural backgrounds, understanding of the Scriptures, and levels of literary sophistication. When one is dealing with a translation in a major language with a long literary tradition and with many competent judges of stylistic adequacy and semantic correctness, there is no problem in getting a relatively broad and valid base of reactions. The major difficulty in such circumstances is that often only the "specialists" are consulted, and they tend to be so specialized in their views of communication that they are sometimes insensitive to what is really intelligible to the average reader.

When, however, one is dealing with a "new language" or one with only a relatively limited "literary history," the problems are in a sense much more complicated, for the potential audience cannot react with the same degree of sophistication. In such circumstances one can usually not depend upon written replies to questions about the acceptability of a translation. Therefore, most of the testing of the text must be in an oral setting.

A number of tests have been devised as "rough calculations" of degree of intelligibility and ease of comprehension. Usually such systems for testing the adequacy of a communication depend upon such statistical features as the number of words per sentence, the number of syllables per word, the number of clauses per sentence, the length of paragraphs, and the proportion of so-called abstract nouns. Though some of these systems of testing may have some value for the languages for which they have been specifically developed, they are basically quite useless when automatically and arbitrarily imposed upon languages with different types of structure. Actually the only linguistically sound test of ease of comprehension is the Cloze Technique, which is based on the principle of transitional probabilities. That is to say, the easier it is for the reader to guess the next word, the easier it is to comprehend the word in such a context. This matter of "degree of predictability" (being able to guess the right word is only another way of talking about predictability) is essentially a concept derived from Information Theory.

In its written application the Cloze Technique provides the reader with a text in which every fifth word is deleted and a blank space is left in its place.[1] The reader is then asked to fill in those words which seem to fit the context best. Obviously, the greater the number of correct guesses, the easier the text is to comprehend, for the greater is its predictability. It is not always possible, however, to employ the written form of the Cloze Technique, and so one can use an oral parallel. In such instances one reads a text to a group of persons and simply says "Blank" for every tenth word. The group is then asked to guess until someone hits on the right word, and the fewer the number of total incorrect guesses, the easier the text is to read. In general, one only needs about fifty such blanks in any text, whether in written or oral form, to provide a very satisfactory guide as to the relative comprehensibility of the text.

There are, of course, certain very important precautions which must be followed in applying the Cloze Technique. One cannot, for example, compare people's reactions to a familiar translation with their reactions to a new one. They will quite naturally be able to fill in the words of the familiar translation, even though it may be basically more difficult to comprehend. If one is going to judge two different translations of the Bible, it is essential to use persons who are equally unfamiliar with both of the translations.

It is also important to recognize that there is no absolute standard in the Cloze Technique. This can only be a comparative judgment, and hence one should always test two different types of material on the same individuals.

---

[1] It is possible to omit every fifth, sixth, seventh, eighth, ninth, or tenth word, but it seems not to make any appreciable difference in the results, provided one has approximately fifty blanks which have to be filled in.

Perhaps the greatest advantage of the Cloze Technique is that it tests so many features of the translation at the same time: (1) syntactic patterns, (2) semotactic appropriateness, (3) cultural backgrounds, and (4) thematic relevance. As a result, one may have a combined "judgment" of a translation which is exceptionally reliable. On the other hand, the analyst who wishes to use the Cloze Technique for improving a translation must be extremely careful to determine precisely why at certain points in the test the individuals had such difficulties in responding correctly.

It is also possible to set up some rough calculations of frequency of usage of certain grammatical and lexical features and to employ these to test a translation. For example, it might be found that in the receptor language, one normally employs the passive construction only 5 percent of the time and the active 95 percent. If, however, in any passage in a translation the passive is used as much as 20 percent of the time (one in five, rather than one in twenty), it is obvious that the translation is unnatural in this particular feature. One may also make statistical analyses of such features as average length of sentences, number of clauses in a sentence, hypotactic vs. paratactic arrangements, nouns to express events in contrast with verbs to express events, and average number of preposed or postposed attributives to nouns. In fact, any such feature which is amenable to statistical evaluation may be studied in receptor language texts and also in the translation, and the results can then be compared. If there is more than a 10 percent deviation, one should be alerted to the possibilities of unnaturalness.

In applying such mechanical statistic methods to the analysis of a translation, it is important, however, to recognize that these are only very rough calculations. That is to say, they are essentially quantitative, not qualitative, judgments, and in no way as valid as the results of using the Cloze Technique. Moreover, to make any really satisfactory statistical judgments it is important to have a considerable body of text material and of different discourse types, *e.g.*, conversation, narration, argument, description, poetry, etc. One cannot lump together all the various styles of language. Moreover, one must also apply such statistical counts to a sufficiently large sample of the translation so as to make comparison valid. Often such statistical methods are wrongly applied to too little data.

The advantage of the Cloze Technique is that the reactions of persons to the "blanks" actually represents an incredibly larger body of "stored data" (the total language experience of the individuals in question) than could ever be collected by statistical linguistic methods.

Practical Tests

As fine as the Cloze Technique may be, it is often difficult to administer and the results are sometimes cumbersome to analyze. It is, therefore, important that one also make use of other more practical tests to provide important clues as to the adequacy of the translation and also to help the translator make satisfactory corrections in what he has done. The following tests have proved to be very helpful, practical, and easy to apply:

Reactions to alternatives

It is obviously impossible to obtain satisfactory responses if one merely reads a translation to people and then asks such questions as: "Do you like it?" "Do you understand it?" and "Is there anything wrong with this translation?" Most people are simply too polite to find fault with a translation, since it generally comes with all the prestige of those who have been chosen to do the work and whose competence is not easily challenged by others. Moreover, a person does not usually like to imply, at least not in public, that he does not understand something, especially when other people assume that he does or should. Therefore, if a translator really wants to obtain satisfactory replies to direct questions on specific problems, the only way to do so is by supplying people with alternatives. This means that one must read a sentence in two or more ways, often repeating such alternatives slowly (and, of course, in context), and then ask such questions as: "Which way sounds the sweetest?" "Which is plainer?" "What words will be easiest for the people back in the villages to understand?"

One must often avoid any implications that the persons listening to such alternatives have any difficulty in understanding either expression. They will often insist that they can understand anything and that all alternatives are clear to them, but they will usually admit that some of the "ignorant people" deep in the jungle, out in the grasslands, or back in the villages would have more difficulty with one of the alternatives than with the other. In this way one can readily determine just which of the expressions is actually more comprehensible, even to the audience in question.

In obtaining reactions to such alternatives, it is important that the materials be read to people by someone who is not responsible for the draft of the particular book in question. In fact, the translator should probably not be present, for people are often quite quick to sense just which alternative he favors and will so often respond in terms of what they know he wants rather than on the basis of what they actually think. This must not be regarded as deception. It is only that for many peoples politeness in such matters has greater value than causing loss of face.

Explaining the contents

A second very important way of testing a translation is to have someone read a passage to someone else and then to get this individual to explain the contents to other persons, who did not hear the reading. It is most important that the person not be asked to explain the meaning back to the one who has done the reading, for almost inevitably the explanation comes back more or less in the same words as the translation, and there are few if any significant modifications. On the other hand, when a person is asked to explain such a translation to other people, and especially to persons who have had less educational background and are not acquainted with the contents of the Scriptures, it is most helpful to note (1) the lexical modifications which take place, (2) the extent of built-in redundancy, (3) the distortions in meaning which may be introduced, and (4) the syntactic alterations which are automatically made.

The primary purpose of this type of test is to find out how well the meaning comes across, both in terms of the total content and in terms of the correctness of understanding. However, any lexical substitutions should also be carefully noted, and any important syntactic restructuring may be a clue as to how the translation itself may be made more readily comprehensible.

Reading the text aloud

One of the best tests of a translation is to get several different people to read a text aloud. Such reading should take place before other persons, so that the reader will presumably be trying to communicate the message of the text.

As the text is read, the translator should note carefully those places at which the reader stumbles, hesitates, makes some substitution of another grammatical form, puts in another word, or in any way has difficulty in reading the text fluently. Of course, some of the problems in reading may be due to inexperience in public reading, but if two or more persons have difficulty at the same point in the reading of a translation, this is a warning signal that something is likely to be wrong. Perhaps it is an awkward grammatical form, perhaps a difficult semotactic arrangement, perhaps a problem of word order. But whatever the problem may be, it should be carefully analyzed.

Hesitations or stumbling in reading are not, however, the only signals of problems. The substitution of other grammatical or lexical forms provides important clues to the problems of transitional probabilities. If the reader has automatically put in another word or grammatical form, it is a sign that something is awkward about the text of the translation. Perhaps more built-in redundancy is required so as to build the context up to the point where the proper expression will appear more natural.

Publication of sample material

Despite all the tests that one might wish to make of a translation it seems that only the actual publication of sample materials can provide the kind of test necessary to judge the acceptability of a translation. But even the analysis of reactions to a published text is not a simple matter. The popularity may be for a number of different reasons: (1) reasonable price, (2) illustrations, (3) attractive format, (4) special distribution programs, and even (5) quality of paper. Of course, the extent of the demand for a translation is an important factor, but much more important than the number of copies distributed is the number of "reader hours" spent by its recipients. In fact, the ultimate judgment of a translation must be calculated in terms of reader hours per copy, not extent of distribution. This is especially true of the Bible, which is so often bought as a prestige symbol or as a kind of "fetish of the faith." The fact that a Bible with particularly small type sells well may not mean that it is greatly read (in fact, some small-type Bibles are practically illegible); it may mean only that people can more conveniently carry such Bibles to church.

Perhaps the best ways of judging the published sample material are

(1) to determine the extent to which people buy copies of such translations in order to share them with friends, (2) the amount of time people read such translations outside of church or regular times of worship, and (3) the degree of involvement the indivdual shows when he is reading such a translation: How long does he read it before putting it down? Does his face show real interest and understanding (or is he only going through a devotional practice)? To what extent does he talk to other people about the translation?

THE ULTIMATE BASIS FOR JUDGING A TRANSLATION

What is a good translation? Perhaps we can answer this question by contrasting a good translation with bad translations of two kinds:

Bad	Good	Bad
Formal correspondence: the form (syntax and classes of words) is preserved; the meaning is lost or distorted	Dynamic equivalence: the form is restructured (different syntax and lexicon) to preserve the same meaning	Paraphrase by addition, deletion, or skewing of the message

On the one hand, it is possible to make a bad translation, as in column 1, by preserving the form at the expense of the content. On the other hand, it is possible to make a bad translation, as in column 3, by paraphrasing loosely and distorting the message to conform to alien cultural patterns (see pp. 110, 134). This is the bad sense of the word "paraphrase." But, as in column 2, a good translation focuses on the meaning or content as such and aims to preserve that intact; and in the process it may quite radically restructure the form: this is paraphrase in the proper sense.

The ultimate test of a translation must be based upon three major factors: (1) the correctness with which the receptors understand the message of the original (that is to say, its "faithfulness to the original" as determined by the extent to which people really comprehend the meaning), (2) the ease of comprehension, and (3) the involvement a person experiences as the result of the adequacy of the form of the translation. Perhaps no better compliment could come to a translator than to have someone say, "I never knew before that God spoke my language."

APPENDIX

Organization of Translation Projects

The plan of operation suggested here is designed for the situation in which a team, composed largely or exclusively of native speakers and representing all or most of the Christian constituencies in a given language, is given the task of translating the Bible. The day is fast disappearing when a missionary, working on his own initiative and with a minimum of regard for what is happening around him, can select a language and launch and carry to successful conclusion a translation of the Bible. There are several reasons for this.

One reason is the increasing role of the churches in deciding what languages require translations and who should do the work. Closely allied to this reason is the fact that more and more translations are being done by native speakers of the receptor languages. Even in cases where foreigners are still crucially involved, it is increasingly recognized that only fully fluent and competent native speakers can master the subtleties of semotactic and stylistic structures sufficiently to produce idiomatic translations. Thus, the native speakers in such cases are being recognized as the real translators, while the foreigners who participate are exegetical informants and assistants. A third reason, partly stemming from the fact that communications between various churches and missions are improving steadily, is that considerations of priority and of collaboration are increasingly important.

The more traditional plan of operation, in which a missionary translates with the aid of an informant who is a native speaker of the receptor language, still obtains in a fairly large number of pioneer first translations in various parts of the world; but even in these cases, there is happily a strong tendency to upgrade the role of the "informant." Inasmuch as this situation is rapidly becoming outdated and involves a number of quite specialized techniques, it will not be considered here.

One more thing should be said before we proceed to describe the plan of operations recommended by the United Bible Societies: the best plan must always be implemented intelligently and flexibly in the light of the facts of each situation. After all, it is people who are doing the job, people with varying gifts and personalities, people who are used to working at cooperative projects under all sorts of systems provided by their various cultures. No plan of operation, simply followed in a literal and mechanical manner, can lead to good results in all cases. What follows, therefore, represents a kind of pragmatic consensus based on the experience of Bible Societies in hundreds of projects around the world. It is intended to be adapted as required to the needs and possibilities of each specific case.

At various points in this outline, we refer to the United Bible Societies translations consultant. He is the technical specialist made available by the Bible Societies to the churches to assist them in following the steps which are suggested here for organizing a translation project. He normally continues to cooperate with the translators until their work is complete.

Determining the Need for a Translation

Before any translation project is undertaken, it is essential that the need for such a project be thoroughly investigated. This is true both for languages in which no Scriptures at all exist and for languages which have only some Scriptures, or which have Scriptures in a form which is not fully satisfactory.

In an earlier day, it was commonly supposed in Christian circles that translations of the Scriptures would be required for all the languages of the world. The most recent guesses, based on reliable though fragmentary data, suggest that there are somewhere between 4,000 and 5,000 languages and significantly different dialects now spoken in the world. The Bible has already been translated into some 1,500 languages, and these represent fully 97% of the world's population. If the old concept of our task is correct, we must still translate the Scriptures into some 2,500 to 3,500 languages, even though their speakers represent less than 3% of the world's population.

But are we really translating for languages? Are we not rather translating for people? People not only speak languages, but often they speak more than one language fluently, and they have various attitudes about the languages they use. It is not enough, then, to note the existence of a speech community in order to justify a Scripture translation. One must investigate linguistic diversity, sociolinguistic attitudes, and religious need. In many cases, people can use the Scriptures which already exist in another language, because, for example, the languages in question are closely related or the people are largely bilingual. In such cases, there is no real need for proliferating translations. On the other hand, if the people use their own language regularly in worship and do not have ready access to the Scriptures in some other language, they should surely have a translation of their own.

Where the Scriptures already exist in a language but the translation is not fully satisfactory, it is important to study the situation carefully in order to determine just what may be needed. If thorough investigation by the translations consultant shows that the problem is merely one of unfortunate choices for one or two key lexical items, but that the general language and style of the translation are fully adequate, then a revision may be satisfactory. But in the majority of cases, where Scriptures are not used as they ought to be, the problem is more fundamental. In some cases, the orthography is so poor that people have great difficulty in reading. In other cases, the translation is excessively literal, many of the phrases are unnatural and heavy, and the language is archaic, so that people give up trying to use the Scriptures. Such deficiencies can be discovered by a detailed examination of the existing texts, using proven linguistic techniques.

In such cases, it is preferable to make a new translation rather than a revision. In many constituencies the very word "revision" often troubles people, for revision of the Bible means changing it, and this seems to call into question its inspiration and authority. Furthermore, since revision means changing details, specific changes are easy to spot and can be readily attacked by the traditionalists who are found in all societies. A new translation is so different from the old that it more or less disarms the attacks of the traditionalists. If the new translation has been done well, other people will be so pleased with it that their approval will largely offset the disapproval of the traditionalists.

There are also technical problems involved in revising an existing translation. In the first place, because changes are made in terms of details, endless time is spent in debating the pros and cons of changing this or that detail, and the effort spent on each one will rarely be proportionate to its intrinsic importance. In the second place, many of the really significant problems with the existing translations have to do with their overall style and structure, rather than with the selection of specific vocabulary items. In other words, it is the coherence of the text as a whole and the flow of information which need to be corrected. This can never be done on a piecemeal or bit-by-bit basis. Revising an unsatisfactory translation has been compared to painting over the dirty spots on a wall. The spots of new paint do not harmonize with the rest of the wall and are no more satisfactory than the dirty spots they cover. It is much better to repaint the entire wall.

Priorities in Translation

No matter how the task is defined, it is obviously enormous and will occupy the resources and energies of Christians for some years to come. Given this fact, it becomes important to establish some kind of priorities so that the limited means and personnel available at any given time can be used to the greatest advantage. This is particularly true for those cases in which the Bible Societies are actively involved. For their own guidance in establishing priorities, the Bible Societies have developed a formula which takes into consideration the situation in which a language is used, the planning involved in the potential project, and, for those projects which are already in progress, the quality of the performance.

1. *The Situation*

In assessing the situation, three types of considerations are evaluated. The first has to do with the *size and role of the language*. Other things being equal, priority is given to the larger of two languages, or to a language designated as national or official, or to a language spoken by an appreciable number of people who cannot communicate effectively in any other language. The significant use of a given language in the public communications media, such as radio and the newspapers, is an additional plus factor. Thus, the criteria considered involve not only the absolute demographic size of a language, but also its official and sociological status. The formula also recognizes the fact that in many cases people are functionally bilingual and are differently predisposed to receive or reject printed material in one or other of the languages they use effectively. The use of this formula does not mean, of course, that the United Bible Societies are attempting to prevent the translation of the Scriptures into the many small languages of the world. It means simply that the size and role of a language constitute one important factor in establishing priorities for the use of limited resources.

A second factor in evaluating the situation is *distribution potential*. Obviously, it is of no use to make and publish a translation which no one will buy and read. Here figures for literacy and, if available, for distribution of other publications are taken into consideration.

A third and related factor is that of *Christian opportunity*. Under this heading the Bible Societies attempt to evaluate the interest and motivation of the Christian community, the evangelistic opportunities, and the possible intensity of use which is anticipated for the translation.

2. *Planning*

A second broad area which is evaluated in establishing priorities is that of planning. Here again three factors are considered. Among *types of translation*, a priority is given to first or new translations as opposed to revisions of old ones. With respect to the *level of language* to be used in the translation, priority is given to common language or popular language translations over translations made in literary language. Translations in traditional ecclesiastical language are given still lower priority. Finally, an effort is made to evaluate the *qualifications and training* of the potential translators and the soundness of their *organization and procedure*.

3. *Performance*

Once a project is under way, it is continually evaluated in terms of the quality of the translation and the efficiency with which the work is pursued.

Clearly, the Bible Societies cannot establish these priorities in a vacuum. Rather, the criteria are applied in consultation with the churches, and the desires and intentions of the churches are among the most important considerations which the Bible Societies weigh.

INVOLVING THE CHRISTIAN COMMUNITY

In most parts of the world, especially in all but the very smallest language areas, it is commonly true that two or more Christian groups are actively at work. In such situations it is highly desirable that all Christian groups be involved in a project. This is important not only to avoid the waste of duplicated effort, but more fundamentally because, whatever their differences of doctrinal emphasis, all Christian groups subscribe to the same Scriptures as authoritative. It can create confusion which militates against effective evangelization and Christian teaching to have two or more similar or competing translations in a given language. For these reasons, in every case where it is possible, the Bible Societies strongly urge the churches involved to cooperate at least for the purpose of translating the Scriptures. It should be emphasized, however, that in no case are the Bible Societies in a position to compel churches to do so. This is not their role as servants of the churches. Nor are the Bible Societies as an organization concerned to take any official position on the question of cooperation for any purpose other than that of the translation, publication, and distribution of the Scriptures.

Increasingly, Roman Catholics and Protestants are working together on joint Bible translation projects. In order to facilitate such cooperation, a document has been prepared entitled *Guiding Principles for Inter-confessional Cooperation in Translating the Bible*. This document, issued jointly by the United Bible Societies and the Vatican's Secretariat for Promoting Christian Unity, spells out in considerable detail the way in which such cooperation can be made to work harmoniously. The document is available in a number of languages, and can be obtained from the Bible Societies.

Finding the Right Persons to Do the Work

As we have already stated, the plan of operation recommended by the Bible Societies involves a team approach rather than an individualistic approach to the translation of the Bible. Various members of the team play different roles in the total operation.

Finding the right persons to do the work is undoubtedly the most important step in the entire procedure. But this cannot be done simply by asking various constituencies formally to elect or appoint persons to various positions. Rather, preliminary investigations should be carried out by the translations consultant in discussion with the churches and the Bible Societies. The consultant will ask various Christian leaders for suggestions as to who might be the most able people. He will become acquainted with these people as individuals and assess their potential. Gradually, certain promising individuals will begin to stand out in his thinking. In workshops or seminars he will have occasion to observe them individually under working conditions. He will then communicate his observations to the Bible Societies and to the churches involved, and will informally suggest who might be appointed. When agreement is reached between the Bible Societies and the churches on this informal basis, each church involved in the project may then officially nominate those translators and reviewers which are its own members. All of the translators and reviewers for a given project should be officially appointed by the Bible Society in the area concerned. It is by this same procedure that agreement should be worked out on the conditions of employment and the way in which the translators and reviewers will be released from their ordinary duties to work on the translation project. If at all possible, it should be stipulated that the translators will work full time.

1. *The Translators*

Experience has indicated that the ideal number of translators is between three and five. When the group is larger, its procedures become excessively cumbersome. These translators are selected primarily for competence, rather than on the basis of political representation of the total spectrum of the Christian constituency. The abilities involved are primarily of two sorts. Some members of the team need to be especially capable in the Biblical languages and exegesis, though it is not necessary that all should be equally expert in this area. On the other hand, while all of the translators should be fully competent and at home in the receptor language, some may be selected especially for their excellence as creative writers and communicators to the general public. It is essential, however, that all the translators be of such outstanding ability that they are acceptable to the constituencies involved and that they have a mutual respect for one another. One markedly weak translator can easily ruin the work, because his very lack of capacity may make him tendentious, argumentative, and divisive in his approach.

If at all possible, the translators should be able to give all or a major part of their time to the translation. In case after case it has proved virtually impossible to make satisfactory progress when translators are working only part time. In view of the urgency of the task and the priorities involved, the most effective approach should surely be followed. If the churches really need or desire a translation, they must be prepared to release people to do the work.

In an earlier Bible Society terminology the translators were called the "Editorial Committee," but this label proved so misleading that it has been abandoned, and they are sometimes referred to simply as the "working group." In reality the translators function as a committee for only a small part of the time. Most of their work is done individually, each working in his own manner. From time to time they meet together as a group to compare and evaluate their work and to decide the final form of the translation.

2. The Reviewers

The reviewers usually number eight to ten and are especially chosen either because of their competence in the original languages and in Biblical studies, or because of their ability as writers in the receptor language. They are often persons who have the technical capability to translate but who, because of other responsibilities or because they do not work well in a team, cannot serve effectively as translators.

In some projects, one individual in particular is designated as the stylist. It is his role to take the draft which is submitted to the reviewers and to make recommendations for stylistic improvements. The role of such an individual is discussed in part on pages 103 and 104. However, since all the reviewers in any case provide their judgments largely by correspondence, there seems to be no reason for considering the stylist to be anything other than one of the reviewers.

In the earlier terminology, the reviewers were called the "Review Committee." But their role as a committee is so restricted that the term is being abandoned as misleading. From time to time the reviewers may be called together to discuss a specific agenda covering points on which the translators need guidance, but they should not meet as a committee to discuss in detail all that the translators have done. It should be emphasized that their function is supplementary and advisory. They do not constitute a committee of censors.

3. *The Consultative Group*

The consultative group normally consists of from 25 to 50 persons, depending upon the size and complexity of the Christian constituency. Its role is essentially in the area of public relations and it is constituted for the express purpose of representing the various parts of the Christian constituency. Its members are sharply distinguished from the translators and reviewers, who are selected primarily for their competence. Accordingly, one should include in the consultative group any persons who by virtue of their position or influence should be related to such a major undertaking, and whose good will is necessary to the public acceptance of the translation.

Though the consultative group should be kept informed of progress in the translation, they will receive drafts only at a fairly late stage of the proceedings, and they communicate their suggestions only in writing. It is not the collective decisions of such a group which are important, but rather their individual reactions.

4. *The Project Secretary or Coordinator*

In order for the project to proceed efficiently, it is necessary that one person be designated as secretary or coordinator of the project. This person may, if necessary, be one of the translators, but for major undertakings it is generally useful to have a secretary who can give considerable time to several different phases of the undertaking: (a) preparing the duplicated copies of the manuscript to be sent to the various participants; (b) receiving, analyzing, and classifying the suggestions which come from the reviewers and the consultative group so that the translators can deal with them quickly and effectively; (c) proofreading the manuscripts for content and orthographic accuracy and preparing final copy for the printers; (d) carrying out the routine correspondence for the work; (e) making arrangements for meetings, etc.

At the beginning of a translation program, the secretary usually serves only on a part time basis; but as the project progresses, he should be free to give an increasing amount of time to the work. Otherwise valuable time of the various other participants will be unnecessarily wasted. It is not necessary that the secretary produce all the copies of the manuscripts and do all the proofreading personally. Other persons may be engaged for typing and proofreading. But the secretary should oversee the work and be responsible for it.

Working out Basic Principles and Procedures

Once the translators and reviewers have been selected, it is crucial that they set up effective principles and procedures to guide them in their work. This needs to be done in sessions with a translations consultant in which they can explore the problems fully. These sessions, especially the early ones, are training sessions as well, in which the theory and practice of translation are discussed.

Through translation exercises based dn various typical and difficult passages (for example, Genesis 1, Psalm 1, Isaiah 53, Matthew 5-7, Mark 1, John 1, Romans 1, and Ephesians 1), the consultant and the participants in the project gradually develop principles that will guide them. It is not enough to adopt the Bible Societies' general rules, for these are stated in such broad terms that they cannot easily be applied to a particular problem. Rather, the principles must be worked out in sufficient detail and be sufficiently specific to the language in question to give guidance to the translators and reviewers in their work as they face concrete problems. However, the stated principles should not be so detailed and voluminous as to be unwieldly and cumbersome. They must be a help in making decisions rather than a straightjacket to inhibit creativity. The principles are of course subject to change, but if a principle is changed at some point in the translation process, it is then essential that all the work that has been done before be revised with this changed principle in view.

A typical set of principles for translation was worked out at a translators' seminar held in Turfloop, South Africa, in July 1967. These are given below, simply as an illustration of what can and should be done to assist the translators and reviewers in their work.

It will be noted that the principles cover four major aspects of the translation: text, exegesis, form of language, and supplementary features. As might be expected, the principles involving form of language are the most numerous and detailed, since they deal with so many different features. Obviously, the statement of principles for each translation will differ because languages are different. Even within a particular language, each translation should be designed to meet the needs of a specific type of constituency and hence will require a distinctive set of principles.

A Sample Set of Principles of Translation
Prepared for Use in a So-Called "Southern Bantu" Language

Text
1. For the Old Testament the committee should base its work on the Masoretic text as given in Kittel's third edition, with the provision that in certain particularly difficult passages the committee may follow a reading supported by versional evidence, alternative Hebrew traditions, or, as a last resort, an emendation.
2. For the New Testament the text published by the United Bible Societies is recommended. For those passages which lack adequate textual authority but which occur in traditional texts of the Scriptures, it is recommended that the words be included in half-brackets, with an introductory statement, indicating that these passages do not occur in the earliest and best manuscripts.

Exegesis
3. Exegesis should be based upon the commentaries recommended and supplied by the Bible Society.

4. The following translations may be used for help in exegesis: *The Revised Standard Version*, *The New English Bible*, *Today's English Version*, and *The Translators' Translation*.

Form of Language

5. In vocabulary and grammatical forms every attempt is to be made to reflect the different styles of language in the Scriptures.
6. Content is to have priority over style.
7. The level of style should be formal (not technical), except in those passages in which informal usage would be more in keeping with the content.
8. The language of persons from twenty-five to thirty-five years of age is to have priority.
9. The translation must be intelligible to non-Christians as well as to Christians.
10. Contextual consistency is to have priority over verbal consistency.
11. Long, involved sentences are to be broken up on the basis of receptor-language usage.
12. Idioms are to be changed when they make no sense or are likely to lead to misunderstanding.
13. Receptor-language idioms are to be employed when there is no danger of misinterpretation and when this is in keeping with the content.
14. Nouns expressing events should be changed to verbs whenever the results would be more in keeping with receptor-language usage.
15. Grammatical forms should be employed with approximately the same frequency with which they are used in receptor-language texts.
16. Nouns should be used for pronouns wherever the pronominal usage would be obscure or ambiguous.
17. Answers to rhetorical questions should be introduced unless the following expressions clearly imply the proper answer.
18. Pleonastic expressions such as "answering, said" should be avoided.
19. Introductory expressions such as "verily, verily," must be related to the content of what is said, not to the fact of saying.
20. Introductory particles such as "behold" should be altered to fit the context, *e.g.*, "listen."
21. The sources of direct discourse should be clearly marked, *e.g.*, Mark 1:2, where "God" as the source of the statement must be introduced.
22. Discourse markers should be employed, in keeping with receptor-language usage.
23. The basic unit of translation should be the paragraph, with such shifts in verse content or order as may be required.
24. Transitions between sentences should be marked in keeping with receptor-language usage.
25. Third-person references to the first person should be changed to first person wherever ambiguity might result.
26. First-person plural references to the first-person singular should be changed to first-person singular.
27. In narrative style the present tense forms may be used to indicate the "liveliness" of the narrative.
28. Wherever in passive constructions there is serious ambiguity or obscurity in the receptor language as to who the agent is, one should either add the agent or change the construction to the active.
29. Concord classes should only be shifted in the case of titles.
30. In the case of genuine ambiguity, either in the source or receptor texts, one alternative should be given in the text and the other in the margin.
31. Ellipses may be filled out, in accordance with receptor-language requirements.
32. Proper names should in general be transcribed on the basis of receptor-language phonological structures, taking into consideration syllabic patterns, sequences of vowels, and length of words. However, for common proper names already in wide usage the spelling may follow the usage of the dominant language of the area.

Supplementary Features

33. Wherever supplementary information is required, *e.g.*, in the case of plays on words, historical details, or cultural differences, this should be provided in marginal notes, to be included on the page where the problem occurs.
34. All technical terms should be explained in a glossary.
35. All unfamiliar terms for weights and measures should be explained in a Table of Weights and Measures.
36. Maps listing the principal geographical features should be prepared.
37. Section headings should be based on the series published by the United Bible Societies.
38. Pictures of special relevance and interest to the receptors should be employed.
39. Titles of books should be given in their full form, *e.g.*, not "Gospel of Matthew" but "Good News about Jesus Christ as Written by Matthew."
40. A limited reference system should be employed, following the model provided by the United Bible Societies.

In addition to a statement of principles, it is essential that each translation project have a well-defined set of procedures. Agreement on procedures at the beginning of the program will avoid a great deal of misunderstanding and will facilitate enormously the progress of the undertaking. The statement of procedures must cover a number of basic aspects of the work: (1) the responsibility and authority of the various persons and groups related to the program, (2) the means by which the work of the various participants is to be coordinated, (3) the order in which the different parts of the task are to be taken up, and (4) the methods for decision-making. Some of the different aspects of these procedures are discussed in the following sections.

PREPARING THE BASIC DRAFTS

Two important principles are involved in the work of preparing the basic drafts. First, everyone who is officially designated as a translator must be involved in preparing the drafts, for no one should have the privilege of criticizing the work of others without having his own efforts criticized also. Second, the basic drafts are prepared by translators working individually, rather than as a committee. Translating in committee is not only highly inefficient and wasteful of time, but it rarely produces an acceptable style.

The most effective procedure is usually to assign a different portion to each translator, taking into consideration his preferences, his aptitudes, and the amount of time he will be able to devote to the task. The translator will then, by himself, work out a first draft of this portion. It is important not to break up books of the Bible and assign parts of them to different people, for the resulting style will be too uneven. It is also important not to have more than one translator translate the same passage and then try to hammer out a compromise text. This is a hopeless procedure, due to the natural tendency of each person to be both defensive and aggressive in such situations. In assigning responsibility for various books, it is usually not wise to divide up the entire New Testament or Old Testament at once; rather, the books should be assigned a few at a time, for some persons may not prove to be as capable as was expected, and some may be unduly slow in producing their quota. The progress of the work should not be hampered by advance decisions governing the assignment of responsibility.

Particularly in those projects in which the Bible Societies are financially involved, it has proved to be necessary to establish some means by which a steady outflow of work from the translators may be assured. At least two approaches have been used in various cases with fair to excellent results. Both involve a quota of work (that is, a given amount of work to be accomplished in a given amount of time) as a standard. In one approach, the translator is given, at the time he is assigned a portion, a deadline by which that portion should be drafted. In the other approach, actual financial incentives are offered for work which goes beyond the quota set up as the standard. Whichever method is used, it is essential that the translators be given specific guidance as to the amount of time that is expected to be spent on their work.

Checking the First Drafts

As soon as the first drafts have been made, copies should be sent to the other translators for their study. This means that as the project advances, the translators will divide their time in varying proportions between doing original creative work and studying the drafts of others. Here again, to avoid delay, the translators should be given deadlines for completing their comments on the work of each of the others. The comments from his fellow translators should be returned to the original drafter, who will then incorporate all the suggestions that are corrections of obvious minor errors or are so evidently within the scope of the statement of principles that they do not require further discussion. When the translators meet, as they do from time to time, discussion can focus on those recommendations not accepted by the original drafter or on the alternative suggestions made by the other translators.

In the first instance, the translators meeting in committee should go over the problems which have been classified for their use by the project secretary. This insures the most efficient use of time. Subsequently, it is useful to have the committee read the entire text together so that anything missed in individual study can be brought to the attention of the group. It is not necessary, however, that in their first discussion of a passage the translators attempt to make final and binding decisions. Many of the same questions will reappear when the reviewers and the consultative group have had opportunity to study the drafts. In any case, some of these passages will come back to the attention of the translators in the process of checking for consistency in the rendering of parallel passages.

As often as possible, the translators meeting in committee should attempt to reach consensus, but this is not always possible. In dealing with relatively minor questions, it is sometimes useful to adopt a voting procedure to come to a decision. However, when a serious issue strongly divides the group, it is often advisable to set the problem aside until it can be discussed with a translations consultant. If the problem passages are reviewed just before the meeting with the consultant, it will often be found that most of them are now readily resolved and do not need to be brought to his attention. The reason is that in the heat of argument, the issues seem much more important than they do several days or weeks later when more experience has been gained and the problems are seen in a wider perspective.

It is important for the translators to remember that they always have available the services of a translations consultant to help them solve their problems, whether these be technical or organizational. The translations departments of the Bible Societies do not attempt to dictate what should be done, but they are prepared to provide translators with guidance based upon experience with a number of other projects which have met the same or similar problems.

THE ROLE OF THE REVIEWERS AND THE CONSULTATIVE GROUP

Once the translators have, by the steps outlined above, worked out a "stage 2 draft," this is duplicated and sent to the reviewers, who are expected to study it and return their comments within a stipulated period of time. In some cases, the draft at this stage will also be circulated to the consultative group, though in other cases the consultative group is brought in at a later stage.

It is quite true that not all reviewers will give as much time to this work as they should, and many members of the consultative group will not respond at all. However, if the reviewers have been properly selected and briefed, their work can be extremely helpful.

For the translators to receive the greatest value from the contributions of the reviewers and the consultative group, it is useful to have the comments carefully studied and classified by the project secretary or coordinator, if there is one; otherwise by one of the translators designated for this task. In this way the translators can consider systematically and at one time all the comments on a particular verse, or all the suggestions relating to a particular type of wording or syntactic construction.

One or more of the reviewers may be particularly competent to make comments on style. It is important that the comments from these stylists be considered seriously, especially in the elaboration of the final draft. The translators should exercise restraint in making changes after the stylist's recommendations have been considered, for much of the value of his comments can be destroyed by subsequent alterations in the form of the translation.

It should be noted again that the work of the reviewers and the consultative group is advisory and supplementary to that of the translators. By definition the translators are the only persons who are able to devote their full time and attention to the translation, and if they have been properly selected, they are the most competent persons in the project and have contributed the most work; therefore they should make the final decisions. It is an important principle that responsibility to do the work and authority to make decisions should rest with the same individuals. If the translators should prove to be obdurate in resisting the advice of a large majority of the reviewers, the translations consultant may need to be called in to arbitrate.

In some projects the reviewers have insisted on meeting together as a committee and going over the whole draft verse by verse. This is rarely a desirable approach. Not only can such a committee spend endless hours debating over details, but the end results are rarely as good as the work of the translators which was the basis of the discussion. The reviewers and the consultative group should remember that it is not their work to be censors.

Final Preparation of the Manuscript

In preparing the final manuscript for the printers it is most important to follow carefully the instructions laid out by the Bible Society covering this process, for care at this stage can save a great deal of time and result in a much more satisfactory publication. The translations consultant will make available to the translators a small brochure entitled *Preparing the Manuscript*. It spells out in detail the procedures to be followed and the style and format which are desired.

Reading the Proofs

The manuscript should be prepared with such care that there are not likely to be any significant editorial changes in the proof sheets. Corrections introduced in galley proofs are expensive and in page proofs much more so. Therefore only the absolutely necessary editorial changes can be accepted at this stage.

Reading the proofs should be done at least twice; first for content (one person reading the manuscript aloud and another person following the printed proofs) and then for details of form, e.g. numeration, indentation, punctuation, spelling, etc. Full instructions on the best methods for reading and marking proofs are supplied to the translators by the Bible Societies.

Conclusions

It would, of course, be wonderful if satisfactory results in a translations project could be guaranteed merely by laying down valid principles and setting up standard procedures. Such statements of principles and procedures do help, but they will fail utterly unless there are other intangible features which are even more important than the formal rules. These basic ingredients in the work of Bible translating include (1) humility (the essential quality of true scholarship), (2) openness to suggestion, (3) spiritual sensitivity, (4) deep reverence for the message, and (5) evangelistic spirit, which alone makes possible such a degree of empathy with the intended reader that a truly creative and meaningful translation can be produced. The real problems of the translation are not technical, they are human. The ultimate solutions involve the transformation of the human spirit.

BIBLIOGRAPHY

The following bibliography is selective, in that it includes only books and articles which (a) are most pertinent to the topics discussed in this book and (b) were not included in the bibliography of *Toward a Science of Translating* (1964). The titles of three frequently cited journals are abbreviated, as follows:

IJAL = International Journal of American Linguistics
PA = Practical Anthropology
TBT = The Bible Translator
Other references are cited in full.

Bible Texts and Versions Cited

American Standard Version. 1901.
Amplified New Testament, The. 1958. Grand Rapids, Mich.: Zondervan Publishing House.
Good News for Modern Man: The New Testament in Today's English Version. 1966. New York: American Bible Society.
Greek New Testament, The. 1966. Edited by Kurt Aland, Matthew Black, Bruce M. Metzger, and Allen Wikgren. New York: American Bible Society; London: British and Foreign Bible Society; Edinburgh: National Bible Society of Scotland; Amsterdam: Netherlands Bible Society; Stuttgart: Württemberg Bible Society.
King James Version. 1611.
Living Letters. 1962. Tr. by Kenneth N. Taylor. Grand Rapids, Mich.: Tyndale House Publishers.
New English Bible: The New Testament. 1961. London: Oxford University Press and Cambridge University Press.
New Testament in Modern English, The. 1958. Tr. by J. B. Phillips. London: Geoffrey Bles, Ltd.
New Testament in the Translation of Monsignor Ronald Knox, The. 1944. New York: Sheed and Ward; London: Burns and Oates, Ltd.
Revised Version, The. 1881.

General Bibliography

Ackroyd, Peter R. and Knibb, Michael A. 1966. Translating the Psalms. TBT 17.1-11.
Alt, Franz L. and Rhodes, Ida. 1964. Reconnaissance des propositions et des syntagmes dans la traduction automatique des langages. In E. Delaveney, ed. Traduction Automatique et Linguistique Appliquée. Paris: P.U.F., pp. 121-141.
Andreyev, N.D. 1964. Linguistic aspects of translation. In H. G. Lunt, ed. Proceedings of the Ninth International Congress of Linguists. The Hague: Mouton and Co., pp. 625-637.
Aoki, Haruo. 1966. Nez Perce and Proto-Shahaptian kinship terms. IJAL 32. 357-368.
Arrowsmith, William, and Shattuck, Roger, eds. 1964. The Craft and Context of Translation. Garden City, New York: Doubleday, Anchor Books.
Asch, Solomon. 1955. On the use of metaphor in the description of persons. In Heinz Werner, ed. On Expressive Language. Worcester: Clark University Press., pp. 29-38.
Bach, Emmon. 1967. *Have* and *be* in English syntax. Language 43.462-485.
Bar-Hillel, Yehoshua. 1967. Review of Jerry A. Fodor and Jerrold J. Katz, eds. The Structure of Language. (Englewood, N.J.: Prentice-Hall, Inc., 1964). Language 43.526-550.
Barton, J. 1964. L'emploi de l'article en anglais. In E. Delaveney, ed. Traduction Automatique et Linguistique Appliquée. Paris: P.U.F., pp. 231-241.

Bateson, Mary C. 1968. Linguistics in the semiotic frame. Linguistics 39.5-17.

Beekman, John. 1966. 'Literalism' a hindrance to understanding. TBT 17.178-189.

Bendix, Edward Herman. 1966. Componential Analysis of General Vocabulary: The Semantic Structure of a Set of Verbs in English, Hindi, and Japanese. IJAL 32, No. 2, Part II. Publication 41 of the Indiana University Research Center in Anthropology, Folklore, and Linguistics.

Benveniste, Emile. 1939. Nature du signe linguistique. Acta Linguistica 1.94-103. Reprinted in Hamp, Householder, and Austerlitz, eds. Readings in Linguistics II. Chicago and London: University of Chicago Press, pp. 104-108.

——, 1954. Problèmes sémantiques de la reconstruction. Word 10 251-264.

——, 1966. Problèmes de Linguistique Générale. Paris: Gallimard.

Berlin, Brent. 1963. Some semantic features of reduplication in Tzeltal. IJAL 29.211-218.

——, 1967. Categories of eating in Tzeltal and Navaho. IJAL 33.1-6.

——, and Romney, A. Kimball. 1964. Descriptive semantics of Tzeltal numeral classifiers. In A. Kimball Romney and Roy G. d'Andrade, eds. Transcultural Studies in Cognition. Special Publication of American Anthropologist 66, No. 3, part 2, pp. 79-98.

Bloomfield, Leonard. 1927. Literate and illiterate speech. American Speech 2.432-439. Reprinted in Dell Hymes, ed., Language in Culture and Society. New York: Harper and Row, pp. 391-396.

Bolinger, Dwight. 1965. The atomization of meaning. Language 41.555-573.

——, 1966. Transformulation: structural translation. Acta Linguistica Hafniensa 9.130-144.

Bratcher, Robert G. 1962a. Review of the Twentieth Century New Testament (Chicago: Moody Press, 1961). TBT 13.231-234.

——, 1962b. Review of New American Standard Gospel of John (La Habra, Calif.: The Lockman Foundation, 1960). TBT 13.234-236.

——, 1963a. "The name" in prepositional phrases in the New Testament. TBT 14.72-80.

——, 1963b. Review of Gerrit Verkuyl, The Berkeley Version of the New Testament (6th ed.) (Grand Rapids, Mich.: Zondervan, 1945). TBT 14.140-143.

——, 1964. Review of New American Standard New Testament (Chicago; Moody Press, 1963). Eternity, June, 1964, pp. 43-45.

——, 1966. Good News for Modern Man. TBT 17.159-172.

Brown, Roger W. and Gilman, Albert. 1960. The pronouns of power and solidarity. In Thomas A. Sebeok, ed. Style in Language. Cambridge and New York: M.I.T. Press and John Wiley, pp. 253-276.

Brown, Roger W. and Ford, Marguerite. 1961. Address in American English. Journal of Abnormal and Social Psychology 62.375-385. Reprinted in Dell Hymes, ed., Language in Culture and Society. New York: Harper and Row, pp. 234-244.

Burce, Willard L. 1965. Sentence structures in Mark: Greek and Enga. TBT 16.128-141.

Burling, Robbins. 1964. Cognition and componential analysis: God's truth or hocus-pocus? American Anthropologist 66.20-28. With discussion by Dell Hymes and Charles Frake and a rejoinder by Burling, 66.116-122.

Caillé, Pierre-François. 1967. Traduire c'est choisir. Babel 13.7-13.

Casagrande, Joseph B. 1963. Language universals in anthropological perspective. In J. H. Greenberg, ed. Universals of Language. Cambridge: M.I.T. Press. pp. 220-235.

Catford, J.C. 1965. A Linguistic Theory of Translation. London: Oxford University Press.

Chafe, Wallace L. 1965. Meaning in language. In E. A. Hammel, ed., Formal Semantic Analysis. Special Publication of American Anthropologist 67, No. 5, Part II, pp. 23-36.

——, 1968. Idiomaticity as an anomaly in the Chomskian paradigm. Foundations of Language 4.109-127.

Chao, Yuen Ren. 1956. Chinese terms of address. Language 32.217-241.

——, 1959. How Chinese logic operates. Anthropological Linguistics 1(1).1-8.

——, 1964. Translation without machine. In H. G. Lunt, ed. Proceedings of the Ninth International Congress of Linguists. The Hague: Mouton and Co., pp. 504-510.

Charney, Elinore K. 1964. L'interprétation sémantique d'entités linguistiques à fonctions structurales. In E. Delaveney, ed. Traduction Automatique et Linguistique Appliquée. Paris: P.U.F., pp. 103-120.

——, 1966. Structural Semantic Foundations for a Theory of Meaning. Chicago: Mechanical Translation Group, University of Chicago.

Cherry, Colin. 1966. On Human Communication, 2nd edition. Cambridge, Mass.: The M.I.T. Press.

Chomsky, Noam. 1965. Aspects of the Theory of Syntax. Cambridge, Mass.: The M.I.T. Press.

——, 1966. Topics in the theory of generative grammar. In Thomas A. Sebeok, ed., Current Trends in Linguistics, Vol. III: Theoretical Foundations. The Hague: Mouton and Co., pp. 1-60.

Clements, Ronald E. 1966. Divine Titles as a problem of Old Testament Translation. TBT 17.81-84.

Colby, B.N. 1966. Ethnographic Semantics: A Preliminary Survey. Current Anthropology 7.3-32.

Covell, Ralph. 1964. Bible translation in the Asian setting. TBT 15.132-142.

Culshaw, Wesley J. 1967. William Carey—then and now. TBT 18.53-60.

Darbelnet, J. 1967. Composantes sémantiques. Canadian Journal of Linguistics 13.15-19.

Deer, Donald. 1965. Procedures followed for translating the book of Acts into Kituba. TBT 16.120-122.

Delaveney, Emile, ed. 1964. Traduction Automatique et Linguistique Appliquée. Choix de communications présentées à la Conférence Internationale sur la Traduction Mécanique et l'Analyse Linguistique Appliquée. Paris: Presses Universitaires de France.

Deutsch, Martin. 1965. The role of social class in language development and cognition. American Journal of Orthopsychiatry 35.78-88.

Doke, Clement C. 1966. The translation of 'the Holy Spirit' in Bantu languages. TBT 17.32-38.

Emeneau, Murray B. 1948. Taboos on animal names. Language 24.56-63.

——, 1958. Oral poets of South India—the Todas. Journal of American Folklore 71.312-324. Reprinted in Dell Hymes, ed., Language in Culture and Society. New York: Harper and Row, pp. 330-340.

——, 1966. Style and meaning in an oral literature. Language 42.323-345.

Enkvist, Nils Erik, Spencer, John, and Gregory, Michael J. 1964. Linguistics and Style. London: Oxford University Press.

Evans-Pritchard, E. E. 1948. Nuer modes of address. Uganda Journal 12.166-171. Reprinted in Dell Hymes, ed., Language in Culture and Society. New York: Harper and Row, pp. 221-225.

Fehderau, Harold W. 1964a. Defining the Kituba language for a translation project. TBT 15.27-30.

——, 1964b. A Translator's Handbook on Mark in action. TBT 15.76-79.

Ferguson, C.A. 1959. Diglossia. Word 15.325-340.

Fillmore, Charles J. 1967. The case for case. In E. Bach and R. Harms, eds., Proceedings of the 1967 Texas Conference on Language Universals. New York: Holt, Rinehart and Winston.

——, 1968. Lexical entries for verbs. Foundations of Language 4.373-393.

Fischer, John L. 1958. Social influence in the choice of a linguistic variant. Word 14.47-56. Reprinted in Dell Hymes, ed., Language in Culture and Society. New York: Harper and Row, pp. 483-488.

——, 1963. Linguistic class indicators. Current Anthropology 4.1.116.

——, 1966. Interrogatives in Ponapean: some semantic and grammatical aspects. In Francis P. Dinneen, ed. Report of the Seventeenth Annual Round Table Meeting on Linguistics and Language Studies. Georgetown University Monograph Series on Languages and Linguistics No. 19, pp. 1-18.

Flydel, Leiv. 1964. Signes et symboles dans les grandeurs les moins complexes du plan du contenu. In H. G. Lunt, ed. Proceedings of the Ninth International Congress of Linguists. The Hague: Mouton and Co., pp. 537-546.

Fodor, Jerry A. and Katz, Jerrold J., eds. 1964. The Structure of Language: Readings in the Philosophy of Language. Englewood Cliffs, N.J.: Prentice-Hall, Inc.

Frake, Charles O. 1964. Notes on queries in ethnography. In A. Kimball Romney and Roy G. d'Andrade, eds. Transcultural Studies in Cognition. Special Publication of American Anthropologist 66, No. 3, part 2, pp. 132-145.

Frantz, Donald G. 1966. Person indexing in Blackfoot. IJAL 32.50-58.

Garvin, Paul L. 1944. Referential adjustment and linguistic structure. Acta Linguistica 4(2).53-60.

——, 1959. The standard language problem: concepts and methods. Anthropological Linguistics 1(2).28-31. Reprinted in Dell Hymes, ed., Language in Culture and Society, New York: Harper and Row, pp. 521-523.

——, 1964. L'analyse linguistique automatique: un problème heuristique. In E. Delaveney, ed. Traduction Automatique et Linguistique Appliquée. Paris: P.U.F., pp. 1-21.

——, Brewer, Jocelyn, and Mathiot, Madeleine. 1967. Predication-Typing: A Pilot Study in Semantic Analysis. Language 43, Number 2, Part II. Language Monograph No. 27.

Gedney, William J. 1963. Special vocabularies in Thai. In M. Zarechnak, ed., Report of the Twelfth Annual Round Table Meeting on Linguistics and Language Studies. Georgetown University Monograph Series on Languages and Linguistics No. 14, pp. 109-114.

Gleason, H. A., Jr. 1963. Some contributions of linguistics to biblical studies. The Hartford Quarterly 4(1).47-58.

——, 1964. The organization of language. In C. I. J. M. Stuart, ed. Report of the Fifteenth Annual Round Table Meeting on Linguistics and Language Studies. Georgetown University Monograph Series on Languages and Linguistics No. 17, pp. 75-96.

——, 1965. Linguistics and English Grammar. New York: Holt, Rinehart and Winston.

Glick, Leonard B. 1964. Categories and relations in Gimi natural science. In James B. Watson, ed. New Guinea: The Central Highlands. Special Publication of American Anthropologist 66, No. 4, part 2, pp. 273-280.

Goodenough, Ward. 1957. Cultural anthropology and linguistics. In P. L. Garvin, ed., Report of the Seventh Annual Round Table Meeting on Linguistics and Language Study. Washington: Georgetown University Monograph Series on Languages and Linguistics No. 9, pp. 167-173.

Graham, Albert and Sue. 1966. Charting character referent ties in Satéré texts. TBT 17.14-26.

Greenberg, Joseph H. 1963. Some universals of grammar with particular reference to the order of meaningful elements. In J. H. Greenberg, ed. Universals of Language. Cambridge: M.I.T. Press, pp. 58-90.

——, 1966. Language universals. In Thomas A. Sebeok, ed., Current Trends in Linguistics, Vol. III: Theoretical Foundations. The Hague: Mouton and Co., pp. 61-112.

Greimas, A.J. 1966. Sémantique Structurale. Paris: Librairie Larousse.

Grice, H.P. 1968. Utterer's meaning, sentence-meaning, and word-meaning. Foundations of Language 4.225-242.

Grimes, Joseph E. 1967. Positional analysis. Language 43.437-444.

Guillaume, Gustave. 1964. Langage et Science du Langage. Paris: Librairie A.-G. Nizet; Quebec: Presses de l'Université Laval.

Guillebaud, Philippa. 1965. Some points of interest and difficulty experienced in translating Genesis into Bari. TBT 16.189-192.

Gumperz, John J., and Hymes, Dell, eds. 1964. The Ethnography of Communication. Special Publication of American Anthropologist 66, No. 6, Part II.

Güttinger, Fritz. 1963. Zielsprache: Theorie und Technik des Übersetzens. Zürich: Manesse Verlag.

Hall, Edward T. 1960. Linguistic models in the analysis of culture. In Wm. M. Austin, ed. Report of the Ninth Annual Round Table Meeting on Linguistics and Language Studies. Georgetown University Monograph Series on Languages and Linguistics No. 11, pp. 157-164.

Hall, Robert A., Jr. 1966. Pidgin and Creole Languages. Ithaca, N.Y.: Cornell University Press.

Halliday, M.A.K. 1961. Categories of the theory of grammar. Word 17.241-292.

——, 1964. The linguistic study of literary texts. In H. G. Lunt, ed. Proceedings of the Ninth International Congress of Linguists. The Hague: Mouton and Co., pp. 302-307.

——, 1966. Some notes on 'deep' grammar. Journal of Linguistics 2.57-68.

——, 1967-1968. Notes on transitivity and theme in English. Journal of Linguistics 3.37-81, 199-244; 4.179-216.

Hammer, Muriel. 1966. Some comments on formal analysis of grammatical and semantic systems. American Anthropologist 68.362-373.

Hamp, Eric, Householder, Fred, and Austerlitz, Robert, eds. 1966. Readings in Linguistics II. Chicago and London: University of Chicago Press.

Harris, Zellig S. 1965. Transformational theory. Language 41.363-401.

Hendricks, William O. 1967. On the notion 'Beyond the sentence.' Linguistics 37.12-51.

Hess, Harwood. 1964. A study of glossa in the New Testament. TBT 15.93-96.

Hjelmslev, Louis. 1954. La stratification du langage. Word 10.163-188.

Hockett, Charles F. 1960. Ethno-linguistic implications of studies in linguistics and psychiatry. In Wm. M. Austin, ed., Report of the Ninth Annual Round Table Meeting on Linguistics and Language Studies. Georgetown University Monograph Series on Languages and Linguistics No. 11, pp. 175-193.

——, 1963. The problem of universals in language. In J. H. Greenberg, ed., Universals in Language. Cambridge: M.I.T. Press, pp. 1-22.

Hopkins, Nicholas S. 1963. Dogon classificatory systems. Anthropology Tomorrow 9(1).48-54.

Hymes, Dell. 1964a. Directions in (ethno-) linguistic theory. In A. Kimball Romney and Roy G. d'Andrade, eds. Transcultural studies in Cognition. Special Publication of American Anthropologist 66, No. 3, part 2, pp. 6-56.

——, ed. 1964b. Language in Culture and Society: a Reader in Linguistics and Anthropology. New York: Harper and Row.

Ikegami, Yoshihiko. 1967. Structural semantics. Linguistics 33.49-67.

Jakobson, Roman. 1963. Implications of language universals for linguistics. In 'J. H. Greenberg, ed., Universals of Language. Cambridge: M.I.T. Press, pp. 208-219.

——, 1966. Grammatical parallelism and its Russian facet. Language 42.399-429.

Joos, Martin. 1960. The isolation of styles. In R. S. Harrell, ed., Report of the Tenth Annual Round Table Meeting on Linguistics and Language Studies. Georgetown University Monograph Series on Languages and Linguistics No. 12, pp. 107-113.

——, 1962. The Five Clocks. IJAL 28, No. 2, Part V. Publication 22 of the Indiana University Research Center in Anthropology, Folkore, and Linguistics.

——, 1964. The English Verb. Madison, Wis.: University of Wisconsin Press.

Katz, Jerrold J. 1966. The Philosophy of Language. New York: Harper and Row.

Kennard, Edward A. 1963. Linguistic acculturation in Hopi. IJAL 29.36-41.

Koch, Walter A. 1967. A linguistic analysis of a satire. Linguistics 33.68-81.

Kurath, Hans. 1963. The semantic patterning of words. In M. Zarechnak, ed. Report of the Twelfth Annual Round Table Meeting on Linguistics and Language Studies. Georgetown University Monograph Series on Languages and Linguistics No. 14, pp. 91-94.

Kuryłowicz, Jerzy. 1936. Dérivation lexicale et dérivation syntaxique. Bulletin de la Société Linguistique de Paris 37.79-82. Reprinted in Hamp, Householder, and Austerlitz, eds., Readings in Linguistics II. Chicago and London: University of Chicago Press, pp. 42-50.

——, 1949. Linguistique et théorie du signe. Journal de psychologie 42.170-180.

Reprinted in Hamp, Householder, and Austerlitz, eds., Readings in Linguistics II. Chicago and London: University of Chicago Press, pp. 227-233.

Labov, William. 1966. The Social Stratification of English in New York City. Washington, D.C.: Center for Applied Linguistics.

Lamb, Sydney M. 1964a. On altneration, transformation, realization, and stratification. In C. I. J. M. Stuart, ed. Report of the Fifteenth Annual Round Table Meeting on Linguistics and Language Studies. Georgetown University Monograph Series on Languages and Linguistics No. 17, pp. 105-122.

——, 1964b. The sememic approach to structural semantics. In A. Kimball Romney and Roy G. d'Andrade, eds. Transcultural Studies in Cognition. Special Publication of American Anthropologist 66, No. 3, part 2, pp. 57-78.

——, 1965. Kinship terminology and linguistic structure. In E. A. Hammel, ed. Formal Semantic Analysis. Special Publication of American Anthropologist 67, No. 5, Part II, pp. 37-64.

——, 1966. Outline of Stratificational Grammar. Washington, D.C.: Georgetown University Press.

Landar, Herbert J. 1962. Fluctuation of forms in Navaho kinship terminology. American Anthropologist 64.985-1000.

——, Ervin, Susan M., and Horowitz, Arnold E. 1960. Navaho color categories. Language 36.368-382.

Langendoen, D. Terence. (Forthcoming). On selection, projection, meaning and semantic content. To appear in Leon Jakobovits and Danny Steinberg, eds., Semantics: an Interdisciplinary Reader in Philosophy, Linguistics, Psychology, and Anthropology.

Law, Howard W. 1966. Grammatical equivalences in Bible translating. TBT 17.123-127.

Loewen, Jacob A. 1960. Spanish loanwords in Waunana. IJAL 26.330-344.

——, 1964a. The Chocó and their spirit world. PA 11.97-104.

——, 1964b. Culture, meaning and translation. TBT 15.189-193.

——, 1965. Language: vernacular, trade or national. PA 12.97-106.

——, 1967. Toward a New Testament in Guarani Popular. TBT 18.33-39.

——, Buckwalter, Albert, and Kratz, James. 1965. Shamanism, illness, and power in Toba church life. PA 12. 250-280.

Lotz, John. 1955. On language and culture. IJAL 21.187-189. Reprinted (with slight changes by author) in Dell Hymes, ed., Language in Culture and Society. New York: Harper and Row, pp. 182-184.

Lounsbury, Floyd G. 1964. The structural analysis of kinship semantics. In H. G. Lunt, ed., Proceedings of the Ninth International Congress of Linguists. The Hague: Mouton and Co., pp. 1073-1093.

Lyons, John. 1966. Towards a 'notional' theory of the 'parts of speech'. Journal of Linguistics 2.209-236.

Markham, Robert P. 1966. The Bible Societies' Greek New Testament: the end of a decade or the beginning of an era? TBT. 107-113.

——, 1967. The Bible Societies' Greek New Testament: A symposium: The critical apparatus. TBT 18.3-11.

——, and Nida, Eugene A. 1966. An Introduction to the Bible Societies' Greek New Testament. New York: American Bible Society.

Marrison, Geoffrey E. 1965. The art of translation and the science of meaning. TBT 16.176-183.

——, 1966. Style in Bible translation. TBT 17.129-132.

Martin, Samuel. 1964. Speech levels in Japan and Korea. In Dell Hymes, ed., Language in Culture and Society. New York: Harper and Row, pp. 407-413.

Martinet, André. 1961. Eléments de Linguistique Générale, 2e éd. Paris: Librairie Armand Colin.

Mathiot, Madeleine. 1967. The place of the dictionary in linguistic description. Language 43.703-724.

Meek, Theophile J. 1965. Translating the Hebrew Bible. TBT 16.141-148.

Moore, Bruce R. 1964. Second thoughts on measuring 'naturalness.' TBT 15.83-87.

Moulton, Harold K. 1967. The Bible Societies' Greek New Testament: A symposium: C. The punctuation apparatus. TBT 18.16-19.

Mounin, Georges. 1963. Les problèmes théoriques de la traduction. Paris: Gallimard.

Mowvley, H. 1965. The concept and content of 'blessing' in the Old Testament. TBT 16.74-80.

Nadel, S. F. 1954. Morality and language among the Nupe. Man 54.55-57. Reprinted in Dell Hymes, ed., Language in Culture and Society. New York: Harper and Row, pp. 264-266.

Neill, Stephen C. 1967. The Bible Societies' Greek New Testament: A symposium: B. Review. TBT 18.12-15.

Newman, Barclay M. 1966. The Meaning of the New Testament. Nashville, Tenn.; Broadman Press.

Newman, Stanley and Gayton, Ann. 1940. Yokuts narrative style. In Gayton and Newman, Yokuts and Western Mono Myths. Berkerley: University of California Press. pp. 4-11. Reprinted in Dell Hymes, ed., Language in Culture and Society. New York: Harper and Row, pp. 372-381.

Nida, Eugene A. 1964. Toward a Science of Translating. Leiden: E. J. Brill.

——, 1966. Bible translation in today's world. TBT 17.59-64.

——, 1967. Translating the New Testament into Haitian Creole. TBT 18.27-30.

Öhman, Suzanne. 1953. Theories of the "linguistic field." Word 9.123-134.

Osgood, C. E. 1963. Language universals and psycho-linguistics. In J. H. Greenberg, ed., Universals of Language. Cambridge, Mass.: M.I.T. Press, pp. 236-254.

——, 1964. Semantic differential technique in the comparative study of cultures. In A. K. Romney and R. G. d'Andrade, eds. Transcultural Studies in Cognition. Special Publication of American Anthropologist 66, No. 3, part 2, pp. 171-200.

Parker-Rhodes, A. F. 1964. Is there an interlingual element in syntax? In H. G. Lunt, ed., Proceedings of the Ninth International Congress of Linguists. The Hague: Mouton and Co., pp. 176-190.

Percival, Keith. 1966. A reconsideration of Whorf's hypothesis. Anthropological Linguistics 8(8).1-12.

Pfeifer, David E. 1966. The question of reference in the writings of J. A. Katz and J. J. Fodor. Foundations of Language 2.142-150.

Phillips, J. B. 1965. The problems of making a contemporary translation. TBT 16.25-32.

Pickett, Velma B. 1964. Those problem pronouns: we, us, and our in the New Testament. TBT 15.86-92.

Pottier, Bernard. 1964. Vers une sémantique moderne. In Travaux de Linguistique et de Littérature publiés par le Centre de Philologie et de Littératures Romanes de l'Université de Strasbourg, Vol. II (1), pp. 107-137.

Reiling, J. 1965. The use and translation of kai egeneto 'and it happened', in the New Testament. TBT 16.153-163.

Reyburn, William D. 1960. The message of the Old Testament and the African Church—I. PA 7.152-156.

——, 1963. Christianity and ritual communication. PA 10.145-159.

Richert, Ernest L. 1965. How the Guru-Samane cult of 'poro' affects translation. TBT 16.81-87.

——, 1965. Indigenous reactions as a guide to meaningful translation. TBT 16.198-200.

Roberts, J. W. 1964. Some aspects of conditional sentences in the Greek New Testament. TBT 15.70-76.

Rodd, Cyril S. 1967. The family in the Old Testament. TBT 18.19-26.

Romney, A. Kimball, and d'Andrade, Roy G. 1964. Cognitive aspects of English kin terms. In A. K. Romney and R. G. d'Andrade, eds. Transcultural Studies in Cognition. Special Publication of American Anthropologist 66, No. 3, part 2, pp. 146-170.

Samarin, William J. 1965. Controlling elicitation of equivalents. TBT 16.36-38.

——, 1967. Field Linguistics. New York: Holt, Rinehart and Winston.

Sapir, Edward and Swadesh, Morris. 1946. American Indian grammatical categories. Word 2.103-112. Reprinted in Dell Hymes, ed., Language in Culture and Society. New York: Harper and Row, pp. 100-107.

Sarles, Harvey B. 1966. The dynamic study of interaction as ethnoscientific strategy. Anthropological Linguistics 8(8).66-70.

Sebeok, Thomas A., ed. 1966. Current Trends in Linguistics, Vol. III: Theoretical Foundations. The Hague: Mouton and Co.

Shimkin, Dmitri B. 1947. On Wind River Shoshone literary forms: an introduction. Journal of the Washington Academy of Sciences 37.329-352. Abridged in Dell Hymes, ed., Language in Culture and Society. New York: Harper and Row, pp. 344-351.

Smalley, William A. 1961. La Version Populaire: a new version in simplified French. TBT 12.181-186.

——, 1965a. The place of linguistics in Bible translation. TBT 16.105-112.

——, 1965b. Phillips and NEB: some comments on style. TBT 16.165-170.

Snaith, Norman H. 1965. The meanings of a word. TBT 16.44-48.

Southworth, Franklin C. 1967. A model of semantic structure. Language 43.342-361.

Stankiewicz, E. 1954. Expressive derivation of substantives in contemporary Russian and Polish. Word 10.457-468.

Stewart, William A. 1963. The functional distribution of Creole and French in Haiti. In E. D. Woodworth and R. J. DiPietro, eds., Report of the Thirteenth Annual Round Table Meeting on Linguistics and Language Studies. Georgetown University Monograph Series on Languages and Linguistics No. 15, pp. 149-159.

Sturtevant, William C. 1964. Studies in ethnoscience. In A. Kimball Romney and Roy G. d'Andrade, eds., Transcultural Studies in Cognition. Special Publication of American Anthropologist 66, No. 3, part 2, pp. 99-131.

Swellengrebel, J. L. 1966. Puzzles in Luke. TBT 17.118-122.

Taber, Charles R. 1964. French Loan Words in Sango: A Statistical Analysis of Incidence. Hartford, Conn.: The Hartford Seminary Foundation, Hartford Studies in Linguistics No. 12.

——, 1966. The Structure of Sango Narrative. Hartford, Conn.: The Hartford Seminary Foundation, Hartford Studies in Linguistics No. 17, parts I and II.

Thompson, R. A. 1968. Transformational theory and semantic analysis. Journal of Linguistics 4.73-78.

Tosh, Wayne. 1964. Content recognition and the production of synonymous expressions. In H. G. Lunt, ed. Proceedings of the Ninth International Congress of Linguists. The Hague: Mouton and Co., pp. 722-729.

Travers, Robert M. W. 1964. The transmission of information to human receivers. AV: Communication Review 12.373-385.

Trubetzkoy, N. S. 1939. Le rapport entre le déterminé, le déterminant et le défini. Mélanges de Linguistique Offerts à Charles Bally, pp. 75-82. Reprinted in Hamp, Householder, and Austerlitz, eds., Readings in Linguistics II. Chicago and London: University of Chicago Press.

Tyler, Stephen A. 1966. Context and variation in Koya kinship terminology. American Anthropologist 68.693-707.

Ullmann, Stephen. 1963. Semantic universals. In Joseph H. Greenberg, ed. Universals of Language. Cambridge: M.I.T. Press, pp. 172-207.

Ure, Jean. 1964. Types of translation and translatability. Babel 10.3-11.

Videbeck, R. and Pia, J. 1966. Plans for coping: an approach to ethnoscience. Anthropological Linguistics 8(8).71-77.

Vinay, J.-P. and Darbelnet, J. 1958. Stylistique comparée du français et de l'anglais: Méthode de traduction. Paris: Didier; Montréal: Beauchemin.

Vygotsky, Lev Semenovich. 1962. Thought and Language. Ed. and tr. by Eugenia Hanfman and Gertrude Vakar. Cambridge, Mass.: The M.I.T. Press.

Weinreich, Uriel. 1958. Travels in semantic space. Word 14.346-366.

——, 1963. On the semantic structure of language. In Joseph H. Greenberg, ed., Universals of Language. Cambridge, Mass.: M.I.T. Press, pp. 114-171.

——, 1966. Explorations in semantic theory. In Thomas A. Sebeok, ed., Current Trends in Linguistics, Vol. III: Theoretical Foundations. The Hague: Mouton and Co., pp. 395-477.

Werner, Heinz, ed. 1955. On Expressive Language. Worcester, Mass.: Clark University Press.

Werner, Oswald. 1965. Semantics of Navaho medical terms: I. IJAL 31.1-17.
——, 1966. Pragmatics and ethnoscience. Anthropological Linguistics 8(8).42-65.
Williams, Gerald E. 1966. Linguistic reflections of cultural systems. Anthropological Linguistics 8(8).13-21.
Wilson, W.A.A. 1964. 'But me no buts'. TBT 15.173-180.
Winburne, John N. 1964. Sentence sequence in discourse. In H. G. Lunt, ed., Proceedings of the Ninth International Congress of Linguists. The Hague: Mouton and Co., pp. 1094-1099.
Wolff, Hans. 1959. Intelligibility and inter-ethnic attitudes. Anthropological Linguistics 1(3).34-41. Reprinted slightly revised by author in Dell Hymes, ed., Language in Culture and Society. New York: Harper & Row, pp. 440-445.
Wonderly, William L. 1961. La Version Popular: a new version in simplified Spanish. TBT 12.169-177.
——, 1963. Some factors of meaningfulness. TBT 14.114-125.
——, 1968. Bible Translations for Popular Use. London: United Bible Societies.
——, and Nida, Eugene A. 1964. Linguistics and Christian missions. TBT 15.51-69, 107-116, 154-166.
Yngve, Victor H. 1964. Génération aléatoire de phrases anglaises. In E. Delaveney, ed. Traduction Automatique et Linguistique Appliquée. Paris: P.U.F., pp. 143-156.

GLOSSARY

The terms contained in this glossary are those which are either inherently technical or are being used in this book in a sense other than their everyday sense. Words which are not defined are to be understood in their common meaning in the kinds of contexts represented by this book. It should be pointed out that technical terms have various meanings in the literature or in other disciplines, as well as ordinary words. Therefore, the terms used in this book are to be understood in the sense defined in this glossary, and the definitions given in the glossary are to be applied to this book; they are not necessarily transposable to other contexts or other authors.

The entry term, in boldface, is given in that grammatical form which occurs most often and/or which is easiest to define. Terms formed on the same root but belonging to other grammatical classes are not separately defined, but are placed in boldface at the end of the definition, unless the meaning is not clear from the definition of the entry term. Alternative forms of the entry term, if they occur at the same alphabetical place, are given together; otherwise they are entered at their proper alphabetical place with a cross-reference in small capitals. Other cross-references, also in small capitals, lead to terms having either the same meaning or a related meaning.

The first definition of each meaning is of the so-called substitutable kind, appropriate to the grammatical class and subclass of the entry. If the needed information is too cumbersome to fit into a single substitutable phrase, it is added in the form of further substitutable phrases separated from the first by a semicolon (;), or of a whole sentence separated from the basic definition by a period (.). When an entry has more than one meaning, the separate definitions are numbered.

Two kinds of information are given in italics, in parentheses: words which typically accompany an entry, and which specify its uses and applications, are given immediately after the entry word; and illustrative examples, which are given within the definition at the appropriate place.

The order of the entries is strictly alphabetical, and ignores all spaces and word boundaries; thus, **semantics** is found between **semantic field** and **semantic space.**

abstract: a member of a category of semantic elements found in all languages and which refer to qualities or quantities which are properties of an object or event, but which can be conceptually separated from the elements whose properties they are. Many languages have one or two grammatical classes which typically represent abstracts, i.e. ADJECTIVES and ADVERBS; others represent some abstracts by a special class of verbs (e.g. *be-red*). Some languages which have adjectives and adverbs can also represent abstracts by nouns derived from them, i.e. abstract nouns (*length, redness*).

abstract noun: in some languages, a kind of noun, usually derived from an adjective or a verb, which refers not to an object but to an event (*repentance, faith*) or to an abstract (*redness, liberty*)

accurate: same as FAITHFUL

active language: see PRODUCER LANGUAGE

active voice: in many languages, the grammatical form of a verb and/or clause in which the grammatical SUBJECT represents the semantic AGENT; opposed to PASSIVE VOICE

adjective: in some languages, a word of a grammatical class which typically modifies a noun. Typically, adjectives represent certain kinds of ABSTRACTS (*red, tall, funny*)

adverb: in some languages, a word of a grammatical class which typically modifies a verb, an adjective, or another adverb. Normally, an adverb represents a semantic ABSTRACT (*fast, soon, greedily*)

affix: a MORPHEME which cannot stand by itself, but which is added to a word, either to change its grammatical class (i.e. derivation), to serve as a grammatical MARKER, or to add an element of meaning. An affix can come before the root word (i.e. a prefix), in the middle (i.e. an infix) or at the end (i.e. a suffix).

agent: the object which accomplishes the action designated by an event, or which causes or initiates the event, or which is affected by a process event; not to be confused with a grammatical SUBJECT, which is the representation of the agent in the KERNEL and in the ACTIVE VOICE

ambiguous: having more than one meaning; **ambiguity**

ambivalent: same as AMBIGUOUS; **ambivalence**

anacolouthon (plural **anacoloutha**): a sentence which begins with one grammatical structure and ends with another; a sentence with interrupted syntax

analysis: the first of the three stages of TRANSLATION; the set of procedures, including BACK TRANSFORMATION and COMPONENTIAL ANALYSIS, which aim at discovering the KERNELS underlying the source text and the clearest understanding of the meaning, in preparation for the transfer

analytical expression: an expression comprising several words which has the same meaning as a given single word. A good dictionary definition is often an analytical expression; see also SYNONYM

analytical redistribution: restatement in the form of an analytical expression; opposed to SYNTHETIC REDISTRIBUTION

animate: belonging to a semantic category of objects which are conceived to be alive; opposed to INANIMATE; frequently represented by obligatory marking in the grammar

antonym: a meaning which shares at least one COMMON COMPONENT with another meaning but which has an opposite value for a POLAR diagnostic component (*good—bad, tall—short*)

apposition: the placing side by side of two expressions which refer to the same thing in different ways; or, the resulting construction (*General de Gaulle, the president of France*)

archaism: an expression which was used at an earlier period but which is no longer current in the language; opposed both to CONTEMPORARY USAGE and to NEOLOGISM; **archaic**

argument: a type of discourse predominantly organized around a number of events between which LOGICAL RELATIONS are predicated

article: in some languages, a kind of DETERMINER which typically specifies whether the referent of a noun phrase has been previously referred to in a discourse. The definite article indicates that it has been, the indefinite that it has not.

artificial language: a language invented by men for a specific use, usually in symbolic logic or for the use of computers; opposed to NATURAL LANGUAGE

aspect: a semantic category which specifies the point of view taken by the speaker with respect to an event, e.g. completed or incompleted, beginning, continuing, or ending, real or imaginary, etc.; often formally marked in the grammar

aural: pertaining to hearing; specifically, pertaining to the language as heard rather than read

background (*to*): to place an element of a discourse in a status of secondary or tertiary interest and attention; opposed to FOREGROUND; see also FOCUS

back transformation: a grammatical process by which the SURFACE STRUCTURE of a discourse is analyzed, by the application of rigorous rules, into its underlying KERNELS in the same language; one aspect, along with COMPONENTIAL ANALYSIS, of the analysis of a source text in translation; opposed to TRANSFORMATION

casual level: that SITUATIONAL LEVEL of spoken language, partly characterized by the use of slang and frequent ellipses, which is used among close friends

category: a set of semantic elements which share some high-level COMMON COMPONENT, e.g. object, animate. The categories of a language cross-cut the DOMAINS, which are culturally based. The categories are often represented by grammatical MARKERS, e.g. by noun or verb classes, though seldom in a one-to-one manner.

causative: a semantic category relating to events, and in some languages represented by grammatical markers accompanying verbs, which indicates that an agent causes some other object to participate in the event

central meaning: that meaning of a word which is generally understood when the word is given with no CONTEXT; also called unmarked meaning

channel capacity: in communication, the degree of ability which a RECEPTOR has to understand a MESSAGE. Channel capacity is conditioned both by the receptor's personal qualities and by his cultural background, and is a function of the amount of information which the receptor has in common with the author. The narrower the channel capacity, the more REDUNDANCY needs to be introduced to lighten the COMMUNICATION LOAD.

chiasmus: a STYLISTIC device in which successive parts of a sentence contain the same pair of semantic elements, but in opposite order (Ps. 51:5: *I was shapen in iniquity; and in sin did my mother conceive me*)

class (*grammatical*): a SET of words which fulfill essentially the same kinds of grammatical functions, and which in some languages are also distinguished morphologically, e.g. verb, noun, adjective

classification: the system according to which a language distinguishes or groups aspects of experience, as symbolized by words, into DOMAINS which are covered by GENERIC terms

classifier: a term used with another term, often a proper name, to make clear what category and/or class it belongs to (*the city of Jerusalem*)

clause: a grammatical construction typically composed of a SUBJECT and a PREDICATE. An independent clause is one which is capable of standing by itself and constituting a SENTENCE; principal and dependent clauses must combine with other clauses to constitute a sentence.

Cloze technique: a technique for testing the degree of difficulty of a text by deleting every fifth word and inviting persons to guess at the missing words; the fewer the errors, the easier the text

collocation: a structured combination of words with COMPATIBLE semantic components

comment: that part of a clause which says something about the TOPIC; typically the PREDICATE

common component: (1) a SEMANTIC COMPONENT which is shared by one meaning of each of several words, so that these meanings cover at least part of a DOMAIN; (2) a semantic component which is shared by several meanings of a word and which supports the intuition that it is one word rather than a set of HOMONYMS

common language: that portion of the total lexical, grammatical, and stylistic resources of a language which is both understood and accepted as good usage by all who know the language. Excluded are (a) LITERARY and TECHNICAL language, which are understood only by persons specially trained; (b) SUBSTANDARD and VULGAR language, which are unacceptable for serious communication; and (c) features which are preculiar to any local, regional, or social DIALECT

communication: the act of transmitting a MESSAGE to a RECEPTOR; the closer the resemblance between the intent of the sender and the understanding of the receptor, the more effective the communication.

communication load: the degree of difficulty of a message, as measured by the ratio between the number of units of information and the number of formal units (i.e. words). An overloaded message can be made easier by the controlled addition of REDUNDANCY, which makes the ratio smaller.

compatible (*meanings*): which can be combined into an acceptable expression (COLLOCATION) because of the sharing of common components, i.e. which belong to the same domain and/or category

complement: a word or phrase which grammatically completes another word or phrase by being subordinate to it; in a broad sense, includes direct object and indirect object; in a narrow sense, used only of expressions which function as adverbs, e.g. to specify time, place, manner, means, etc.

complex (*structure*): composed of more than one element. The word *dancer* is semantically complex because it comprises an event (*dance*) and an object (*-r*) which is agent of the event; it is also grammatically complex; but it is not necessary that semantic and grammatical complexity go together.

component: (1) a part of a construction; (2) a SEMANTIC COMPONENT

componential analysis: that part of the analysis of a text which aims at discovering and organizing the SEMANTIC COMPONENTS of the words

comprehensibility: see INTELLIGIBILITY

concordance: see VERBAL CONSISTENCY

conjunction: in many languages, a word of a grammatical class which joins words, phrase, clauses, or sentences. Conjunctions may coordinate or subordinate; they represent RELATIONS, but not in a one-to-one manner.

connotation, connotative meaning: that aspect of meaning which concerns the emotional attitude of the author and the emotional RESPONSE of a receptor. It can be good or bad, strong or weak; words with very strong connotations, either good or bad, often become TABOO.

constituent part: same as COMPONENT (1)

consumer language: that range of vocabulary, grammar, and style which a person can understand when he hears or reads it; more extensive than PRODUCER LANGUAGE; also called passive language

contemporary usage: that form of language which is used in the present day; opposed both to ARCHAISM and NEOLOGISM

context: the total setting in which a word is used, including the CULTURAL CONTEXT and the linguistic context, which in turn consists of the SYNTACTIC CONTEXT and the SEMOTACTIC CONTEXT. One function of the context is to select for each word the single appropriate meaning, and so to avoid ambiguity in a discourse.

contextual conditioning: the placing in the context of information which is needed to make the meaning clear to a receptor. Typically, it involves making explicit something which is implicit in the original message, as by the use of classifiers.

contextual consistency: the quality which results from translating a source language word by that expression in the receptor language which best fits each context rather than by the same expression in all contexts (which is called VERBAL CONSISTENCY); one aspect of DYNAMIC EQUIVALENCE

contrastive component: see DIAGNOSTIC COMPONENT

coordination: the joining of grammatical elements of the same sort, as by a conjunction

copula: in some languages, a special kind of verb which simultaneously represents certain relations (e.g. class membership, identity) and serves as the principal word of a predicate. In English, *be* is a copula in *He is a man*; this usage is not to be confused with *be* as a verb of existence (*God is*) or as an auxiliary (*He is coming*).

correct: same as FAITHFUL

countable: belonging to a category of objects which can be isolated and counted. Typically, a noun representing a countable object can be marked for singular and plural; opposed to MASS.

cultural context: that part of the CONTEXT which includes both the total culture within which a communication takes place and the specific nonlinguistic circumstances of the communication

cultural focus: that aspect of a culture which is most central, most fully developed, and most constantly in the conscious thinking of the people; consequently, that part which is represented by the richest and most precise kind of vocabulary

cultural translation: a translation in which the content of the message is changed to conform to the receptor culture in some way, and/or in which information is introduced which is not linguistically implicit in the original; opposed to LINGUISTIC TRANSLATION

decoding: that operation by which a receptor interprets a discourse and understands its message; opposed to ENCODING

definite article: see ARTICLE

denotation, denotative meaning: see REFERENTIAL MEANING

dependent clause: see CLAUSE

derivation: see AFFIX

description: a type of discourse predominantly organized around an object or set of objects and the predication of relations and abstracts with respect to the object(s)

descriptive substitute: same as ANALYTICAL EXPRESSION

determiner: a grammatical element accompanying a noun to help specify its reference, e.g. demonstrative, possessive, indefinite, article, etc.

diagnostic component: a SEMANTIC COMPONENT which serves to distinguish one meaning from another, whether the meanings belong to one word or several; also called distinctive component, essential component, and contrastive component

dialect: one of a number of varieties of a language, especially as differentiated by geographical region or by social class

direct discourse: the reported actual words of one person embedded in the discourse of another person; in English, typically marked in writing by quotation marks; opposed to INDIRECT DISCOURSE. Some languages prefer direct discourse, some indirect.

direct object: a noun phrase directly subordinate to a verb; typically, the direct object represents the semantic GOAL.

discourse: a specimen of linguistic material displaying structural and semantic coherence, unity, and completeness, and conveying a message; also called text

distinctive component: see DIAGNOSTIC COMPONENT

ditransitive (*verb*): requiring two grammatical objects, typically one direct and one indirect (*He gave me a book*); see also TRANSITIVE and INTRANSITIVE

domain: a definable area of cultural experience covered by a set of related terms; the defining features of the domain are represented by the COMMON COMPONENTS of the meanings of the terms in the domain; also called semantic field.

dynamic equivalence: quality of a translation in which the message of the original text has been so transported into the receptor language that the RESPONSE of the RECEPTOR is essentially like that of the original receptors. Frequently, the form of the original text is changed; but as long as the change follows the rules of back transformation in the source language, of contextual consistency in the transfer, and of transformation in the receptor language, the message is preserved and the translation is faithful. The opposite principal is FORMAL CORRESPONDENCE.

efficiency: in communication, the maximum understanding by the receptor at the cost of the least effort; opposed to SPECIAL EFFECTS

ellipsis: the patterned omission of some information from a discourse; the leaving of some information IMPLICIT

encoding: that operation by which a sender plans a message and composes a discourse to convey it; opposed to DECODING

endocentric (*expression*): in semantics, whose meaning is derivable from the meanings of its constituent words; opposed to EXOCENTRIC

epistolary formula: the set forms which are used in a letter to mark that it is a letter

equivalence: a very close similarity in meaning, as opposed to similarity in form; see DYNAMIC EQUIVALENCE and FORMAL CORRESPONDENCE

esoteric (*dialect, language*): intended to be used and understood only by initiated persons, as a mark of their being initiated and as a device to exclude unitiated persons from the communication

essential component: see DIAGNOSTIC COMPONENT

euphemism: a word or expression which is used in ordinary circumstances as a substitute for a TABOO word

event: a category of semantic elements in all languages which refer to actions, processes, etc., in which objects can participate (*run, fall, grow, think*). In most languages, there is a grammatical class of words called VERBS which most appropriately but not obligatorily represent events; some languages also have a special class of nouns (abstract nouns) which can represent events (*faith* < *believe, repentance* < *repent*). In a KERNEL, each event is represented by a verb.

exclusive first person plural: a first person plural form which includes the speaker and other persons but specifically excludes the person addressed; opposed to INCLUSIVE FIRST PERSON PLURAL

exegesis: that discipline whose methods and techniques aim at understanding a text

exocentric (*expression*): in semantics, whose meaning cannot be derived from the meanings of its constituent words; see also IDIOM; opposed to ENDOCENTRIC

expansion: same as ANALYTICAL REDISTRIBUTION

explicit (*information*): which is formally represented in a discourse, as by words, morphemes, order of elements, etc. Explicit information is always completed in the mind of a competent receptor by that information which is IMPLICIT to reconstitute the total MESSAGE.

expressive (*function of language*): which expresses the emotional attitudes of the author and evokes corresponding responses in the receptor; related to CONNOTATION

faithful (*translation*): which evokes in a receptor essentially the same response as that displayed by the receptors of the original message. The receptor understands the same meaning in it, reacts to it emotionally in the same way, and comes to analogous decisions and actions as the original receptors; faithfulness is primarily a quality of the MESSAGE rather than of the FORM, i.e. it results from DYNAMIC EQUIVALENCE rather than from FORMAL CORRESPONDENCE.

figurative (*meaning, expression*): which is used in place of another meaning or expression which is not its synonym but with which it has an association of ideas often mediated through a SUPPLEMENTARY COMPONENT; e.g. a METAPHOR

flashback: reference in a narrative to events prior to the time of the body of the narrative

focus: the center of attention in a discourse or portion of a discourse. In some languages, focus is indicated by grammatical markers, in others by special words, altered word order, etc., as in *the glory of God* versus *the God of glory*; see also BACKGROUND and FOREGROUND

foreground (*to*): to bring an element of a discourse in FOCUS, to place emphasis on it, to make it the center of attention; opposed to BACKGROUND

form (*of a discourse*): the overt structure of a discourse in terms of its words, grammatical classes, and syntactic and stylistic patterns; the vehicle by which the MESSAGE is conveyed

formal correspondence: quality of a translation in which the features of the form of the source text have been mechanically reproduced in the receptor language. Typically, formal correspondence distorts the grammatical and stylistic patterns of the receptor language, and hence distorts the message, so as to cause the receptor to misunderstand or to labor unduly hard; opposed to DYNAMIC EQUIVALENCE; see also LITERALNESS

formal level: that SITUATIONAL LEVEL of spoken language, partly characterized by a high degree of orderliness and complexity at all levels of structure, which is used by competent persons in addressing an audience on a solemn occasion; it is the form of spoken language which most closely resembles LITERARY LANGUAGE.

forward transformation: see TRANSFORMATION

generic (*word, meaning*): referring to a broad, inclusive DOMAIN or experience, as opposed to SPECIFIC; e.g. *animal* is generic, while *cat, dog, camel* are specific; see also INCLUSION and TAXONOMY

genitive (*construction*): in which one noun is related to another by subordination, sometimes in a possessive sense. In some languages, the subordinate noun is in a special form.

genius (*of a language*): the unique qualities at all levels of a language which distinguish it from other languages. It is the differences between the genius of a source language and a receptor language which require a faithful translation to follow the principles of dynamic equivalence rather than of formal correspondence.

glottochronology: the statistical analysis of the basic vocabulary items shared by two dialects or related languages in an effort to determine, by the application of a formula, the length of time since their divergence from the same parent form

goal (*semantic*): that object which undergoes or submits to the action of a transitive event; not to be confused with the direct object or grammatical goal of a verb, by which it is often represented, especially in a kernel

grammar: that part of the structure of a language which specifies the structure of words, phrases, clauses, and sentences; distinguished from semantics and phonology. That part of grammar which deals with the structure of phrases, clauses, and sentences is called SYNTAX, that dealing with the structure of words is called MORPHOLOGY.

harmonization: the act of changing the form and/or meaning of one passage to

make it resemble more closely another passage considered parallel, as between two
or three synoptic accounts of an episode; or, the result of this act

heaviness: quality of style which makes a discourse unduly difficult to understand
through the use of very complex or unnatural forms; in translation, often results
from LITERALNESS

hierarchy: see TAXONOMY

highlight: see FOREGROUND

homonym: a word which is written and/or pronounced in the same way as another, but which has an unrelated meaning

honorific: a form used to express respect or deference; obligatory in some languages
in referring to or addressing certain kinds of people

hypotactic: pertaining to the grammatical relationship between a principal CLAUSE
and a dependent clause; opposed to PARATACTIC; *hypotaxis*

idiom: an expression consisting of several words and whose meaning cannot be
derived from the meanings of the individual words, e.g. *kick the bucket* for *die*; also
called exocentric expression

idiomatic: see NATURAL

ideophone: a word or expression, often unusual or irregular in phonology (e.g.
through the use of SOUND SYMBOLISM) and in its syntactic constructions, which
expresses primarily a highly specific connotation usually with reference to a highly
select set of words

imperative (*function of language*): which has the effect of inciting a receptor to
appropriate action

implicit (*information*): which is present in a message, and is so intended by the
sender and understood by a competent receptor, without being formally present in
the discourse; e.g., an agent is implicit with each event. Information which was
clearly implicit for original receptors may need to be made EXPLICIT for subsequent
receptors if they are to understand the message.

inanimate: see ANIMATE

inclusion: the relation in semantic space between a SPECIFIC meaning and a more
GENERIC meaning which entirely covers all aspects of experience covered by the
first meaning and other aspects as well; as, *walk* is included in *move*. A set of
meanings standing in a hierarchy of inclusions is a TAXONOMY.

inclusive first person plural: a first person plural form which includes at least
the speaker and the person addressed; opposed to EXCLUSIVE FIRST PERSON PLURAL

indefinite article: see ARTICLE

independent clause: see CLAUSE

indirect discourse: the reported words of one person embedded in grammatically
transformed form in the discourse of another person. Typically, references to the
original speaker and persons addressed by him are in the third person, and some
languages use other formal devices to distinguish between indirect discourse and
DIRECT DISCOURSE.

indirect object: a noun phrase subordinated to a verb, usually through a preposition, typically co-occurring with a DIRECT OBJECT, and often expressing the
object benefited by the action (*He gave the book to John*)

infix: see AFFIX

information: the total meaning which constitutes a MESSAGE, especially conceived in its distinct parts. Information may be either EXPLICIT or IMPLICIT.

informative (*function of language*): which conveys meaning in such a way that the
receptor understands the message; related to REFERENTIAL MEANING

intelligibility: quality of a discourse in which a receptor can understand the message

intimate level: that SITUATIONAL LEVEL of spoken language, partly characterized
by a high proportion of privately coined expressions and the use of ellipses, which
is used among persons bound by the closest ties of affection and shared experience,
e.g. the members of a family

intransitive (*verb*): used without a direct object or indirect object; see also TRANS-
ITIVE and DITRANSITIVE

kernel: a SENTENCE pattern which is basic to the structure of a language, and
which is characterized by (a) the simplest possible form, in which OBJECTS are
represented by NOUNS, EVENTS by VERBS, and ABSTRACTS by ADJECTIVES, ADVERBS,

or special verbs (according to the GENIUS of the language), (b) the least ambiguous expression of all RELATIONS, and (c) the EXPLICIT inclusion of all INFORMATION. Each language has only 6-12 types of kernels. Kernels are discovered in a SURFACE STRUCTURE by BACK TRANSFORMATION; they are converted into a surface structure by TRANSFORMATION.

levels: see SITUATIONAL LEVELS

lexical: pertaining to the selection and use of words as units bearing meaning; related to SEMOTACTIC, but often more arbitrary than systematic

linguistic context: that aspect of the CONTEXT which comprises the SYNTACTIC CONTEXT and the SEMOTACTIC CONTEXT

linguistic translation: a translation in which only information which is linguistically implicit in the original is made explicit and in which all changes of form follow the rules of back transformation and transformation and of componential analysis; opposed to CULTURAL TRANSLATION. Only a linguistic translation can be considered FAITHFUL.

literal (*meaning*): which is based on the most commonly understood meanings of the diagnostic components; opposed to FIGURATIVE. The CENTRAL MEANING is literal, but there may be other literal meanings as well.

literalness: quality of a translation in which the form of the original has been reproduced in the receptor language in such a way as to distort the message and/or the patterns of the receptor language; see also FORMAL CORRESPONDENCE

literary genre: any one of several types of discourse defined in terms of generally accepted linguistic and stylistic criteria, e.g. the fable, the parable, the lyric, etc.

literary language: that form of language, sometimes but not always written, in which texts are composed and transmitted which are intended to be esthetically pleasing; characterized by careful, often elaborate use of words and grammatical and stylistic devices; in unwritten languages, most closely resembles the FORMAL LEVEL of spoken language; often not understood by uneducated persons

logical relation: a relation between two events which is discovered by reason rather than by direct observation, e.g. cause and effect and condition

marginal note: in Bible Society usage, a purely objective, factual note added beside the text to permit the reader to understand information which was implicit for the original receptors but which is not otherwise accessible to him

marker (*grammatical*): a device, e.g. affix, copula, preposition, determiner, etc., which indicates the grammatical nature or function of a word or construction

mass: belonging to a category of objects which cannot be individually isolated and counted, but from which indefinitely bounded quantities can be removed, e.g. *sand, water*; opposed to COUNTABLE; typically incapable of having a plural

message: the total meaning or content of a discourse; the concepts and feelings which the author intends the reader to understand and receive

metaphor: a FIGURATIVE expression used instead of another to make an implicit comparison between the items referred to by the two expressions, often based upon SUPPLEMENTARY COMPONENTS. An expression in every way similar except that the comparison is explicit is a simile.

morpheme: the smallest grammatical piece in a language. Some words, especially particles, are composed of only one morpheme; others are composed of several morphemes, e.g. *un-shak-able*. Morphemes are often classified as stems and AFFIXES.

morphology: see GRAMMAR; **morphological**

narrative: a type of discourse predominantly organized around a chain of events in temporal sequence, together with participants and circumstances

natural: characterized by the use of grammatical constructions and combinations of words which do not violate the ordinary patterns of a language; opposed to TRANSLATIONESE, HEAVINESS

natural language: a language which has developed through the normal processes as the speech form of a community of people; opposed to ARTIFICIAL LANGUAGE

neologism, neologistic expression: an expression which has been newly created, often expressly to give an effect of novelty or of individuality; opposed to ARCHAISM and CONTEMPORARY USAGE

noise: in communication, any factor (e.g. physical noise, radio static, fatigue, deafness, lack of interest, etc.) which hinders effective understanding. In order to overcome noise, REDUNDANCY is introduced into the communication.

nominal (*phrase, expression, construction*): see NOUN PHRASE

nominalization: the kind of TRANSFORMATION by which constructions of various kinds (especially verb phrases) are converted into noun phrases; or, the resulting noun phrase; e.g. *She sings beautifully → her beautiful singing* (where → symbolizes a transformation)

noun: in most languages, a grammatical class of words which can function as subject, direct object, or indirect object of a verb. In some languages, nouns are also distinguished by their morphological form. The traditional definition of a noun as the name of a person, place, or thing derives from the intuitive similarity between the grammatical noun and the semantic OBJECT; but in some languages there are nouns which do not represent objects; in a KERNEL, a noun does represent an object.

noun phrase: a phrase which functions grammatically as a NOUN; often, a phrase having a noun as its principal word

object: a member of a semantic category which in all languages refers to persons, animals, places, things, etc., e.g. *man, horse, mountain, table, spirit*. In most languages, there is a grammatical class called NOUNS which most appropriately but not obligatorily represent objects.

objective (*genitive, possessive*): in which the relation between the object represented by one noun phrase and the event represented by the other noun phrase is that of a goal, e.g. *the salvation of man*; opposed to SUBJECTIVE

oral literature: a body of texts composed according to the standards of literary language and transmitted from person to person in essentially unchanged form orally rather than in writing; typical of all unwritten languages

ordinary level: that SITUATIONAL LEVEL of spoken language, partly characterized by a relatively low degree of organization above the sentence and by rather frequent anacoloutha, which is used in normal conversation between acquaintances

overlapping: pertaining to the relationship between two meanings which share one or more COMMON COMPONENTS and which are not in POLAR contrast, but which also have components not in common. If the overlapping area is fairly extensive, the terms are SYNONYMS.

parallel: a passage from one book which deals with the same topic or episode in similar terms as a passage from another book; or, a passage which formally ressembles another to such an extent that quotation or allusion may be involved

parallelism: the use in successive parts of a text of expressions which are similar in sound, grammar, or meaning, or combinations of these; characteristic of POETIC LANGUAGE

paraphrase: the restatement of a meaning in a different form. Various transforms of a kernel are typically paraphrases of each other, e.g. *The dog bit the man* and *The man was bitten by the dog*; see also SYNONYM

paratactic: pertaining to the relationship between two CLAUSES of equal rank; *parataxis* is COORDINATION between clauses; opposed to HYPOTACTIC

participant: an object in its relation to an event, e.g. agent, goal, instrument. The object is said to **participate** in the event.

participial (*phrase, construction*): in which a participle is the main word

particle: a small word which does not change its form, e.g. a preposition, a conjunction

passive language: see CONSUMER LANGUAGE

passive voice: in some languages, that grammatical form of a verb and/or a clause in which the grammatical subject expresses the semantic goal and the semantic agent is expressed either by an agent complement or by nothing; opposed to ACTIVE VOICE. Many languages have no passive voice, and in translating a passive voice into such languages implicit agents must be made explicit.

phonology: that part of the structure of a language which deals with sound units, and consequently with pronunciation patterns; significant in translation proper only as regards the spelling of words (mainly proper names) which are transferred untranslated from the source language into the receptor language, and which must usually be spelled in accordance with the patterns of pronunciation and spelling of the receptor language

phrase: a grammatical construction such that the entire phrase can typically fulfill the same functions in a clause as the principal word or words, e.g. a noun phrase, a verb phrase, an adverb phrase

play on words: an expression with potentially more than one meaning and used as a stylistic device; the intentional exploitation of an ambiguity or chance resemblance between expressions

pleonasm, pleonastic expression: an expression in which for structural reasons information is explicit more than once which is not necessary for communication, e.g. Job 33:2, *The tongue in my mouth speaks*

poetic language: language characterized by the use of PARALLELISM, FIGURATIVE LANGUAGE, conciseness and condensation, etc., and typically used in poems

polar (*contrast*): in which there is the possibility of only two, completely opposite values. ANTONYMS are related by having at least one common component and one component on which there is a polar contrast.

possessive (*construction*): consisting of a possessive noun or pronoun and a noun; the semantic nature of the relation represented depends upon the nature and meaning of the terms involved.

predicate: one of the divisions of a CLAUSE, the other being the SUBJECT. Typically, the principal part of a predicate is a verb phrase.

predicate (*to*): to make of some semantic element the predicate of a clause, as in *The copula predicates a relation of identity*

predicate (*adjective, noun, phrase*): in English and some other languages, which occurs in a predicate following a copula, as in *He is tall* and *He is a boy*

prefix: see AFFIX

preposition: in some languages, one of a grammatical class of words which join two nouns, two verbs, or a noun and a verb. Prepositions represent semantic RELATIONS, but not in a one-to-one manner.

prepositional phrase, prepositional expression: a phrase introduced by a preposition and typically functioning as an adverbial complement of a verb or as the genitive complement of a noun

primary (*element, structure*): which occupies the center of focus, which is FORE-GROUNDED in a discourse; opposed to SECONDARY and TERTIARY

principal clause: see CLAUSE

process event: an event which refers to a change of state occurring through time

producer language: that range of vocabulary, grammar, and style which a person can actively and correctly use in speaking or in writing; opposed to CONSUMER LANGUAGE; also called active language

proper (*noun, name*): specific to an individual object rather than to a category, e.g. *John* versus *man*

receptor: a person receiving or intended to receive a message

receptor language: the language into which a message is translated from the original or SOURCE LANGUAGE

redundancy: the expression more than once of the same units of information, either to overcome NOISE or to lighten the COMMUNICATION LOAD; not to be confused with TAUTOLOGY or PLEONASM

referent: that to which the referential meaning points in the nonlinguistic world

referential meaning: that aspect of the meaning of a term which most closely relates the term to the portion of the nonlinguistic world which it symbolizes, and which can be defined by COMPONENTIAL ANALYSIS; also called denotation; opposed to CONNOTATION

relation, relational, relationship: a semantic element which specifies the meaningful connections between objects, events, and abstracts, e.g. agent, goal, identity. In the grammar, relations are variously represented in different languages by word order, affixes, prepositions, conjunctions, copulas, etc., but there is not a one-to-one connection between relations and grammatical MARKERS.

relative pronoun: a pronoun which simultaneously stands in one clause for a noun in a preceding clause and subordinates the clause to the noun, e.g. *This is the man who came to dinner*

rendering: the form of a portion of a translation which is intended to represent a corresponding portion of the original text

response (*of a receptor*): the sum of the reactions of a receptor to a message in terms of understanding (or lack of it), emotional attitude, decision, and action

restructure: to change the form of a discourse without changing the contents of the message; specifically, to transform the raw results of the transfer process into a stylistic form appropriate to the receptor language and to the intended receptors

rhetorical: see STYLISTIC

rhetorical question: an expression cast in the form of a question not to elicit information but for the stylistic effect of evoking a more active response from he receptor; often to be translated by emphatic statement

secondary (*element, structure*): which is somewhat backgrounded in a discourse; opposed to PRIMARY and TERTIARY

semantic area: that aspect of experience which is covered by a term or by a set of related terms

semantic component: a structural part of the REFERENTIAL MEANING of a word, discovered by COMPONENTIAL ANALYSIS. Semantic components may be common components, diagnostic components, or supplementary components.

semantic field: see DOMAIN

semantics: that part of the structure of a language which deals with the meanings of words and expressions and also with the meaningful structure of discourse. One aspect, componential analysis, deals with referential meaning; another deals with connotation; distinguished from grammar and phonology

semantic space: a conceptualization of the universe of experience in which meanings and domains are said to be near or far from each other according to the number and similarity of shared components or the degree of cultural and/or psychological association of ideas between them

semotactic context: that aspect of the LINGUISTIC CONTEXT which pertains to the meanings of terms surrounding a given term. The semotactic context acts with the SYNTACTIC CONTEXT to select for each word the most appropriate meaning.

sentence: a grammatical construction composed of one or more CLAUSES arranged according to a prescribed pattern, and capable of standing by itself as a complete unit. Grammatical completeness does not imply semantic completeness, however, as many sentences, especially those other than the opening sentence of a discourse, are semantically dependent on preceding sentences (e.g. all of those containing third person pronouns).

sequence of tenses: the patterned way in which the tenses and other forms of verbs follow each other throughout a discourse

set: a group of units, e.g. words, which share some feature (semantic, grammatical, or phonological) in common. Where the shared features are semantic, the terms constitute a CATEGORY or a DOMAIN; where they are grammatical, the terms are a CLASS; and where they share only phonological or spelling similarity, they are HOMONYMS.

simile: see METAPHOR

situational levels (*of language*): levels of usage between which an individual, in speaking, shifts in accordance with the socio-cultural situation in which he finds himself. Five levels are distinguished: the technical level, the formal level, the ordinary level, the casual level, and the intimate level

slang: a special vocabulary, typically used by adolescents to distinguish themselves from adults and to avoid being understood by adults, often characterized by extreme figurative language and sound symbolism; usually very temporary

sound symbolism: the use of special sounds either to imitate or to represent conventionally certain meanings, especially certain connotations; frequently found in ideophones and slang

source language: the language in which the original author of a message formulated it, and the point of departure for translation

spatial relations: relations of distance, relative order, or position between objects, parts of objects, and objects and speaker/audience; typically represented by PREPOSITIONS

special effects: in communication, the impact of those features of vocabulary, grammar, and style which tend to arouse curiosity, heighten emotion, and otherwise strengthen receptor interest, even at the cost of some loss of EFFICIENCY

specific (*word, meaning*): referring to a narrow semantic area, as opposed to GENERIC. The more specific a term, the smaller the set of items it covers and the more components are required to define it; specific terms are INCLUDED in generic terms.

structure: (1) the patterns and rules according to which words, phrases, clauses, sentences, and discourses are built up out of their constituent parts. This is the structure of a language. (2) the characteristic form of a discourse built according to sense (1). This is, e.g., the structure of a sentence, of a discourse.

style: the patterning of choices made by a particular author within the resources and limitations of the language and of the literary genre in which he is working. It is the style which gives to a text its uniqueness and which relates the text personally to its author.

stylistic (*device, speciality*): (1) pertaining to STYLE; (2) pertaining to the use of certain recognized features of form which characterize specific styles or literary genres

subject: one of the major divisons of a CLAUSE, the other being the PREDICATE. Typically, the subject is a noun phrase; not to be confused with the semantic AGENT.

subjective (*possessive, genitive*): in which the relation between the object represented by one noun and the event represented by the other is that of agent, e.g. *His shooting is accurate*; opposed to OBJECTIVE

subordinate (*clause*): same as dependent CLAUSE

subordinate (meaning): in a TAXONOMY, a meaning which is included in the meaning of a more GENERIC term; opposed to SUPERORDINATE; see also SPECIFIC

subordination: the joining of two grammatical elements in such a way that one is dependent on the other; *to* **subordinate**

substandard language: that portion of a language which is commonly used by persons of low prestige and/or poor education, and which is judged by the language community as being inferior and unacceptable for serious communication; characterized by "incorrect" grammar, VULGAR LANGUAGE, etc.

substitution: the use of one term or expression for another; as pronouns, euphemisms, synonyms, metaphors, etc.

suffix: see AFFIX

superordinate: in a TAXONOMY, a meaning which includes the meaning of a SUBORDINATE term; also GENERIC

supplementary component: a SEMANTIC COMPONENT which is typically present in the meaning of a term but which is not required to distinguish it from other meanings. Some supplementary components are variable, some are purely arbitrary or conventional, some relate to the connotation.

surface structure: the grammatical form of a discourse as it is actually spoken or written; often characterized by complexity, stylistic elaboration, potential ambiguity, the presence of information in implicit form, and the shift of class membership of many semantic elements. Rigorous translation requires that the surface structure be BACK TRANSFORMED into the underlying KERNELS before the transfer.

symbol: a form, linguistic or nonlinguistic, which is arbitrarily and conventionally associated with a meaning. Linguistic symbols are words and idioms.

synonym: a word or expression which has essentially the same diagnostic components as another and which can therefore be substituted for it in many but not all contexts. PARAPHRASES and ANALYTICAL EXPRESSIONS and specialized kinds of synonyms.

syntactic context: that aspect of the linguistic context which pertains to the grammatical setting in which a term is used. Because the syntactic context determines the grammatical class and function of a word, it assists the SEMOTACTIC CONTEXT to select the appropriate meaning of each word.

syntax: see GRAMMAR

synthetic (REDISTRIBUTION): the translation of a complex expression by a single word comprising the same diagnostic components

taboo: which is forbidden, either because it is dangerously powerful (positive taboo) or because it defiles or saps one's life force (negative taboo). Words are often taboo, in which case they are replaced in ordinary usage by EUPHEMISMS.

tautology: an expression in which the same components are stated twice with no justification in terms of either structure or communication; often, an expression in which the predicate simply restates the subject; not to be confused with PLEONASM or REDUNDANCY

taxonomy: a set of meanings so structured that the GENERIC, SUPERORDINATE terms at the top define a DOMAIN and include at several levels increasingly SPECIFIC, SUBORDINATE meanings. A taxonomy reflects a system of CLASSIFICATION of experience; also called hierarchy

technical (*term, terminology*): pertaining to a definite field of specialization. Technical terms are typically more precise, and technical terminologies more rigorously organized, than ordinary vocabulary; but because they are not understood by nonspecialists, they are inappropriate in texts intended for general audiences.

technical level: a SITUATIONAL LEVEL of language, partly characterized by the use of technical terminology, which is used among specialists in talking about their specialty; typically obscure to outsiders

temporal relations: relations of time between events

tense: a grammatically marked representation of the time, absolute or relative, of an event

tertiary (*element, structure*): which is completely BACKGROUNDED in a discourse; distinguished from PRIMARY and SECONDARY

text: see DISCOURSE

topic: the part of a clause about which something is predicated in a COMMENT; typically the SUBJECT

transfer: the second stage of translation, in which the message is actually reproduced in the receptor language

transform (*to*): to convert a KERNEL or several kernels into a SURFACE STRUCTURE by the application of transformations

transform: the surface structure resulting from the transformation of a kernel

transformation: A grammatical process by which kernels are restructured into a surface structure of appropriate style, following transfer; also called forward transformation, in opposition to BACK TRANSFORMATION

transition, transitional features: the marked passage from one major portion of a discourse to the next

transitive (*event, verb*): semantically, requiring a goal; grammatically, requiring a direct object; see also INTRANSITIVE and DITRANSITIVE

translation: the reproduction in a receptor language of the closest natural equivalent of the source language message, first in terms of meaning, and second in terms of style. Translation which aims at dynamic equivalence comprises three stages: ANALYSIS, TRANSFER, and RESTRUCTURING.

translationese: an artificial form of a RECEPTOR LANGUAGE, in violation of normal grammatical and semotactic patterns, caused by an excessive effort toward FORMAL CORRESPONDENCE; see also LITERALISM

unmarked meaning: see CENTRAL MEANING

verb: in most languages, a word of a grammatical class which function most typically as the principal word of a predicate. In some languages, verbs are morphologically distinctive; they are often marked for such categories as tense, aspect, person, and number. The traditional definitions of a verb derived from the intuitive similarity between the grammatical verb and the semantic EVENT; but in some languages, events may also be represented by a special class of nouns; and some languages have specialized verbs to represent certain relations and certain abstracts.

verbal consistency, verbal concordance: quality resulting from the effort to translate a given word from the original consistently by a single word in the receptor language; opposed to CONTEXTUAL CONSISTENCY, which is a far sounder principle

verb phrase: a phrase which functions grammatically like a simple verb, and in which a verb is the principal word. A verb phrase is the principal part of a predicate.

vulgar language, vulgarism: a linguistic form which is considered substandard and arouses feelings of disgust

GENERAL INDEX

BIBLICAL INDEX